POKER

HOW TO WIN AT THE GREAT
AMERICAN GAME

POKER

HOW TO WIN AT THE GREAT
AMERICAN GAME

DAVID A. DANIEL

Barricade Books, Inc.

Published by Barricade Books Inc.
150 Fifth Avenue
Suite 700
New York, NY 10011

Book design and page layout by Ling Lu, CompuDesign

Printed in the United States of America.

Library of Congress Cataloging-in-Publication Data

Daniel, David (David A.)
      Poker, how to win at the great American game /
by David Daniel.
            p.   cm.
      ISBN 1-56980-093-6
      1. Poker.   I. Title.
GV1251.D35   1997
795.41'2—DC20   96-21024
                                                        CIP

10 9 8 7 6 5 4 3 2 1

This book is dedicated to my wife
Monica
who has put up with
a poker player
for a couple of decades
(and become a pretty good one herself)

and to the memory of
Andrew Light Daniel
Pop
who never played high-stakes poker
but who played a heck of a game of life
and cashed in too early.

I would like to give special thanks to
Van S. Welch
poker mentor of years gone by
who has always been a better friend to me
than I have been to him.

Medicine is my lawful wife and literature is my mistress.
When I get fed up with one, I spend the night with the other.
Though it is irregular it is not monotonous, and besides,
neither of them loses anything through my infidelity.

—*Anton Chekhow (in a letter to his friend Suvorin)*

If you want to play poker
your wife needs to be happy.

—*David Spanier*

Why? You wanna buy a Bible
and see if it improves your game?

—*Tom, in a $20–$40 Hold 'em game
at the Mirage in Las Vegas when I
asked if he knew where the nearest
bookstore was.*

CONTENTS & OUTLINE

Preface

Why This Book?

There are a lot of poker books out there, and now there's one more. Well, the genre was needing one more and here's why. With very few exceptions, it seems that all the fun has gone out of poker books published in the last twenty years or so. This is principally, I believe, because the majority of these books have been written by the new breed of computer-techy pros who are writing to impress—and sell to—their professional brethren. What we are getting in these books would be the equivalent of a technical manual teaching fishermen the most effective methods of catching tuna. This is fine if you are or plan to be a professional fisherman, but even so: where's the adventure on the sea? Where are the storms? The rocky shoals? Weathered faces, sharp eyes, and muscles straining against the nets? Where are the families on shore wondering if, this time, Papa may not make it home?

If I were starting out today as a poker player and picked up one of these professional manuals, I'd think "Yuck, what a bore!" and find something else to do. I have *fun* playing poker! Doesn't anyone else these days?

Make no bones: as you will quickly discover in the following pages, poker is business for me too; but it's also a fascinating, wonderful, intricate adventure on the high seas of human nature. And you can make money at it! What could be better? When I play poker, I feel like a kid must feel when he's just discovered he can make money trading comic books. Some sportswriters must feel like this: somebody is actually paying them to spend their afternoons at the ball park! Heaven!

I recently read something that irritated the hell out of me. It was in one of the pros' books and said: "Just don't put too much stock in other author's (sic) strategy recommendations. Most don't play for a living. I do." This is typical of the pros' inflated opinion of what they do and how they do it. In fact, because most of us *don't* make a living at poker, the pros' manuals are basically irrelevant to us. (Except, as discussed in Chapters 6 and 9, to find out what they're thinking.) To put their recommendations to use, you would have to play like they do—all day every day—and be prepared to make a pretty boring living for yourself. I am an amateur (who nonetheless often consorts with pros). I win money playing poker but I do it because it's fun. If I've done my job with this book—and you do yours by studying it—you'll be able to have fun and win money, too.

Now, just because I feel recent "computer-techy" books have gone overboard on the technical side doesn't mean there *isn't* a technical side. Of course there is. In fact, being of the computer generation myself, my friend/partner Ricardo Pessanha and I have developed a poker simulation program, called The PokerWiz, which is the dream-come-true of any serious poker player. With it, the user can set up just about any poker situation he or she wants to, run off a hundred thousand or a million hands, and see the results in minute detail. The various references in this book to million-hand computer runs are all from The PokerWiz. This is great. This is wonderful. If one is not mathematically inclined there is no longer any need to suffer through excruciating calculations of probability or to memorize endless, eye-glazing charts.

It is essential, however, to keep in mind that probability, math, computers, etc. are all just backup; the essence of poker is people as, I hope, you will learn in the following pages. Good luck!

Chapter 1

Whiskey, Cordite,
and Loose Women

Whether you haven't played the game in years, play occasionally, or are a semi-serious player with a regular weekly or monthly game, or are an active or aspiring pro or semi-pro, if you are American and over the age of ten it is almost impossible that you have never played poker. Poker is as much a part of America as baseball, softball, football, Monopoly, Scrabble and cheating on income tax: the entire population is either doing it now, or has done it in the past, or will do it at some time in their lives.

If you are like most people, you've played poker around the kitchen or dining table for toothpicks and buttons, for chips with pretend value, for pennies, for nickels and dimes. And you've probably felt vaguely, well, rather risqué while doing it; cowboyish; Doc Holiday; Maverick; daring and ever so slightly sleazy. This is the flavor of poker.

Baseball tastes like a sultry summer afternoon: Sun, women in short shorts and halter tops perspiring just enough to glow, long grass where the outfield ends, children, bees and mosquitoes, beer, fried chicken and hot dogs. Mickey Mantle. Tobacco. Chewing tobacco. Spitting and scratching disdainfully as you look the pitcher in the eye and sneer, just before you wallop the winning home run into the cheap seats in the bottom of the ninth.

Not many of us chew tobacco, spit, scratch, and sneer as we step up to the plate, and rare is the opportunity to smash in the winning home run, but the essence is there as we stick our collective nose in the glass to savor the bouquet before we sip. It's the company picnic, the softball game, and you're up. There are two on, two out, you're losing by two, and it's the bottom of the ninth. Are you thinking about why sales at the Houston office

17

are off 3 percent? Are you convinced you are a hopeless putz at bat? Or does a fleeting image, slightly out of focus, of Jose Canseco putting a ball in the parking lot flash through your mind and the roar of the crowd momentarily fill your ears?

So what if you *have* been a hopeless putz at your last 150 at bats; this time you're going to send it to the moon.

Poker tastes like whiskey and sweat and cordite. Cigar smoke. Loose women and bad guys; honky-tonk nights and hot, still desert mornings-after. Dangerous Dan, six foot eight and three hundred pounds, is sitting across from you having just come in from an evening of pillaging and murdering half the population of the town. He squints up his face, scarred from fifty-six successful defenses of his world heavyweight knife-fighting title. He bets $5,000 into your pitiful, scrawny little one-card draw. If you win this hand, you can buy that ranch you and the little woman have always dreamed of. If you lose, it's back to cleaning out spittoons with your socks because you can't afford a rag, and your little tow-headed, five-year-old daughter, Molly, will never have a new pair of shoes.

You look at your hand and you've pulled the Q♠, giving you a straight flush to the queen! Your entire future depends upon whether Dan can beat this almost unbeatable hand. Your hands tremble as you reach for your money. Dan begins picking his blackened teeth with a twenty-four-inch bowie knife, and behind him three of his flunkies cock their double-barreled street howitzers. You call. Dan shows down four kings and starts to rake in the pot. You say, "GET YOUR HANDS OFF MY MONEY," show down your straight flush, simultaneously draw your peacemaker, waste the flunkies, and stuff the barrel in Dan's left ear. Dan's eyes begin to water as, whimpering and sniffling, he gets on his knees and begs you to let him leave town with his brains intact. You grant him this small favor and give him a final shove out the splintered swinging doors into the heat, dust, humiliation, and horse shit.

So what if the bet was fifty cents and the guy who made it was your buddy Fred, the day manager at Burger King? For a while there, it felt like, well, it *could* have been Dangerous Dan.

The point of all this is that if you are American and haven't been living under a rock, then you have grown up with poker and its mystique; it is the stuff of American legend. If you've bought this book, or are perusing it in the bookstore, then you probably have more than just a simple, penny-ante, passing interest in poker. If that's the case, if you are or are planning to be serious about poker, *forget the mystique*. That poker aura is one of the factors that has been luring a continuous string of losers to poker tables for more than a century and a half. All of which leads us to two questions: What kind of poker player are you? and what kind of poker player do you want to be?

My Dad played in a 5-10-25-cent monthly game with his buddies for decades, was perfectly happy with that, was a regular winner, swaggered for a week if he won $15, and never aspired to more. That is, at a *participatory* level he didn't appear to aspire to more. However, when I began playing poker for hundreds or thousands of dollars (not really when I began, but when I first told him about it), he became transfixed with curiosity and a fount of questions. He wanted to know everything, and his desire to know was matched only by the wistful look that overcame him as we talked.

You see, even if you've been playing nickel and dime poker for twenty years, at some deeply personal level of pretense and fantasy, you're betting the ranch and Molly's new shoes against Dangerous Dan. To whom does fantasy not apply? Who hits the golf ball and doesn't picture Arnold Palmer? Who struts onto the tennis court and doesn't see images of Boris Becker? Who gets behind the wheel and doesn't wish he were Mario Andretti for a day? Who digs his ten-year-old body or his middle-aged pot belly into the batter's box and doesn't think of Joe DiMaggio? Who plays round ball after work down at the Y and doesn't fleetingly pretend to be Michael Jordan? Here's who: Arnold Palmer, Boris Becker, Mario Andretti, Joe DiMaggio, and Michael Jordan. They may, almost certainly, have had their heroes and fantasy figures when first starting out, but by the time they became heroes and fantasy figures themselves, I'll wager my house against a knothole that it was all cold, hard business.

This is not to say that one shouldn't enjoy what one is doing. I doubt you'll find a top player or doer of anything who doesn't enjoy what he's doing. If you don't enjoy it, you won't want to put the required time and effort into it to become really good. I suppose there may be exceptions to this, like a tennis champ who was forced into tennis at the age of two by his neurotic father and is constipated for weeks if he loses a match. But as a general rule, if you talk to, let's say, the top fifty players of the NBA, one thing you'll probably hear from all fifty is, "I love basketball." If you don't enjoy poker, forget it; it's going to be drudgery.

Me, I love poker, love it with a passion. I would rather play poker than . . . well, do *almost* anything else. I am vocationally and avocationally in love with two women: I love my work—my wife, and I love poker—my mistress.

A friend of mine had the habit at one time of telling his wife that he was going out for a drink and would be back in a couple of hours. He would, in fact, show up three days later (he's not married anymore). When he did this, he was with women. I have, on far, far more than one occasion, told my wife that I was going to play poker for a few hours—and shown up three days later. When I did this, I was in fact playing poker, and my wife knew it and knew where to reach me (which she did, every few hours) to see if I was still alive. Perhaps this is why I'm still married (aside from the fact that I'm a fantastic guy): my wife knows who my mistress is—poker. She also knows that for twenty years my mistress has been paying me to go and see her—a nice bonus.

So, my Dad may have wanted to read this book. His game was only recreation, but it was also fantasy—and he wanted to be good at it. He used to come home and tell me about Larry who was "a really sharp player." I used to think that, well, how sharp do you have to be to play in a nickel and dime game? That was truly obtuse of me because, of course, I was completely missing the point. As far as they were concerned, that was *the* game, and Larry was good at it, a winner. Interestingly, my Dad and most of the people in the game had superior positions to Larry's in their company hierarchy, but Larry's ability at the poker game was envied and respected.

Why are *you* reading a poker book? Curiosity? Not very likely. You're probably (1) a serious poker player—at whatever stakes— who reads poker books like a doctor reads medical journals, or (2) not doing as well as you would like at your current level of play, or (3) doing very well at your current level and are thinking of moving up into the big time. Big time, by the way, is relative. There's a discussion of what constitutes high and low stakes in the next chapter. My Dad would have been in category 2. He would never seriously have considered moving into bigger games, but he wanted to win at the game he was in. Whatever your situation, define it to and for yourself; know what you want.

You can make money playing poker. Is that what you want? You can even make a living for you and your family by playing poker, though this is very, very difficult. Is that what you want? Perspectives vary. If you're the chairman of General Motors, you probably aren't terribly interested in poker as a livelihood. If you're flipping burgers at McDonald's, you may be interested in taking a look.

"But McDonald's pays me a guaranteed salary! Poker is a tremendous risk!" That's true. If you're a lousy poker player, you're not going to make money at it. On the other hand, if you're a lousy flipper of burgers, your days may be numbered at McDonald's, too. You decide. If you are a world-class burger flipper—which still doesn't pay squat but is steady—maybe you should stick with burgers and try poker on the side. If you turn out to be a winner at poker, perhaps the extra income would allow you to save up and open your own burger place, whereat, being a world-class burger person, you would make a fortune.

In any case, if you are thinking of dedicating your life to poker—don't. Dedicate your life to God, to your family, to opera, to world peace, to making the perfect burger, whatever. If you discover that you can make a satisfactory income from poker, fine. But don't make it your life. By far, the most likely scenario for the vast majority of would-be, or established, serious poker players is that, if you're good and careful and if you pay attention to the advice herein (and in lots of other poker books), you may be able to *supplement* your income by playing poker. I do it all the time and, hell, I put my pants on one leg at a time, just like you.[1]

If you are determined to try to make a living exclusively at poker, you're in for a rough time, but it certainly can be done, and we'll examine it later. But, think of golf (or baseball, or basketball, or just about anything else): millions play it, a few hundred make their living at it—often not a very good living—and only a tiny handful make really big money at it. Same thing, with one difference: at poker you can *lose* money. That paycheck can go very quickly through the poker black hole and end up in someone else's pocket. What you want, of course, is for someone else's paycheck to end up in *your* pocket.

Sounds kind of ugly, doesn't it? It isn't really. It's only as ugly as basic capitalism. People like Donald Trump and their stockholders and their bankers *count* on other people's paychecks ending up in their pockets. If you have a Ford dealership, are you sure that the guy buying a new car is not blowing the kids' college money on a whim? Taking someone's money at poker *seems* different, but it isn't. People risk money at poker for all sorts of reasons, and they aren't always doing it to win Molly's shoes.

Some people just like to gamble. In fact, a *lot* of people just like to gamble as evidenced by the perpetual throngs in Las Vegas and similar places, and by the equally perpetual profits of the casinos. Do you like to gamble? If you do, please send me your name and address because I'd love to meet you. A gambler is a serious poker player's greatest asset. Sound poker playing isn't

---

[1] For you skirt wearers out there, sorry, I can't relate. I haven't worn a skirt since . . . Well, actually I guess it was Carnival last year in Rio.

gambling; it's science, art, and psychology all mixed with good doses of patience and horse sense. Me, I hate to gamble. To illustrate this, let me give you the history of my life as a casino gambler.

When I was sixteen years old, in 1967, I lost $20 playing roulette in Monte Carlo. (How I got into the casino at age sixteen is another story.) I was sick to my stomach for a week—How could I have been so stupid?—and swore I would never go into a casino again. I kept my oath for seventeen years. Then, in 1984, my wife dragged me kicking and screaming to a casino in Deauville, France. Still, I didn't gamble; instead, I stood behind my wife as she blew $400 playing twenty-one (blackjack). When the four-hundredth dollar went down the shoot, I pretty much took her by the elbow and dragged her, kicking, and screaming, out of the casino, trying to escape before I vomited all over some Frenchman's tuxedo.

Ten years later, I was stuck over a weekend, all alone on business, in the Intercontinental Hotel in Bogotá, Colombia. As I lay on my bed watching CNN, I considered my options for that evening: I could stay lying on my bed watching CNN and thus become an authority on world events; I could wander the streets of Bogotá and risk being shot or kidnapped by terrorists; I could take fifty dollars to the casino in the basement of the hotel and try to convince myself to part with it. I finally got it narrowed down to a choice of risking fifty dollars in the casino or risking being kidnapped and ultimately, reluctantly, decided on the fifty-dollar option.

Once in the casino, I really didn't want to be there, so I hung around for about an hour watching the roulette tables, trying to build enthusiasm to play. One of the roulette tables caught my eye. I watched it and watched it and, lo, that wheel was coming up black numbers four out of six times. I watched it some more. Sure enough, that wheel, or perhaps the cosmos, wasn't right that Saturday night in Bogotá. The wheel was coming up black so often that gamblers were flocking around and—you guessed it—betting red. Makes you just want to shake your head and pity the human condition.

Well, I bought some chips, started betting black and various combinations of black numbers—while the folks all around me were betting red—and shortly had won $1,000. With that thousand dollars, I figured casinos and I were even for this lifetime, and I went back to my room to find out what had happened in the world in the last three hours.

When I tell you poker isn't gambling, take it from a guy who loves to play poker and hates to gamble. Casino gambling doesn't even tempt me (except as an alternative to being shot). I recently spent nine days playing poker in Las Vegas and never once, *not once,* wagered a single penny at craps or blackjack or roulette or slot machines or any other casino game.[2]

Speaking of Vegas, I usually play public poker in California. The reason is that there is a hundred times more poker action in California than there is in Las Vegas. Poker in Las Vegas is treated as kind of a stepchild by the casinos, and, frankly, they wish it would just go away. In equivalent floor space, it is much more lucrative to set up slot machines than poker tables.

In California, poker is the name of the game. You either play poker or you go to Disneyland. The card room staff treat you like a king (or queen). Some places give you free food, free transportation, and some will even send a masseuse around to your table to rub your shoulders. And there are lots more players playing lots more games a lot more of the time.

Recently, however, I've been increasing the frequency of my forays to Las Vegas. Why? Well, for one thing, Vegas is Vegas. After flying over hundreds of miles of brown, barren nothingness, all of a sudden there's a sparkle and excitement in the atmosphere: you're approaching Las Vegas! The air feels different. It's narcotic. Let's get out there and gamble! And therein lies one of the advantages of playing poker in Las Vegas: the place is full of gamblers. They'll go from the craps tables, to the black-

---

[2] There are, of course, people who can win regularly and scientifically at blackjack, which means that, for them, blackjack is not gambling. The problem is that as soon as the casinos discover these people, they throw them out and ban them from playing. So what's the point?

jack tables, to the sports book, to the poker tables. So, Vegas is electric; Vegas is magic; Vegas is full of people who think it's fun to throw money away; Vegas is a serious poker player's paradise even though it's sometimes harder to find a good game than it is in California. We'll see more about casino poker in Chapter 9.

At whatever level and for whatever reason you play, this book is replete with information that will help you along. You will be able to use this information to win at poker, whether you play the game as a sideline or as a profession, at small stakes or big stakes, in private or public games, regularly or occasionally—if you pay heed and apply what you learn. A word of warning, however: Most poker books concentrate their advice on the cards—what cards to play when, what cards not to play when. This is fine, as far as it goes, and we'll certainly be talking some about cards here, but it isn't far enough. My Dad used to say that a college degree was nothing but a license to start learning. How true. We get out of college and think we know it all—until we come face to face with the real world. All of a sudden we find out we're dealing with people who knew twenty or thirty years ago what we know now and have expanded on that basic knowledge with a lifetime of experience. If you've studied and learned poker of the never-stay-unless-you-think-you-have-top-hand variety, then you have your degree. Now it's time to get out into the world and learn what poker is really about, namely, people.

Chapter 2, coming up, goes over some basic vocabulary and discusses some of the concepts this vocabulary invokes. Chapter 3 quickly runs down the games, variations of poker, used illustratively in this book. Chapter 4 talks about you, you as a poker player, and the people you play poker with. Together, these two factors, you and the people you play with, represent 99 percent of whether you will be a winner or a loser at poker, at whatever stakes and for whatever reason you play. As you will see throughout this book, in the long run cards matter practically not at all. If you put a World Champion of Poker at a table with a three-year-old kid and deal them each a thousand hands face up, the kid is going to get just as many winning hands as the champion. Winners and losers all play with the same cards, but the winners win and the losers lose. It isn't the cards that matter, it's the player.

Good luck!

Chapter 2

Conceptual Vocabulary

et's not have a lot of tsk-tsking and weight-of-the-worldly wringing of hands out there among grammarians. I write grammatical Standard American English for a living and this, by God, is a vacation. Significant sections of this book are written in Standard Poker English, a recognized subdialect spoken around poker tables from Anchorage to Miami and beyond. *Two pairs,* for example, is anathema to Standard Poker English; prefer *two pair.* *"Goodness! He bet all his money on an ace and king!"* This is a bell-ringing shibboleth to native speakers of Standard Poker English; prefer, *"Shit! Sumbitch tapped on Big Slick!"* In recounting personal poker exploits, only the historical present tense is used, no matter that the incident occurred an hour or fifty years ago: *"There I am, it's the winter of '45, we're playin' stud, Bill has two jacks showin', and I know I should just fold, but . . ."* Cropping the *ing* endings is optional. Finally, one's Poker Players Union membership card would be immediately and irretrievably revoked should one ever be caught using *beaten* in any context as the past participle of the verb *to beat;* viz., "I flop six titties and get *beat* on the river by a gutshot."

In terms of vocabulary, a complete glossary is provided in Appendix 4 for nonnative speakers of Standard Poker English. However, a few explanations of some vocabulary along with their related concepts will be useful before we get too far.

Several relatively esoteric terms are cited above. For example:

Big Slick:

This refers to your first two "hole" or "pocket" cards in Hold'em and indicates an ace-king off-suit. Why *Big Slick* was reserved especially for cards that are not suited, I don't know. Ace-king suited would seem to have been a better choice for linguistic distinction. Some people call this *Super Big Slick* or *Super Slick,* but this is relatively rare. Mostly, as far as I can discern, ace-king suited goes nameless except, sometimes, as *Big Slick Suited,* which is kind of a cop-out.

The nice thing about Big Slick is, of course, that if you wind up with top pair, you also wind up with top kicker; if you wind up with a straight, it's top straight; if (suited) you wind up with a flush, it's top flush; and, thus, most players, including me, feel that it is worth a raise or two before the flop. The problem is, however, that it is such a promising-looking hand that many players are reluctant to dump it, even when the flop has missed their Big Slick and has clearly hit another player's Junk. If it's not *clear* that other players have made pairs and/or other stuff on the board, Big Slick on its own may be worth seeing through to the end as it will beat any other no-pair hand. In other words, if your Big Slick hits, great, you'll win more often than not; if your Big Slick misses, it sometimes requires a lot of very acute judgment whether to dump it or see it through. In sum, Big Slick is a great starting hand, but it isn't as good as it seems. After all, heads up, a pair of 2s is about a 53 to 47 favorite over Big Slick. Proceed with caution.

Tap:

This is a verb that means either (a) to bet all one's money in a table-stakes game: "I knew I had the best hand by the fourth card so I *tapped*"; or (b) to force another player to bet all *his* money: "John only had about $500 left so my bet would have *tapped* him." This latter meaning, to force someone to bet all his money, can be a powerful psychological tool when bluffing, or defensive bluffing a marginal hand (see Chapter 6), in a pot-limit or no-limit game. It can be very difficult to call a bet which, if you are wrong, will bust you out of the game. For this reason I *never* put all my playing money on the table when sitting down to a pot-limit or no-limit game.

Let's say I show up to a game with $2,000 in my pocket. Depending, of course, on the minimum buy-in, I will rarely put more than, say, $500 on the table. That way, if it comes to tapping, I can make a judgment based solely on the merits of the bet itself; I don't have the additional worry of knowing I'll have to hit the road if I call and lose. What if the minimum buy-in is $2,000? Easy: I wouldn't play. I'd either (a) find another game with a smaller buy-in, (b) go home and read a book instead of playing, or (c) go get $6,000 more to play with.

Assuming the $500 buy-in and $2,000 in your pocket, how you put that $500 on the table is also very important. Wait a minute. How many ways can there be to put money on a table? Well, in this case, there are at least two. Depending on my read of the players, I may want to appear timid, shy, and worried about the money. This would mean that I had read the players as being the sort who will easily underestimate me and try to bully me with big, tapping bets. In this case, out of sight of the table, I would separate $500 from my wad and put it in a pocket by itself or, preferably, in my wallet. Then, sitting down at the game, I would make a big show of reluctantly, painfully, taking all my money—$500—out of my wallet, making sure the other players saw that this was all I had. I then sit back and wait for them to try to bully me.[3]

If I'm—and there's irony in this—less confident about my ability in relation to the other players, I will do the opposite. I will establish a defensive, you-can't-push-me-around posture by making sure I flagrantly wave my wad about and disdainfully pull off the measly $500 buy-in. This makes the players less

---

[3.] Though this has been a tactic of mine for years, I recently saw an article in a magazine advising players to keep an eye out for the "nerds" and "dorks" who reluctantly "pinch" money from their wallets. These players, said the article, will be easy to bluff and bully. I can only hope that a whole lot of my future opponents read that article. Finding out what the "experts" think certain behavior implies and then doing the opposite is a valuable tool in private or public poker. We'll see more of this later.

likely to try to bully and bluff me with tapping bets since they know I have plenty of backup. Therefore, when one of them bets a lot of money at me he'll be more likely than not to have a strong hand.

Fold:

Now, this is silly. Everyone knows what it means to fold a poker hand, right? So why include it here? Because almost no one *really* understands. Imagine a group of old farts sitting around the cracker barrel in the general store exchanging bits of country wisdom. One says, "Yep, welp," chaw-smack-spit, "life's just like cards: ya gotta play the hand yer dealt." Well, that's true for bridge, gin, canasta, cribbage, rummy, hearts, old maid, and life—but it's not true of poker. Imagine playing, say, Monopoly or backgammon. You roll the dice and say, "Well, I don't like that roll. I'm going to keep rolling until I get some numbers I like." You can *do* that in poker! Imagine a batter in baseball saying, "If it takes a hundred pitches, I'm just gonna stand here till I get a nice easy one right down the middle." If he had that luxury (as, in fact, in the earliest days of baseball he did), he would be an idiot to swing at anything but a perfect pitch, right?

This should be so easy to understand, yet it seems 99 percent of poker players will effectively say to themselves, "Even though this wonderful game affords me the incredible luxury of not having to play if I don't want to, of not having to bet my money if I don't want to, of waiting till I have a really good chance of winning, I'm gonna go ahead and throw my money away on crappy hands that don't have a hope in hell of winning just because I'm stupid and I feel like losing my house."

Is that clear enough? Imagine again our lucky batter explaining to his coach why he swung at three pitches in the dirt and struck out, when all he had to do was stand there and wait for his perfect pitch. Really dumb. If you don't like your chances this time around, just FOLD! There will be a whole new potential opportunity arising for you in about two minutes when you get your next hand.

Flop, etc.:

The *flop* are the first three common cards turned up in Hold'em. Common cards on the table are often called the *widow,* but now they are more frequently referred to as the *board,* perhaps because *board* is gender-neutral. In a blow to political correctness, however, see *titties,* below. So, the first three board cards in Hold'em are the *flop,* the fourth is the *turn,* and the fifth and last is the *river.* To *flop,* the verb, refers both to what the dealer does in creating the *flop,* i.e., he *flops* the *flop,* as well as to the particular hand created for a player by the cards in the *flop.* "I *flopped* a straight," therefore, means that the three *flop* cards plus the two in your hand made a straight. "I *flopped* a set," means that you have, say, a pair of 8s in the pocket, got an 8 on the flop, and therefore now have a *set,* which is more hip poker jargon for three of a kind.

    River is also a verb and can be either active: "I knew he had me beat on the *turn* (fourth board card), but I *rivered* him with a heart flush," means that with the last (fifth board) card, your hand became a winner; or passive: "I had him beat on the *turn,* but he *rivered* me with a heart flush," means exactly the opposite—you were winning through the fourth board card, but the last card made your hand a loser. (This can also be stated in the more classically passive " . . . I *was rivered* by a heart flush.")

    The truth is that *to river* in the active sense—"*I rivered* him . . ."—is rarely used. This is because *rivering* has the connotation of "lucking out." As we all know, whenever a poker player wins a hand, it is due to his consummate skill, vast experience, and superior intelligence, but whenever he loses a hand, it is always because some moronic opponent got lucky. Therefore, it is extremely rare to hear a poker player say "I *rivered* him . . ." as that would be the same as saying "I got lucky." "I *was rivered* . . ." is, however, heard constantly. (Another expression that is the equivalent of *to river* is *to draw out on,* but this can imply that more than one card was involved. "I had him beat before the flop, but he *drew out on* me" can mean that any or all of the subsequent five cards created the winning hand.) The fourth board card, the *turn,* has not yet acquired full verb status as in "I turned two pair." Standard Poker English still usually requires "I got (or made) two pair *on the turn.*"

Titties:

Well, these come in pairs, and the expression has been attributed to Amarillo Slim[4] whereby *two titties* equal one queen. Therefore, by extension, you have *two titties, four titties, six titties,* and *eight titties,* which represent the maximum possible number of *titties,* unless, of course, you're playing with wild cards in which case you could have a maximum total of *ten titties.* To my knowledge, jacks and kings have yet to be assigned any anatomy-specific nicknames. Perhaps it's time for a little equal-opportunity inventiveness on the part of poker players. Big putz and little putz? You could then have, say, QQQJJ, which would be six titties full of little putzes.

Gutshot:

This almost always refers to the card needed to complete an inside straight draw, as in "I needed a jack for a *gutshot,*" or the act of having tried for or accomplished an inside straight draw, as in "I hit a *gutshot.*" An inside straight is a straight with a hole in it, as 9♦10♥ _ Q♠K♣. Trying to hit that jack has been the ruin of many a man, but it does happen or we wouldn't need a

[4.] In *Big Deal, A Year as a Professional Poker Player;* Anthony Holden; Bantam Press, 1990.

word, *gutshot,* to describe it. Here again, however, you will rarely hear a poker player admit to having tried for, or won with, a *gutshot.* You will always hear something like, "I had thirty-seven *outs* (which see), and the one that came in was the *gutshot.* I never would have stayed in the hand otherwise." Actually, going for a gutshot is quite acceptable if the *pot odds* (which see) are correct—a minimum of eleven to one. Further sweetening the pot, you can frequently count on getting called if you hit a *gutshot* and bet, because opponents will often refuse to believe you've hit it.

Moving on to some as yet uncited, but soon-to-be-helpful vocabulary, we have:

Nuts:

Sometimes called the *lock* or *lock hand,* the *cinch* or *cinch hand,* the *immortal hand,* the *immortal lock,* the *boss hand,* the *weenie,* the *hammer,* and a host of other names, the *nuts* is simply the best possible and, therefore, unbeatable, hand. Some people add a qualifier to this and say *pure nuts,* which leads me to wonder what the *impure nuts* would be. Although sometimes applied to a very powerful hand in games like draw (where the only true *nuts* would be a royal flush), it really only refers to stud games and widow, or board, games like Hold'em and Omaha in which the exposed cards define what the best possible hand is. If the board in Hold'em or Omaha is 2♠ A♥ 6♦ 9♣ K♠, then the absolute best hand possible, the *nuts,* is three aces. If you're playing five stud and have [8]8286 against your opponent's [?]AK55, there's no card in the universe that he could have in the hole that would beat you; you have the *nuts.* If, on the other hand, you have [4]4246 against his [?]AK55, and you have seen no other 5s out, you may well have him beat, but *he* has the *possible nuts* and, therefore, you would normally be unable (if you're sane) to bet into him. Another way of putting it is that, a priori, you are *nutted,* which means that someone other than you is showing the *possible nuts.*

In seven card stud, it's often more difficult to know if one has the *nuts* or not due to the three unknown hole cards being able to hide powerful hands. You have to have more information, like having seen relevant cards exposed around the table. A hand like [??] 2♣ 10♥ J♥ 6♦ [?] could be anything from zip, to a pair of 2s, to four 6s, to a royal flush. You don't know without further information. However, in seven stud low, also known as razz, it's easy to discern the *nuts*. If you have [A3]56KQ[2] and your opponent is showing [??]7499[?], you know you have the *nuts* because his best possible low is a 7-4. Beware, though: many players forget that an opponent only has to use two of his up cards. So, if he's showing [??]7429[?], it *looks* like a seven-low, but in truth *he* has you *nutted* since his 4 and 2 could combine with his hole cards to make a better six-low or even a . . .

Wheel or Bicycle:

When playing lowball, or high-low split poker, there are three main systems employed to rank low hands. The first is called *deuce-to-the-seven* by which the best possible low hand is 7-5-4-3-2 off-suit. So why isn't it called *seven-to-the-deuce*? Beats me.) Straights and flushes are counted strictly as high hands, and the ace is likewise strictly high. Though it is relatively rare to encounter *deuce-to-the-seven* in modern poker, it does crop up often enough for you to need to be aware of it.[5]

In more frequent use is the 6-4 low, usually known as the *sixty-four,* by which the best possible low hand is 6-4-3-2-A off-suit. Though straights and flushes still count only as high hands,

[5.] A useful thing to do with *deuce-to-the-seven* is to introduce it as a novelty in your home game: "OK, we're going to play something different . . . " You'd be surprised how many players, unused to the new system, will go low with an ace in their hands, which, remember, is worse than a king-low. As long as you know what you're doing, you can win some nice pots from these mistakes until the other players either learn the game or get fed up and refuse to play it. What? To be so Machiavellian? Just wait. We have not yet begun to Machiavelli. . . .

the ace has now become mobile and can be considered a "one." But the system most frequently encountered these days is the *wheel*. In this system the best low hand is 5-4-3-2-A, suited or not, and known as the *wheel*, or more antiquatedly as the *bicycle*. Clearly, straights and flushes do not count against a low hand, and the ace has achieved its ultimate mobility as either a "one" or a "thirteen" in the same hand. The hand 6♥ 5♥ 3♥ 2♥ A♥, for example, would be both a 6-5 low and an ace-high flush. The *wheel* is extremely popular in high-low split games for the obvious reason that it is much easier to make a hand that can swing both ways and capture the whole pot.

Whenever you sit down to a new game, ASK WHAT SYSTEM THEY ARE USING FOR LOW and demand a full explanation. If you just ask "Is the *wheel* low?" which *should* imply all the other rules that go with it, you may or may not get a complete answer. "Sure the *wheel* is low," but the fine print in that particular game may say "unless it's suited in which case it's a straight flush and can't be used low." Always, always ask for complete rules. And, as with every other monumental victory or devastating defeat cited in this book, I speak from experience.

When my then-future-father-in-law first invited me to his poker game some twenty years ago, I had been playing in a group that used the wheel. His game was a much more highfalutin affair than I had been used to, not in terms of the money involved, but in its venue and participants: it was held at a pretty exclusive country club, and the players were mostly in the captains-of-industry and society-dons categories. These guys would actually avoid burping and farting and would look contrite and say "excuse me" when they did—at a poker game! Besides, my then-future-father-in-law was involved, and I was a tad nervous, not wanting to appear to be a total dickhead.

As it turned out, my total dickheadedness was proven beyond any doubt on just the second hand of the night, which was five stud high-low split. I had the nuts for low, which had also turned into a flush for high. Delighted, I was about to declare both ways when, in a stunning display of skill and poker acumen, I "knew" that one of my opponents had hit a full house and, therefore, I only went low. Sure enough, those two-pair showing *had* been a full house; I had been right! Trouble was, my then-future-father-in-law had also gone low—with a pair of aces showing! I almost felt sorry for him as I turned over my no-pair. "Ah ha! I *thought* you had a flush!" he said and began to rake in his half of the pot. "Buhbuhbuhbuhbut . . ." I said as I realized what I had done. They were using the *sixty-four,* straights and flushes being high hands only. The game being pot limit, that mistake cost me a pile (actually, I ended up breaking even for the night, which was more than I deserved), but the good news is that that was nearly twenty years ago, and I haven't repeated the mistake since. In a new game, always ask what the rules are, first thing. Ask for the high rules, too. Variations in the rules for ranking high hands are rarer, but you never know, you might run into a group that plays skip-straights or four-flushes or something even more bizarre. Just because a group doesn't detail all the rules to a new player doesn't mean they're trying to trap you. Many poker players just assume that the rules they play by are the rules that everybody plays by, and, therefore, require no explanation. Ask. **Ask**.

Twist or Buy:

In a lot of home or private games, variations of poker are played whereby a player can get replacement cards at or near the end of the hand. These replacement cards are usually called *twists.* Often a price is exacted for the privilege of *twisting,* that is, the player must pay to replace a card, and the *twist* is then sometimes referred to more descriptively as a *buy.*

The first game on record to employ *twists* was five card draw. At the dawn of the poker era, a player received five cards and that was it. The draw was invented to create more action and add an extra betting round. Modern *twists* and *buys* were created for the same purpose. Let's say you're playing five stud.

There was a time when you only had one option. Now you have many: five stud; five stud with a *twist* (or two or three *twists*); five stud low; five stud low with a *twist* (or ditto); five stud high-low; five stud high-low with a *twist;* five stud high-low with a *reversible twist* (you can throw away an up card, turn up your hole card, and take the *twist* down); even "Game 24," which is five card draw, high-low, roll'em with a *reversible twist* (the roll'em makes the game end up like five stud). There are many other variations out there, but these are some of the ones I've played, and in any case, you get the idea.

Usually, a twist in, say, five stud high-low will work thusly: The player is dealt five stud in the classic fashion, that is, one down and four up in four rounds. The player now has five cards but thinks he can, or needs to, improve so he opts to twist, which may be free or paid. He throws away one of his cards, and the dealer gives him a replacement card. There is then an additional betting round once all players have received their twists. That's it. It's not very complicated, but it sure adds to the action and the extra betting round, or rounds, in the case of multiple twists, can build nice pots. The *really* nice thing about *twists* or *buys* is that they keep bad players in to the end, eternally hoping to improve lousy hands.

Limits, Pot Limit, No Limit, Table Stakes, etc.

Taking the last first, *table stakes* defines all poker. Hollywood especially has led many people to believe that if someone bets a million dollars at you and you don't have or can't get a million dollars then you lose.[6] This is utter poppycock; poker has *never* been played that way. *Table stakes* means that you never can be forced to call a bet for more money than you have on the table. If some guy bets a thousand dollars at you and you want to call but only have two hundred on the table, all you have to do is say "I'm all in for two hundred" or "I call for two hundred,"

[6.] Hollywood: the folks who brought you *Krakatoa East of Java* when, in fact, Krakatoa is *west* of Java.

and the other guy has to take back eight hundred of his bet. Simple as that, and it always has been. Many people have been convinced otherwise and forced to write checks or sign over deeds, but those people were conned out of their money, not pokered out of it.

The only, repeat *only,* exception to this is in a game with strict, monetarily defined—as opposed to pot-defined—betting *limits* and a *limited number of raises* per round and then only if it has been agreed upon beforehand that a player can *draw light,* which means owe money to the pot which he doesn't have on the table. (A limited number of raises per round is absolutely essential lest you run into two or more players in cahoots who keep raising back and forth ad infinitum.) In that case, a player can calculate his maximum risk per hand and, therefore, it is somewhat permissible to be obliged to *draw light* if you run out of money on the table. Let's say the maximum bet is $10 with a limit of three raises per round and the game you're playing has five betting rounds. You can calculate that your maximum risk per hand is $10 × 4 bets × 5 rounds or $200. You know, therefore, that your maximum risk beyond the money you have on the table is $200 and you, by playing, "agree" that that is okay. Even that, however, isn't really kosher. There is no purer "business poker" played anywhere than that played in casinos and public card rooms. ("Business poker" means "definitely not friendly, this game is for blood.") And every casino or public card room I've ever played in—and that's a lot—maintains *table stakes* rules even in limit games.

Most poker games in America are *limit* games, probably because the players feel that, with limits, they have a better idea of what their overall risk is going to be when sitting down to play. This is only partly true as we shall see in a minute, but the point here is that the nature of the *betting limit* will be a, if not *the,* determining factor as to the nature of the game. Let's consider some of the variables.

The ratio of the betting limit to the ante: If the ante is high in relation to the *limits,* tight players—the ones who sit for hours and throw hand after hand away waiting for the nuts—are going to be more likely to lose.

As an example, go back to page 32 where I said that poker allows you to keep "rolling the dice," unlike Monopoly or backgammon, until you get a roll you like. Well, as usual, here comes the caveat. Poker does allow you to keep "rolling the dice," but it charges you a "fee" to do so, known as the *ante*. Let's say the fee is one cent per roll, and when you get a roll you like you stand to win $100. Hell, just keep rolling till it's perfect! Now, let's say the fee per roll is $1. Well, you can keep rolling, but you're going to keep your eye on it as the fee builds up. Now let's say the fee is $5 per roll. If you wait for the perfect roll as you did when the fee was one cent, you're going to go broke. You're going to have to get out there and play, accepting less than perfect "rolls" if you hope to make any money. If you misjudge the cost of "rolling the dice" in relation to what you stand to win, you will be playing either too loosely or too tightly, and either way you're in trouble. Therefore, if the betting limit is low in relation to the ante, the game will tend to be loose. If the limit is high in relation to the ante, the game will tend to be tight as it is then worthwhile to sit back and wait for the nuts.

Progressive versus fixed limits: Most modern poker variations have a surfeit of betting rounds. Whereas the old standby, five draw, has two betting rounds, stud games and their variations can have four, five, six, or seven or more. Whether the betting limits are invariable or are progressively increased with subsequent betting rounds will also help determine the nature of the game. As the pot grows, if the bets do not grow with it, you often end up in the last rounds with *pot odds* (which see) so enormous that it pays to draw to just about anything. Let's say the *limit* is invariable at $2. Eight players are playing seven card stud. (see chart on next page)

Already by the third round a player is getting 24 to 1 pot odds. This is more than enough to try for, say, two cards to a flush! By the fourth round a player is getting 27 to 1 for his $2. Even if there are only two cards left in the deck that could help you, it's worth trying! Furthermore, by the last round, you'll

Rounds	Pot
Dealer antes	$2
(1) 6 players call $2 bet + $2 raise	$26[7]
(2) 4 players call $2 bet + $2 raise	$42
(3) 4 players call $2 bet	$50
(4) 3 players call $2 bet	$56
(5) 2 players call $2 bet	$60

never be able to bluff anyone out for $2 against $58 to be won. At 29 to 1, you'd have to be absolutely positive that you were beat in order to fold. Any little doubt would be worth a call.

Now let's look at the same game with progressive bets, $2 capped at $5. (see chart on next page)

In this case, by the third round, the last caller is getting 13 to 1, not good enough anymore to try for two cards to a flush. On the fourth round, the last caller is getting 13.2 to 1—still good enough for an inside straight or to fill two little pair, but just barely. By the final bet, a player is looking at 15.2 to 1. Though this is still pretty good, it's about half the odds offered in the first, fixed limit, example. A player would, therefore, have to be somewhat more circumspect in considering whether or not he is being bluffed. (For those of you who noticed that I dropped a player from the second round, this would be more realistic with the increased betting limit.)

Still, this shows the two basic characteristics (some say flaws) of a limit game:

1. Your pot odds often make it worthwhile to go after hard-to-get hands, especially in a loose game. I've been in $20–$40 Hold'em games in casinos in which eight players have all called

---

[7.] I'm considering the original bettor as a "caller" to simplify the chart.

Rounds	Pot
Dealer antes	$2
(1) 6 players call $2 bet + $2 raise	$26
(2) 3 players call $3 bet + $3 raise	$44
(3) 3 players call $4 bet	$56
(4) 3 players call $5 bet	$71
(5) 2 players call $5 bet	$81

four raises before the flop, which puts at least $800 in the pot. On the flop, which is still a $20 bet, what am I *not* going to draw to at 40 to 1 odds? It's got to be really, truly, bad.

2. You've got to use maneuvering, manipulation and psychology, rather than just money, to make bluffs work. You're not going to "scare" anybody when you miss your flush and throw $5 into an eighty- or hundred-dollar pot. You have to have set up your opponent so that he believes, knows, feels he's beat.[8]

High Limit vs. Low Limit: This is so relative that it is almost impossible even to discuss, but, intrepid soul that I am, I'll do my best. Would you be comfortable playing at the stakes mentioned above, $2 progressive to $5? What do you think your overall risk per session would be? In fact, those are the limits used in one of the home games I play in and are the limits for the "model" limit game used throughout the later chapters of this book. The average wins and losses per eight-hour session (about 100 hands) are in the $300 to $600 range. Is that high stakes, medium stakes, or low stakes? I have the feeling that most players likely to be reading this book would say "medium," maybe those of you who only play in home games with buddies would say "pretty high." It is all so relative to one's wealth, income,

---

[8.] You'll find plenty of examples on how to do this later in the book.

attitude, habits, experience—everything—that it's hard to peg down.

I've found, however, that whether you're playing with middle-class, salaried citizens or Texas oil millionaires, with a few exceptions, there is a point, a level of risk, at which everyone has the feeling "we're playing for real money here." For poker to be poker, you have to be playing for "real money," whatever that means to you. If you're like the Saudi prince who dropped seven million dollars in Monte Carlo and said, "that's what I make in an hour from my wells," a $2–$5 game is just not going to hold your interest. But this is more psychology and attitude than actual wealth. If that Saudi prince actually had to work for his seven million an hour, even he might feel differently about it. A friend of mine, who is quite well off, once told me, "If I lost $100 playing cards, I would shoot myself." For him, apparently, $100 is real money even though he could easily afford it. You have to decide for yourself. On the one hand, for poker to be real poker, the risk must be enough to "matter," to hold your, and the other players', attention.[9] On the other hand, you must be comfortable with the risk. If somebody bets $1,000, or $100, or $10 at you and you start thinking, "Oh dear God, if I call and lose, the family isn't going to eat," then you ought to be home with the family or in a smaller game you can afford. There's nothing wrong with a 25–50 cent game if winning or losing, say, $40 per session is real money to you, and it is for a lot of people.

Therefore, a particular game's limits *as a function of the players' attitudes about the limits* will affect the nature of the game. The closer you get to the players' feelings of "real money," the tighter the game will tend to be. It's true that, as a rule of thumb, the higher the stakes get, in absolute rather than relative

---

[9.] I have a young—seventeen years old—brother-in-law who lives with us occasionally, and I'm teaching him to play poker. Of course, we don't play for money. What, then? Poker without stakes just isn't poker. We decided on the following: each buy-in ($300 in chips) represents one weekend of washing all the household dirty dishes. You should see him sweat when he has to decide to call an all-in bet. A weekend of dirty dishes for him—and for me, too!—is "real money."

terms, the tighter the game gets—and the better the players are. That's because of all the people you're likely to play poker with, there are really very few for whom, say, $1,000 is chicken feed. Move up to $10,000 and there are even fewer. So, you could say, in general, that lower stakes = loose game, and higher stakes = tight game, but, as with everything else in poker, it ultimately depends on the players. I've seen very tight games with five-dollar limits and very loose games with thousand-dollar limits.

Therefore, you need to adapt your playing and your strategies *not necessarily according to the absolute stakes,* but according to the players' attitudes about those stakes. If you're in a "big" game—whatever that means to you—with loose players who are constantly giving you tremendous *pot odds,* but you're playing "tight," then you are wasting opportunities to win money. If you're playing tight because that's your strategy, well, you're wrong, but so be it; you're all grown up and can choose for yourself. But if you're playing tight because the *stakes scare you,* then find another game.

When I say "attitude" is one of the factors, what I mean is that, well, for example, I could not afford to lose, say, $2,000 a week at poker, but at this stage of my poker life, I know that if I get in a game with a $2,000 win/loss potential—I'm probably not going to lose! And if I do lose this week, I'll probably win next week, and so on. You see? I'm comfortable with those stakes because I'm confident of my poker ability. Now, if I ended up in a game with win/loss swings of, say, $100,000, I would be scared shitless. This is because I know that even the greatest of poker players can lose in any given session, and there's no way I want to (or could afford to) lose a hundred grand in one session. Sure, I'm confident, but I'm also confident of my limitations.

Finally, on *limits,* I said earlier that limiting the bets makes people feel they can calculate their overall risk. Well, the *betting limit* is only half the equation; the other half is the *pace* of the game. This, as so many other things, is easy yet so few people realize it. Take the example of the $2–$5 progressive game above, for which the average wins and losses per session of 100 hands are $300 to $600. If the players spent less time discussing politics, grazing at the food table, and generally swapping tales of family and business—if they increased the *pace* of the game— then in one session they might get in 200 hands instead of 100. The average wins and losses per session would then be in the $600 to $1,200 range. The per-session risk would be double! This is why so many people, used to playing in slow, chatty home games, sit down at their first casino game and get the impression that their money has evaporated in a trice, even though they've been playing for similar stakes at home. Whereas the typical home game, between stories of how the kids are doing at school, gets in twelve to fourteen hands an hour, casino games operate at about forty hands per hour. In an eight-hour session you'll have been dealt over 300 hands! So, if your risk-per-session at your home game is, say, $300, you'd have to pick a casino game at one-third the stakes to maintain that ratio. That's pace.

Pot Limit is exactly what it says it is: the most you can bet at any one time is the amount that's in the pot. There are, however, two methods of computing what's in the pot, and this occasion-ally causes confusion. In fact, there aren't *really* two methods; there is one method and one misconception. Let's say there's $100 in the pot. Someone bets $100, making a pot of $200, and you want to raise. The misconception says that you are limited to calling the $100 and raising $200, which is what was in the pot before you called. (There is actually a second misconception that says your entire bet, your call plus your raise, cannot exceed the $200 that was in the pot. This, however, is so utterly mis-conceived that you won't run into it much.) The correct method is to figure that once you have called the $100 bet there is now $300 in the pot, and *that* is your limit for raising, i.e., $100 call + $300 raise for a total of $400 bet. "But we've been using the other method for forty years!" you complain. Well, there's no particular harm in it if you don't mind being considered igno-rant and substandard; if you want to go on playing under a mis-conception, that's up to you.

Pot Limit is always played *table stakes,* and a pot that starts out with one dollar can quickly become thousands. Let's say the game is seven stud high-low. The dealer antes $1. The first bettor bets $1. Two guys call, so we have $4 in the pot. The third guy to call wants to raise, so he calls $1 and raises $5. Ten dollars in the pot. The next guy wants to raise as well, so he calls $6 and raises $16. Thirty-two dollars in the pot. The first bettor calls $21. The next two guys also call $21 each. Ninety-five dollars in the pot. The guy who raised first wants to raise again. He calls the $16 raise and raises $111. Two hundred and twenty-two dollars in the pot. The guy who had reraised him before wants to reraise again. He calls the $111 and raises $333. Six hundred and sixty-six dollars in the pot. The first bettor, the next two guys, and the first raiser all call which is $666 + ($444 × 3) + $333 = $2,331 in the pot—and it was only the first round of betting! This is not an exaggerated scenario for a *pot limit* high-low game, with five players in the hand and two of them raising. You can see why *pot limit* is always played *table stakes.*

No limit simply means that there is, well, no limit on what you can bet or be forced to call, *up to the amount of your table stake.* Even with just $1 in the pot, the first bettor can opt to bet thousands (although this would usually be pretty stupid) if he wants to and if he has that much on the table. Which reminds me, a corollary to *table stakes* is: not only are you limited in what you have to call, you are also limited in what you may bet. Let's say you sit down to a *no limit* game. You have a couple thousand in your pocket, but only put $200 on the table. All of a sudden, you find yourself with a straight flush and start frantically pulling money out of your pocket to bet it up. No, no, no! Uh-uh! Can't do that. You can only put more money on the table between hands, not in the middle of one. You can't have it both ways. If you're going to limit your losses, then you're limiting your winning potential, too.

One of my favorite pastimes at all types of poker, but especially at no limit, is stealing the antes or, ideally, stealing the antes along with the early, exploratory bets. But, I do this with a bet that, although high enough to encourage the frail to fold, is still commensurate with what I hope to win. Players who shove their whole stacks in to win the antes are risking too much to win too little.

In sum, if you're considering playing in a game and it turns out that it is *pot limit* or *no limit,* or if there are monetary *limits* but no limits to the number of raises, make sure that they're playing *table stakes*. If they're not GET OUT OF THERE FAST. Those guys are either lunatics or crooks, and you don't want to be playing with either.

Outs:

The various ways your cards can improve to make a hand are called *outs*. Let's say you're playing seven stud. Your first five cards are A♠ K♠ 10♦ J♠ 6♥, and obviously, you have two cards yet to come. You think your opponent has two low pair at this point, so how are you going to win? Well, you can hit one of four queens for a straight, two of ten remaining spades for a flush, one each of the remaining aces, kings, tens, jacks or 6s to make two higher pair, or two of the remaining aces, kings, tens, jacks, or 6s for trips. These are your *outs* at this point. We'll say your sixth card is the 4♠. You can no longer make two pair or trips, so your *outs* are now limited to getting one of three queens for the straight or one of the remaining nine spades to make the flush. (Two notes here: For simplification I'm not considering that any of your cards have shown, and in the last example, there are only three queens available to make the straight because the Q♠ is being counted as a flush card.)

Using an example from Hold'em, we'll consider that your hole cards are J♦ 10♦. The board is showing 7♦ 9♥ K♦ 2♠, and you are convinced that your opponent has trip kings. You have to hit a straight or flush to win, so you figure your *outs:* you can hit any of nine remaining diamonds, except the 9♦ and the 2♦, which would give your opponent a full house. You can hit any of three 8s for a straight to the jack or any of three queens for a straight to the king (the 8♦ and Q♦ having already been counted as flush cards). And that's it: thirteen cards, *outs,* of the remaining forty-four. (Since you are convinced your opponent has a pair of kings in the hole—or *in the pocket,* or *pocket kings,* to use the jazzier vernacular—you can figure there are forty-four remaining "unknown" cards rather than forty-six.) At this point your opponent is bound to bet and whether or not you call depends upon your . . .

Pot odds:

As alluded to in the discussion of *limits,* this is really easy, and yet so many folks get it wrong. It is also essential, yet so many folks ignore it. In the Hold'em example above . . . tell you what I'll do. You wait around a minute while I go get some coffee, and, meanwhile, I'll run a million-hand simulation of that Hold'em example.

There, all done. In fact, I ran two, million-hand simulations, and they were within .01 percent of each other, so I'll give you the average. Your J♦10♦ won 29.56 percent (call it 30 percent) of the hands, and your opponent's K♣K♠ won 70.44 percent (call it 70 percent). That means the odds against your winning were 2.38 to 1, which we will call 2.4 to 1.[10] So, if there is $100 in the pot and your opponent bets $20, making a total of $120 in the pot, you will be getting *simple pot odds* of 6 to 1 when you call the $20 bet. That's $120 in the pot for you to win if you call and hit, against the $20 you will lose if you call and miss. That is a great deal. That is a marvelous deal. You should call

[10.] If you recall, I said above that you had thirteen cards out of forty-four to win. We could have arrived at the same odds simply by doing a quick calculation: (44–13)/13 = 2.38. Easy. A lot of these calculations of probability are pretty complex, however, and now that I can run off a million-hand simulation in a couple minutes, I prefer to do so. For one thing, there are several situations for which my million-hand simulations *have never* shown the same results as the relevant calculation of the theoretical probability. More about this later.

with joy in your heart and merriment in your manner—and not worry about the 70 percent of the times you will miss and lose. With those *pot odds,* if you make this call 100 times, you will lose $1,400 and win $3,600. No one could ever fault you for "rivering" or lucking out; you have done the right thing.

Now, let's say there's $100 in the pot and your opponent bets $100 for a total of $200 in the pot. If you call the $100, you're only getting *simple pot odds* of 2 to 1. If you make *this* call 100 times, you are going to lose $7,000 and win $6,000. What a chump. If you *do* call and win, then yes, you have "rivered" your opponent, you have lucked out. Your opponent did the right thing and you have done the wrong thing and gotten away with it—this time.

Caveat: *unless you think your opponent will call a big end bet if you do hit.* Now you're in the murky realm of *potential pot odds.*[11] Using the same example, there's $100 in the pot, your opponent bets $100, and you have to decide to call at *simple pot odds* of 2 to 1. But, you figure that if you hit your straight or flush, your opponent will not fold his trip kings against, say, a $200 bet. Now you're in business. Now you can figure that your $100 call is going to win $400 if you hit (the $200 already in the pot plus the $200 your opponent will call), for *potential pot odds* of 4 to 1. Over 100 events, you will win $12,000 for every $7,000 you lose. The problem and the reason *potential pot odds* are murky is that you have to be right about what your opponent will do.

Card odds:

These go hand in hand with pot odds and, once again, are kindergarten-simple. Let's say the game is five card draw, jacks or better to open. Doc opens, and everyone folds to Rube. Rube

---

[11.] Most poker writers call this *implied pot odds,* but I'm not sure what the implication is. I prefer *potential pot odds,* which, to me at least, seems more to the point.

has a pair of 10s and just can't decide whether or not to avail himself of the marvelous opportunity poker affords him, namely, folding like the rest of the players did.

"Whatcha thinking about, Rube?"

"Gosh darn! A pair of 10s is *almost* a pair of jacks, and maybe I could win!"

"Well, do you know how much of a dog you are?"

"Ya wanna step outside?"

"Sorry. *Dog* is hip gambler's lingo for underdog. Let me put it this way. Do you have *any idea* what the likelihood is of your winning?"

"Uh, well, nuh-uh."

"So, let's say Doc does in fact just have jacks, you think your 10s are a good bet?"

"Well, sure, I mean, 10s are just one under jacks."

"Would you draw against jacks if you had a pair of 2s?"

"Of course not. You tink I'm a dummy?"

"What are the odds of beating the jacks by drawing to your pair of tens?"

"Uh, dunno."

"It's about 3.3 to 1. What are the odds of beating the jacks by drawing to a pair of 2s?"

"Uh, maybe a million to one?"

"Close. It's about 3.3 to 1." [12]

"No shit? Ya mean I oughta start drawing to my pairs of 2s?"

"If the ratio of the *money* you stand to win to the *money* you stand to lose is greater than the ratio of the *number of times* you're going to lose to the *number of times* you're going to win, then you can draw to whatever you damn well please. But in order to know that, you have to know what the odds are of improving your hand."

"OK, man, 3.3 to 1."

[12.] 3.3 to 1 are the composite odds of: not improving the 10s (or 2s), of improving and beating the jacks, and of improving and still losing when the jacks improve. It does not include any chance of bluffing to win the pot, which could change the odds depending on the likelihood of the bluff's being successful.

"So, are you going to call and draw to your pair of 10s?"

"Well, uh, lessee. How much money is in the pot?"

"By George, I think he's got it!"

There's more about card odds later in the book and in Appendix 1. But why? Didn't I say that cards are unimportant? Ah. The above is very basic card advice for a very basic player. Were Rube an advanced *people* player, the dialogue would have another ending:

"So, are you going to call and draw to your pair of 10s?"

"No, man. I'm gonna raise."

"Raise?"

"Sure. Look, Doc is a chump and opens early with weak hands, like he did just now—see how his eyes were fluttering when he bet?—then he gets worried and upset if someone raises behind him. So I'm gonna raise, draw one card to my 10s— which makes me about a 6 to 1 dog to actually beat the jacks— then bet the roof at him after the draw. If he doesn't improve the jacks, he won't call 'cause he's afraid of big bets, which means that better than two times outta three this is my pot. Haven't you got somewhere to go?"

"Oops. Sorry for butting in . . . "

The difference between the two endings is the difference between playing poker as a card game and playing poker as a people game—butcha still gotta know the basics, Rube.

Edge odds:

I don't really like the expression *edge odds* in reference to poker. It implies a precise mathematical result for something, which is, in fact, nebulous and fickle: your ability in relation to the other players in the game. I prefer to call it, simply, your *edge*. In *The Advanced Concepts of Poker,* by Frank Wallace, the author has a whole formula worked out for calculating exactly what your overall personal advantage or disadvantage is in relation to the other players in a regular game. Frankly, or Wallacely, I think this is a crock, along with the cartoon persona of John Finn. Wallace says that if you figure your average win or loss over a given number of games compared to the biggest wins over the same games, you'll have your *edge odds.* Well, if you believe that, then there's a bridge in Brooklyn I'd like to sell you.

Your *edge,* whether positive or negative, in any poker game simply means that you are either (a) a better player than those around you, which means that the cards played by you have a better chance of winning than those same cards played by someone else, or (b) the opposite, that is, you are being consistently outplayed and, therefore, stand to lose with cards that a better player might win with. Is that clear? As mud?

The basic principle here is that of all players playing with the same good and bad cards over the long haul. Your superior skill in relation to your opponents simply means that you will win more money with your good cards and lose less money with your bad cards than your opponents. That's your *edge:* the extra weight that tips the scales in your favor.

The reason this is not precisely calculable is that you and your opponents are not machines. There are going to be days when you are in top form, playing like a master, and there are going to be days when, for one reason or another, you're playing like a putz. The vagaries of human nature and human behavior will be discussed *a lot* in coming chapters.

Cards speak, Declare, etc.:

There are two principal uses of the phrase *cards speak.* The first has to do with all poker in general, and the second has to do with high-low split games. We'll take the general sense first.

Let's say you're playing seven stud. Your first five cards are A♣ K♣ A♦ 6♣ K♥. You've got two big pair. However, your opponent is showing a pair of 8s, and you think he might have trips, so you may have to make the full house to win. Assuming that you keep playing, the next card you get is the 4♣. You still only have two pair, and you're still worried about the possible trip 8s. You get your last card down and look at it quickly with high hopes: it's a 3, and you still only have two pair. You check, your opponent bets, and, because you aren't *sure* he has trips, you call just in case he doesn't. Well, he turns over three 8s, and you say, "You win, I only have aces up." Dejectedly, you turn up your cards . . . and another player says, "Wait a minute, you have a flush!" What? A flush?

You were so busy worrying about getting the full house that you failed to notice that the sixth card had given you four clubs, and ultimately you failed even to pay attention to the suit of your seventh card, which you now see was the 3♣. Sure enough, you have a flush. But you've already surrendered the pot! Your opponent has it half raked in! Too late! Nope. You win. Your opponent may be pretty upset as he shoves the pot back at you, but he has no choice: it's your pot. Even if the pot is now securely intermingled with your opponent's stack of chips, the game stops, everyone counts backward to figure how much was in the pot, and your opponent hands it over. That is *cards speak*. Of course, everyone thinks you're a dork, but you can worry about that while you count your money, and, besides, it happens to everybody at some point.

Cards speak is a universal principle of poker, to the point that in casinos and public card rooms you don't have to (in fact, usually shouldn't) announce your hand at all. You just turn it over, and it's the house dealer's job to determine the winner. This doesn't mean you can abandon all responsibility for your own hand; I've seen house dealers make mistakes, and in home games the other players may not always be paying sufficient attention to save your ass. In a home game, it's also discourteous constantly to demand of the other players that they read your hand for you. There's a guy like that in the model home game used throughout later chapters. A principal part of his poker strategy is to be as irritating and obnoxious as possible in order to upset the other players and thereby put them off their games. (For vocabulary purposes, this sort of player is called a *button pusher*. Button pushing can certainly be a useful tactic, if it's done subtly, but more about this later.) At virtually every showdown in which he's involved, he'll just turn over his cards and ask, "What have I got?" Or, he will purposely undercall his hand, knowing full well he's got a winner, and wait for the other players to "correct" him. When the other players complain— "Jeez, Carl, can't you read your own hand?"—he'll say, "*Cards speak,* don't they?" in a smarmy tone of voice. In sum, *cards speak* is meant to be a back-up for an honest mistake. It is *not* meant to relieve you of overall responsibility for your own hand nor is it intended for use as an irritating ploy. If I, for one, see it being used in "Carl" fashion, hell, I just play right along and push his buttons right back at him: "You're right, Carl, you got zip. You lose." Miraculously, he instantly becomes able to read his hand.

The second sense of *cards speak* is that it is one of the three main methods for splitting the pot in high-low games. It is also the most dangerous. It's best explained following the other two, however, so we'll look at *simultaneous declaration* and *verbal declaration* first.

Simultaneous declaration, usually called *chip declare,* is probably the most widely used method in home games. It is accomplished with chips or coins concealed in your fist. At the showdown, the active players each take some chips from their stacks, hide their hands—the flesh-and-bone ones attached to their arms— under the table, and decide whether to put one chip (high), no chip (low), or two chips (high-low) in one of their fists. The appropriate fist is then placed on top of the table and, upon some mutually understood signal, all the players open their fists simultaneously, revealing their intentions. Thus, the *simultaneous declaration.* The only catch here is that if a player decides to go high-low, thus trying for the whole pot, he must win both ways. If he loses *or ties* one way, his hand is dead, and he loses the other way as well.

Going high-low is a risky venture and is often not worth it for the following reason. Say you're playing a game like seven stud high-low, and you have the nuts low, say 65432. Now this is also a straight for high. But, *half of the pot is already yours,* which means that you'd be making an even bet, 50–50, your half of the pot against the other half of the pot, to try for the whole thing. You've got to be right equally as often as you're wrong just to break even. To make a profit, you have to be right at a ratio of 2 to 1 (assuming same-sized pots).[13] Can you do that? If you decide that your 6-high straight, or whatever, is good enough to win high as well as low, will you be right two times out of three? Your theoretical risk is actually even greater. If you just go low and tie, you will still get one-fourth of the pot. If you go high-low and tie for low, you will get nothing.

Simultaneous declaration is certainly the fairest way of declaring for high or low, which is probably why it is the most popular. Least fair, in my opinion, is *verbal declaration*. This is really kind of silly and will probably die out as a method of declaration, if it isn't in its death throes already. What happens is, at the showdown the players announce in turn which way they're going. Clearly, this is a positional game. If you're last and three players ahead of you have declared "high," just by declaring "low," you are guaranteed half the pot. (*Verbal declaration* has its defenders, those who think there is a challenge in jockeying for positional advantage at declaration time. Well, if you're interested, you'll have to talk to one of them because I don't have anything good to say about it.)

Now we can come back to *cards speak,* which is used almost exclusively in casinos and public card rooms, and is used with some frequency in home games as well. *Cards speak,* too, is fair in that there is no outrageous advantage based on position. At the showdown, the players simply, well, show down their hands and the high hand wins high, and the low hand wins low. As I mentioned before, this is exceedingly dangerous in widow games

---

[13.] If you're about to write a huffy letter complaining that the ratio could be 3 to 2 or 5 to 4 or anything over even to show a profit, gimme a break. I know that. We're keeping things simple here. Besides, the bigger the numbers get, the less point there is in trying to swing—unless you're talking about a million pots.

in that if you only have a one-way hand for low, you may end up with just some small fraction of the pot—much less than you put in to it.

Let's say you're playing Omaha, high-low. You have A♣ 2♦ 3♣ 10♥. The board is 4♥ 6♥ 8♠ 10♦ K♥. The ace-deuce in your hand is the nuts for low, but you don't have much for high: a pair of 10s. There has been a lot of high betting, but, from the second round on, there have only been three active players. We'll stipulate that by the end of the hand there's $500 in the pot, of which each of the remaining three players has contributed $160. Comes the showdown. You have an ace-deuce nut for low, but so does the next guy, and so does the next guy! It turns out, however, that the third guy's ace-deuce is suited in hearts. He, therefore, wins the high half of the pot with the heart flush, plus one-third of the low half with his ace-deuce, a total of $333 (two-thirds of the whole pot). You and the second player have to be content with one-third of the low half (one-sixth of the whole pot) each. You and he therefore each "win" $83, which gives each of you a loss of $77 on the hand. The situation is even worse if there are only two of you in the hand. Then, you will have contributed up to *half* of the pot, but your one-way low hand against a two-way hand will only get a quarter of it back. Bummer. Some years ago, I played regularly in a pot limit game in which high-low was determined by *cards speak*. After two or three hits where I "won" but lost money, I basically stopped playing one-way low hands in widow games in which one or two cards in a player's hand can determine the low nuts. I recommend the same to you; low ties are just too common.

Well, you say, you can tie in *simultaneous declaration* and end up with a fraction of the pot there, too! That's true, but it's rarer, and you usually end up with a bigger fraction. Take the same Omaha example above. With *simultaneous declaration*, there could be three possible scenarios: (1) You all go low, in which case you each get a third of the pot and win about $7; (2) The high-low hand goes high only—the most likely scenario unless he's a putz—in which case you and the other guy each get half of the low half instead of just a third, losing $35 instead of $77; and (3) The high-low hand in fact goes high-low in which case you and the other guy each get a full half of the pot, which is what you were after in the first place. In every scenario, you are better off than in *cards speak,* and in two of the three, you actually win money. This, obviously, is because there is no case in which the high-low hand can get two-thirds of the pot.

Another advantage of *simultaneous declaration* is that, if you choose, it allows for the addition of an extra betting round after the declare. Some home games do this and some don't, but I highly recommend it. Your opportunities are greatly enhanced for maneuvering, bluffing, and outwitting your opponents, and the extra betting round makes pots bigger.

The only real advantage of *cards speak* over *chip declare* is that it gives you more opportunities to *back into* a winner. (*Back into* means winning a pot sort of by accident.) You can often be awarded a pot without having to decide first, as you would in *chip declare,* which way to go. Let's say the game is seven stud high-low. You have [A2]A256[8]. You started out good and strong, kept going with a two-way hand, but ended up with a mediocre 8-low and two-pair high. Your opponent is showing [??]774K[?]. Now, does he have a high hand, say trip 7s? Or does he have a low hand, a 7-low? You don't know. If the game is *chip declare,* you're in a quandary about which way to go. If you guess wrong you may lose. In *cards speak,* you've got the nuts. If he has trip sevens, then he can't beat an 8-low. If he has a 7-low, then he can't beat your aces-up. You're guaranteed half the pot without having to think.

One last word about *simultaneous declaration* or *chip declare.* A disadvantage can arise if you have smallish hands and find it difficult to conceal a poker chip in your fist. If this is your situation, you should suggest, no, insist to the other players in your game that coins or dice or whatever—something small—be used instead. I certainly will take advantage of noticing an awkwardly formed fist, and so will any other serious poker player.

Kicker:

In widow games especially, your *kicker* may be the prime determining factor whether you win or lose a hand. It is your next highest card after considering your hand. You're playing Hold'em. You have A♥ 10♦, and the board shows A♠ K♦ 8♣ 6♥ 2♦. You and one other player are in through the last round. He bets, you call and show down your A♥10♦. He shows down A♣Q♦. He wins. Obviously. His hand is A♠ A♣ K♦ Q♦ 8♣. Your hand is A♠ A♥ K♦ 10♦ 8♣. His queen *kicker* beats your 10 *kicker*. (In hipper poker lingo, you can also say that his *kicker outkicked* yours.) If you don't have a good *kicker*, you only have half a hand. This seems so clear, but the amount of money that is thrown away at Hold'em on hands like ace-*rag* (*rag* = lousy card, ergo, lousy *kicker*) would cover the national debt. And the rags start at the 10s; with A–9 you are deep in rag country. But, you say, I might hit a pair of aces—top pair! If you do, you just have to hope and pray that a better player hasn't hit aces as well, because if he has, you lose; he won't be in there with ace-rag. Do yourself a favor and make this your never-to-be-broken rule: At a full Hold'em table, if you're not in late position and your ace-rag isn't suited, pretend it's a 7–2 off-suit and dump it. If you are in late position and your ace-rag is suited, sometimes you can limp in if it's cheap enough. There. Make that your axiom.

Again, how does this fit in with the overall truth that cards don't matter? It is, in fact, an essential part of it. As we saw above with Rube and will see again later on, you have to know enough about cards, the basics, to know that hands like ace-rag are not good hands in and of themselves. But can you win with them? Of course. You can win with rag-rag, you can win without even looking at your cards, if you're a sufficiently expert people player. You can also lose with pocket rockets (a pair of aces—I *love* poker talk!) if you're not.

Position

As with so many of the concepts reviewed above, this too is a very simple yet oft misunderstood notion. My seventeen-year-old brother-in-law (of dishes fame) was playing one of my computer poker games a while back and said, "You know, it's really great being last to decide what to do because you get to see what everyone else does first." Nuff said for now.

In fact, that's enough "vocabulary" for now. There is, of course, a whole slew of poker jargon that you will encounter in the following pages, but this is the main stuff. For the little stuff, use the glossary in Appendix 4.

Chapter 3

Games

There are lots of games called Poker, an infinite variety limited only by human imagination. Therefore, if your group is playing some variation that is not covered here, I'm not surprised. *My* groups play several variations not covered here. However, the varieties we will cover in this book are, I think, representative of the main ones in that they can be used to demonstrate basic principles that apply to all, or at least most, forms of poker. One restriction: I am not specifically including games with wild cards for the reason that wild-card games are *truly* of infinite variety and possibility. OK, I confess, there's another reason: I don't like wild-card games.

In the old days, when only five-card draw was being played in Gardena, a rather dreary little suburb of Los Angeles, it was virtually always played using one joker as the "bug." The bug is a limited wild card, being good only as an ace or to complete a straight or flush for high. (For low the joker was used as an all-purpose wild card.) In other words, K-K-6-6-Jo was two pair, kings and sixes with an ace, whereas A-A-6-6-Jo was a full house, aces over sixes. Similarly, A-Jo-K-Q-9 was simply a pair of aces, whereas A-K-Q-J-Jo was a straight. I liked that. The joker as bug created more action without utterly destroying the usual value of hands. I don't know if anyone plays five-card draw anymore—with or without the bug—but if you do, as far as I'm concerned the best book ever written on the subject is *Play Poker, Quit Work and Sleep till Noon* by John Fox. I recently noticed that this book is in its umpteenth printing, so someone, somewhere, must still be playing Old-Gardena-style five card draw (maybe in Gardena—I haven't been there in years).

However, since Mr. Fox has covered draw with the bug, and since I don't feel like pandering to deuces, one-eyed jacks, suicide kings, 3s and 9s (baseball!), low-hole-card and the like, we'll just have to settle for relatively standard poker variants (is there such a thing as a standard variant?), which, my polls show, are the most widely played among serious players in any case.

So, what makes a poker variant still poker? Well, in both the high and low varieties it is that a poker hand is made up of five cards, regardless of from how many—six, seven, ten, fifteen—cards one may be choosing those five. Next, the standard ranking of poker hands still applies: Royal flush, Straight flush, Four of a kind, Full House, Flush,[14] Straight, Three of a kind, Two pair, One pair, No pair. (Or in reverse for low variations.) Finally, they all share the one factor that makes all poker poker: the best hand doesn't necessarily take the pot. Following are the games we'll be seeing in this book.

High-only Poker

Hold'em: Former World Champion Doyle Brunson calls (no limit) Hold'em the "Cadillac" of poker games. Why he thinks Hold'em is only a sixth- or seventh-rate game, I don't know.[15] This game is so much the essence of modern poker that one's inclination is to write only about Hold'em. It is by far the ultimate game in terms of strategy, tactics, card reading, and people playing. In this chapter, however, we're only going to review the mechanics of the games and a few of their main characteristics. To wit: Each player receives two cards down, followed by a round of betting. Next comes the flop, which, as we have seen, is three cards dealt face up on the table, common to all players. The flop determines the actual and potential value of your hand.

[14.] Around the world many people play poker with a stripped deck, removing cards from the deck depending on the number of players. In these games, a flush beats a full house. For a further explanation and details of stripped-deck poker, see Appendix 3.
[15.] Dear General Motors: Just kidding. Can't you take a joke?

The flop is followed by a round of betting. Next comes the fourth common card, the turn, and a round of betting, followed by the fifth common card, the river, and the final round of betting. To make a hand, each player may use one, both, or neither of his hole cards in conjunction with the "board." Thus, three spades on the board plus two spades in your hand, or four spades on the board and one spade in your hand, make a flush. If the board itself is showing five spades and you think that that is probably the best hand, you can simply "play the board" and might, therefore, tie with other players who are also "playing the board."

Whoever came up with Hold'em—there are many stories—should have a statue erected in his or her honor. The game combines the best aspects of draw and stud while culling their shortcomings. The cards on the board give you general parameters of what hands are possible, while keeping the actual holdings of individual players—within those parameters—a secret. In a stud game you can usually tell, for example, who's got the pairs and who's got the come hand. In Hold'em you don't know who's got what except through a close monitoring of the players' behavior and betting, which is more like draw. But the board limits the possibilities, like stud, and, again like stud, the four betting rounds give you many opportunities to maneuver, parry and thrust, poke around for information, lay low, make a racket, leap out of the bushes as your quarry passes, change your mind, and stay in the bushes because your quarry turned out to be a bigger muthuh than you expected. What a game!

Omaha: The board cards and betting rounds are the same as Hold'em but each player receives *four* cards down to begin the game, and each player *must* use two cards from his hand with three from the board. Thus, four spades on the board and one spade in your hand no longer make a flush; you must use *two* cards from your hand. The *real* difference between Hold'em and Omaha, however, is that, in Omaha, if you're a couple hands off the nuts, you're usually dead. Consider this board:

A♣ 10♣ 5♥ 5♦ 6♣

In Hold'em if you have, say, Q♣J♣ you're going to win much more often than not (about 86 percent of the time in a show-down against four random opponents). In Omaha, however, if you don't have at least one of the possible full houses,[16] you're not usually even in the running. A hand like Q♣J♣ is frequently going to come in about fourth depending, of course, on how many players are left in the hand and how the betting is running (in this case, Q♣J♣ will only win about 41 percent of the time in a showdown with four random opponents). In short, Omaha is much, much more of a lottery than is Hold'em: you either hit the nuts, or close to the nuts, or you don't.

Seven card stud: All right, so anyone reading this book should know how seven card stud is dealt, yes? No? Well, just in case . . . Each player receives two cards down and one card up followed by a betting round. (Just so you don't think this is a complete waste of time, I'll bet many of you don't know that in hip poker lingo this first up-card is called the "door" card. It is "in the door.") Next, each player receives three more cards face up, after each one of which there is a betting round. (More jar-gon: these cards are, respectively, fourth street, fifth street, and sixth street.) The final card (seventh street or, sometimes, the *river* as in Hold'em) is then dealt face down. A complete hand, then, consists of three down cards and four up cards.

Seven stud is a much easier and less stressful game than Hold'em.[17] For one thing, the table is littered with exposed cards, which help you to determine not only your chances of hitting a

---

[16.] For you novices out there, the potential of the board as shown, in descending rank, is: four fives, aces full of fives, tens full of fives, sixes full of fives, fives full of aces, fives full of tens, fives full of sixes, club flushes, trip fives, two pair aces and tens, two pair aces and sixes, two pair aces and fives, [gap], two pair tens and sixes, two pair tens and fives, [gap] two pair sixes and fives, [gap], one pair of fives. The two-pair category has the gaps due to the possibility of pocket pairs (pocket kings and the fives on the board, for example) and all the incomplete hands—those of fewer than five cards—or one-pair hands are further graded by their kickers.
[17.] Bobby Baldwin, in his book, *Tales out of Tulsa,* recommends seven card stud over Hold'em for "beginners" for much these same reasons.

particular hand, but also your opponents' chances of having or hitting particular hands. Furthermore, if in Hold'em you have, say, a pair of queens (four titties!) in the pocket against an opponent's pocket pair of aces (pocket rockets, remember?), well, you're dead unless you flop a set and your opponent doesn't. Your only other outs are fluke hands like 8-9-10-J on the board, or four to a flush, the fifth of which you have and your pocket-rockets opposition has not.

Now, imagine a seven card stud hand in which your oppo nent has a pair of aces and you have a pair of queens, say, on fourth street. You can still hit two pair and beat the aces! You're a dog but not by nearly so much. Say it's sixth street and you still have only the queens and you figure your opposition still has only the aces. If you can determine from the plethora of exposed cards that most of your opponent's two-pair cards are dead, whereas your two-pair cards are mostly live, you're still very much in the running!

The same isn't true in Hold'em. If another pair hits, then it hits you both: you make queens up against your opponent's aces up. If you're not inclined to take my word for this (and why should you be?) then here are the stats: in Hold'em your four titties against pocket rockets are *at best* a 4.2-to-1 dog, and you have virtually no room to maneuver. In seven card stud, you are only about a 2-to-1 dog at the outset, and you have the added possibility of perhaps being able to *convince* your opponent that you have more than just the queens. Thus, you can hit and win, or you can bluff and win. It's really, really tough to bluff out a player with pocket rockets in Hold'em, whereas finishing a seven card stud hand with only a pair of aces is weak enough to be bluffable.

High-Low Poker

High-low, split-pot poker is the name of the game in home games, which is both good and bad as we will see later. High-low poker in casinos and public card rooms is a total woft, if you want my opinion.[18] As to ranking of hands, in all cases herein, unless otherwise noted, the "low" in high-low poker will imply the use of the *wheel* as described in Chapter 2. In the high-low category we have:

Seven card stud: The mechanics of this are, of course, the same as for seven card stud high: a player ends up with three cards down and four cards up. The difference is that now you have flexibility. A starting hand like [A♥ 2♥] 3♥ has tremendous potential both ways. There are dangers, however. If you start out in high-only with [K♠ K♦] 10♥, you're sitting pretty strong. In high-low you could be getting nicely sucked into a trap. In pot-limit or no limit high-low, I usually wouldn't even play such a hand. More later.

Seven card stud, buy the deck: This is a popular variant in home games and works like this: Each player receives two down cards. The dealer then turns up the next card, face up on the table. The player to the dealer's immediate left then has the option of taking that card or of taking the next (unknown) card off the deck. In this version, there is a price to be paid if the player opts not to take the face-up card: he must pay a predetermined amount to receive the next card from the deck. If the player does take the face-up card, the dealer then turns up another card, and it is now the second player's turn to decide whether or not to take it or to pay for a card off the deck. If the first player does not take the face-up card, he pays, is dealt the next card off the deck, and the face-up card remains for the subsequent players either to take or pay not to take. There are two main differences between this and "standard" seven card stud high-low: (a) the winning hands tend to be much better for both high and low since you have a "choice" of cards, and (b) pots

---

[18.] As to whether or not all the high-low games in casinos are a woft, I need in fairness to say that, though I know there are many people who agree with me, in truth, (1) I also know there are a lot of people who would disagree with me, especially where the higher-limit games are concerned, and (2) I haven't bothered to check out those higher limit games, the lower-limit games being such a bore that I have been put off doing so. (Woft—Waste of F—ing Time.)

can reach astronomical proportions, even in a relatively low-limit game, due to each player's "buying" an alternative card each step of the way. (In the limit game described in this book, the purchase price is equal to the betting limit at that round of play; therefore, each "buy" is equal to an additional bet.) Naturally, this is a positional game: if you're going low you want ideally to be behind a couple of players who are going high and who will, therefore, be refusing low face-up cards, and vice-versa.

Twists in high-low

As explained in Chapter 2, twists are extra cards that a player can opt, and pay, to receive after the "standard" hand has been dealt. The games mentioned here with twists are:

Five card stud high-low: Once upon not so many decades ago, standard five card stud was one of, if not *the,* most popular variation of poker. It seems what happened is that everyone learned to play it—it is really a very simple and straightforward game—and it became a bore. As I'm sure everyone knows, it is dealt as: one card down and one card up followed by a betting round, then three cards face up, each followed by a betting round. Five card stud low is even more of a bore, to the point that it is commonly known as "sudden death"—one bad card and you're out of there. Five card stud high-low, however, begins to show some interesting possibilities. With the addition of a twist, it is a very good game, and with the addition of a reversible twist it is a great game. At the end of the standard deal, a player may opt to throw one of his cards in exchange for another. In most cases cited in this book, this twist is paid for at the rate of the betting limit for that round, usually $5. Furthermore, when using the reversible twist, if the player is throwing a face-up card, he may opt to turn up his hole card and take the twist down. This is great for causing confusion and uncertainty. It also builds pots as there is, of course, a betting round after the twist.

English Stud: This is a six-card stud game with two paid-for twists. Each player receives two cards down and one card up, followed by a betting round. Each player then receives three more cards face up, each one followed by a betting round. The twists are "bought" in standard style, one at a time, with each twist followed by a betting round. Now, *this* is a pot-builder! If you figure that each active player is (1) paying a "bet" to receive a twist then (2) betting after receiving the twist, you can see that a lot of dough is flowing into the pot. (English stud is also sometimes played "buy the deck" as described under **seven stud, buy the deck,** above. Big pots.)

Spit-buy: You may recall a game called spit-in-the-ocean, which was a draw game with a wild common card. Well, this game is played like that except that the common card is not wild, it is simply common, and it is high-low with a paid-for twist. Each player receives four cards face down, followed by a round of betting. Everyone's common fifth card is then turned face up on the table, followed by another round of betting. Each player may then discard and draw up to three cards, followed by still another round of betting. At this point, those wishing to buy a twist may do so. The receipt of the twist is followed by yet another round of betting.

The advantages of this game over straight high-low draw are, clearly: (1) four betting rounds instead of two and (2) much looser play due to the addition of the twist. For the inexperienced player, however, it can be dangerous in that hands tend to be *much* better and more hotly contested than in standard five draw. The reasons for this are simple, but not always obvious: (1) Say a 3 turns up as the common card. *All* low hands now have a three. In standard draw, that 3 would go into one hand, and you would have to catch one of the remaining three 3s to make your hand. (2) If that 3 is the, say, 3♥, and it makes you a straight, it can *simultaneously* make someone else a heart flush, or full house, or four 3s, to beat you. In standard draw, that 3♥ would be yours and yours alone, making four 3s impossible, a full house of 3s unlikely, and leaving one less heart for a potential heart flush to catch. (3) If the common card is higher than a 7, then all low players (usually) are playing a four-card game.

Say the common card is a king. It is superfluous to any low hand, and you are now contesting the best (lowest) four cards. In four cards, with the best hand being 4-3-2-A, 6-5 is a dog, 7-low is almost unplayable. (On the other hand, I've won low in this game with a pair, and I've won high with no pair by backing in the right way or bluffing out the competition.)

Model Games

For our basic setup in the following chapters, we're going to consider two home-style games.

The Limit Game

Ante: Dealer antes $5.

Limits: $2 progressive, capped at $5 in the final betting rounds.

Raises: Three per betting round.

High-Low: Wheel low, chip declare, followed by a betting round.

Twists: Paid for at $5 each; a betting round after each twist.

Average wins and losses: ± $400.

Characteristic: Very loose, typically a minimum of six first-round callers out of eight players.

The Pot-Limit Game

Ante: Dealer antes $2.

Limit: Equal to the pot (bet plus call).

Raises: Unlimited to all-in (table stakes).

High-Low: Wheel low, chip declare, no betting round after the declare.

Twists: Free. Betting round after each twist.

Average wins and losses: ± $2,000.

Characteristic: Medium loose, typically three or first-round callers out of seven players.

The people involved in both games are composites of all the people I've ever played poker with. Although every hand or situation described has actually occurred and is taken from some twenty years of notes, names, dates, and venues have been changed to protect the foolish. (I do occasionally use hypothetical examples, but these are identified as such.) Where *I* have been the fool, however, I take the brunt and confess all. Since the characters are composites, three hands attributed to "Jack," for example, actually may have happened with three different people, but people who fit the "Jack" mold. Thus, if you recognize yourself among the cast of poker players, it is due only to the fact that the human experience, especially the human poker experience, is so incredibly standardized. If you recognize yourself in a good light, as one of the winning players, then hooray! If you recognize yourself as one of the not-so-good, losing, players, then hooray! for you, too—you're apparently trying to improve your game or you wouldn't be reading a poker book.

Quite often I'll mention games, hands, and situations that happened in casinos or public card rooms. These, too, all happened exactly as told but, again, I've changed names and some venues. As we'll see later, casino, or "public," poker is *very* different from the typical home, or "private," game, even a high-stake private game. It can best be described as the ultimate poker experience, a poker feeding frenzy that I, who have been both minnow and shark, particularly enjoy—in shark mode, that is; being the minnow is only good as a learning experience, and that's stretching it. However, our main thrust here is toward the home player, which means that the casino examples I have chosen to use are those that, I hope, will be of learning benefit even to someone who is never likely to set foot inside a casino poker room. On the other hand, Chapter 9 takes on public poker for its own sake and, therefore, should be of use to those players who do play or would like to play in casinos or card rooms.

Chapter 4

Know Thyself

We'll start with our two home games. Each game has one sucker, I mean asset, who basically finances the game. One such asset has been showing up at the limit game every week for ten years or so and, week in week out, writing a check for four or five hundred dollars. This is Harry. The other asset, in the pot-limit game, has been showing up every week for twenty years and, week in week out, writing a check for two or three *thousand* dollars. This is Clarence. God bless their masochistic souls, because both games would probably fold up without them, but what the hell are they doing?

Some years ago I got into a game that was over my head. Pay heed: whoever you are and however good you are, there is someone out there who is better. We'll talk more about this later, but the point here is this: I played two times with this group. The first time, I got my butt kicked up one side. The second time, I got it kicked down the other—and that was it; I didn't stick around for more. I saw that these gentlemen were looking for a patsy, some new blood to suck, and it wasn't going to be mine.

Please don't be the sort of player whose ego gets hold of him: "I'm good and I can beat these guys no matter how long it takes." Learn to know when you are outclassed or overmatched. It's nothing to be ashamed of. If you can afford to "take lessons" from a situation like this, fine. Do it and learn, then get out. But (1) most of us are not in that category, (2) you won't have to go looking for it; if you're going to play poker seriously it will happen to you, and (3) most of us don't learn very well while our money is being sucked up by some sharp.

So, what are Harry and Clarence doing in those games, week after week, year after year? Why don't they quit? Enjoying themselves? Companionship? Male camaraderie? Sure, they win every once in a while, which only gives them the spark to keep on losing. Harry and Clarence are both rich, or at least sufficiently well-off that they don't have to worry about their poker losses. And outside of the poker games they seem like reasonable, likable fellows, though both at times could be classified in a mild-oddball category. Well, one thing they are doing is buying "friendship." It's very much like a colleague who invites you and six others for beers every Tuesday after work and *always* pays. After a few weeks of this you begin to wonder if the guy has a problem. In fact, everyone else in those poker games thinks Harry and Clarence are patsies, jerks, suckers, wimps. When the assets are absent from the games, the rest of the players make nasty jokes and snide remarks about what chumps they are.

This is not exactly what Harry and Clarence have in mind, I'm sure. Or maybe it is. Perhaps if poker didn't exist Harry and Clarence would be having once-a-week sessions with Wanda the Whip Lady. I don't know. But from my point of view, I don't care if you play for thousands or if you play for nickels, why sit there and lose? Why play the patsy? I don't play poker, or backgammon, or softball, or tiddlywinks to lose. Should you? (Actually, I did do this when I was living in England and started playing squash with a friend of mine. He thrashed me for six months till I finally started beating him occasionally. But that was okay. I knew I was going to get thrashed; there were no egos involved; there was no money involved, I learned the game, and it was good exercise—though doctors have divergent opinions about this where squash is concerned. Best of all, the squash club had a pub in it where we could quickly replenish the liquids lost during the game. After six months, I started playing with other people I could beat, though I kept up my "lessons" with my friend.)

A case in point, that is of butting one's head against superior play, involves our next protagonist in the limit game, Jack. A fifty-something, early-retired publishing executive, Jack has always thought of himself as a heck of a poker player. In fact,

Jack tends to go through cycles in which he sometimes is pretty good—not great, but pretty good—and at other times, he is so predictable he can be twisted around your pinkie. See, Jack has played a lot of poker, though in limited circumstances, has read a lot of poker books, and applies what he has learned with an obsessive precision. So what's wrong? He doesn't vary his methods, nor does he adapt himself to changing situations, i.e., loose games, tight games, better players, worse players, whatever. His tactics and style are always the same. Once you become predictable in poker, it's all over. Better hang up your visor and your diamond stick pin and take up crochet.

Another problem with Jack is that he has the ego problem mentioned above: he refuses to believe that he is simply being outplayed. Some years ago I played regularly in the limit game, but I had to give it up when I moved out of town. I used to beat Jack's pants off all the time, but he was good enough to withstand that and still win money from the other players. He was sort of the number two in the game. His big problem was that he was in the ego-hold category mentioned above and insisted regularly on playing me heads-up. The game would break up at whatever hour, and Jack would say, "Well, Dave, looks like it's you and me," when he should have said, "I guess I'll go home to bed." I would say "Sure" and fleece him for a bundle. Once, I repeat, once, in two years he actually beat me doing this, and he crowed about it for weeks.

I moved away and was gone for about six years, and Jack became number one. Big frog. I then moved back into town, got into the game again, and started playing regularly. All of a sudden, Jack wasn't winning anymore, and he couldn't figure out why. In a game soon after my return, I had told him why. He was losing and lamenting his fate, and I just laughed and said, "Jack, you can't win if I'm playing. You know that." Unfortunately for him, his ego prevents him from heeding remarks like that; he doesn't believe it, won't believe it, in fact, it upsets him for a while and he plays worse, which is why I said it in the first place.

Believe it. I asked earlier if you wanted to make money playing poker. If that's what you want, then don't stick around in games with better players—unless you want lessons and can afford to go through the learning curve because it's going to cost. Be humble, to yourself, at least, if you can't be humble outwardly. The day you start thinking you're the world's greatest poker player, someone is going to slap you down. Be on the lookout. Have the courage to admit to yourself when you're out of your league. I just read a book that included various interviews with Amarillo Slim. During one interview he looked around, pointed someone out and said, "I'd never want to play stud with *him*." So even a world-famous pro like Amarillo Slim watches out for people who can beat him; it's no admission of weakness if you do the same—it's just smart. A warrior recognizes a worthy opponent—and a superior opponent. The warrior can learn from a superior opponent—or die. He who fights and runs away . . .

This doesn't mean that if you're a beginner you must start off winning right away or give it up. If you're a beginner, unless you're one in a million or some sort of poker prodigy, you're going to start off losing. So, what do you do? Make sure you've got enough playing money to pay your way through the learning curve. Start off in low-stake games that won't break you your first time out, or your first twenty times out.

How do you know whether you're losing because you're a beginner, or whether you're losing because you're a putz? You'll know, if you're objective and truthful to yourself. Are you getting better? Are you losing less and less or winning occasionally? Does a little voice start saying, "You've seen that before and this is how to handle it"? Is the little voice starting to be right? When I say "beginner" I mean a beginner at serious poker. One may have been playing recreational poker for a long time, but there is a big difference between that and seriously playing poker to win money.

The truth is that millions of people play recreational poker for nickels. They win or lose ten dollars and don't care; it was entertainment. They think poker is gambling and depends on the cards you get, sort of like picking a winning lottery number—

pure luck. The serious poker player knows that luck has absolutely nothing to do with it. The guy who loses week after week for five years or twenty years is not unlucky; he is a bad player. If poker were pure chance, then in a, say, eight-handed game over X number of years, each player would win one-eighth of the time, and the profits and losses would be evenly spread. But that doesn't happen.

What happens in a typical eight-handed home game is that one or two guys will win consistently year after year, three to five guys will bounce around between even and up or down a little, and one or two guys will bear the brunt. This will vary somewhat depending upon how good (and bloodthirsty) the good players are and how bad the bad players are. The fact is, however, that most medium- to high-stake home games depend on one or two assets like Harry and Clarence, with their money circulating through the so-so players and going home for keeps with the good players. If Harry or Clarence moves out of town, the game usually breaks up because now it's the so-so players who will start financing the game, and they may or may not put up with that for long.

It takes a combination of three factors to make an "asset": (1) he must be a bad poker player; (2) he must have the financial resources to withstand the constant losses; and (3) he must have the proper psychological make-up to keep coming back for a thrashing week after week, month after month, year after year. Any two of these traits are not sufficient to make an "asset." He must have all three. It is my experience that the most common mind-set for the loser to withstand his thrashings is denial. He doesn't admit to himself what's happening, which is why, of course, some of us read poker books and study and learn to become good players: so we can go home with bad players' money.

This doesn't mean that the skillful, even the great, player can't lose. You can win the World Series of Poker one day and sit down and lose your pants the next. Why? Well, for a number of reasons we'll discuss later, but one of those reasons is luck.

Luck? I confess, I had to say "luck" to get your attention; the truth is that there is no such thing. That which we normally call good or bad "luck" in gambling is actually just the favorable (to us) or unfavorable (to us) outcome of probability. How we feel about the result determines whether that result was "lucky" or "unlucky." The odds against your winning most state lotteries are about 14 million to one. The odds against your dying in an air crash are about 14 million to one. If you win a state lottery, you've been very lucky. If you die in an air crash, you've been very unlucky. (This is one reason I'm reluctant to play lotteries: how can I root for a 14-million-to-one shot to happen to me and then get on an airplane?) Besides, in poker, good and bad luck tend to happen simultaneously. Just the other day I was rivered— long-shot rivered—out of a $3,000 pot. That was very unlucky. Oddly enough, the guy who rivered me thought it was exceedingly lucky.

In any case, both the actual and illusory presence of "luck" in poker is one factor that reinforces the "denial" of the bad player mentioned above. It can even be used as an excuse by normally good or solid players to explain their losses. They can blame it on luck, when, in fact, what caused the losses was bad play or stupidity, or both.

Let's say you're playing Hold'em, pot limit. You have A♥Q♥, and the board shows 3♠ K♥ J♥ 5♥. You have the nuts, the ace-high heart flush, with one card to come. There's $3,000 in the pot and that's what you bet. Not only is that the remainder of your entire stake in the game, it's all the money you have. If you lose that, you'll be broke for the next thirty days and borrowing money to pay the rent. But you have a sure thing, right? Hold on. Your one remaining opponent is Clarence, and Clarence is the guy who has been losing every week for twenty years. Clarence has stuck in there to this point with a 5-3 off-suit. He shouldn't be in there in the first place but there he is—it's Clarence after all—and now he has two pair, 5s and 3s.

Even Clarence must read you for the flush, or perhaps he thinks you're bluffing. Whatever Clarence's tortured mind is conjuring in terms of convoluted rationale, he calls and you are now shaking in your boots. You figure what Clarence is calling on and you know that there are only four cards in the deck, two 3s and two 5s, which can help him. That means the odds are in your favor to win by at least a ten to one margin. So why are you, or should you be, quaking in your boots? Because you have made a big mistake. You have committed the gambler's mortal sin: you have bet *all* your money.

The bet was sound, the bet was great: ten to one in your favor to win. The Bank of England would back that bet—if it didn't represent *all* the bank's money. And just as surely as God made disposable diapers, one time in eleven you are going to lose that bet. It could be this time. It *is* this time! A three comes up on the river, and you are broke, busted, gone, out of there. Clarence, so he doesn't have to admit to having called a ten-to-one bet at two-to-one odds, will probably say something like, "I called because I thought you were bluffing, then my 3 came up. How about that?" Fine. Clarence, in coming weeks, and very likely later that same game, will lose all that money back, and more. But it's too late for you. You're gone.

Bad luck. Clarence drew out on you, Clarence rivered you. Baloney. Given the opportunity, you will be drawn out on a precisely calculable percentage of times. It is indeed what we call "bad luck" that Clarence happened to hit when you had the whole month's family budget in the pot, or is it? If you *know* that Clarence is going to make that hand one in eleven times, then you shouldn't be surprised when it happens! Maybe you set yourself up to be "unlucky" by putting all your money in the pot. Moral: Even at odds of ten-to-one in your favor, or a hundred-to-one in your favor, if you bet *all* your money *all* the time, you will lose *all* your money. And you will call it bad luck.

So, say you, I'm only going to play in limit games; no pot limit or no limit for me. That might be a good idea, but beware. In a limit game the odds often favor making, for example, Clarence's call.

Example: same Hold'em cards as above.

There are eight players in your game. Each player antes one dollar.

Pot: $8

First round bet is five dollars. Seven callers to you (this isn't Vegas, after all, and to have nearly everyone call in Hold'em before the flop in a private game is very common). You raise with ace-queen suited, seven callers:

Pot: $88

Second round bet (the flop) is also five dollars. Seven checks to you. You bet (you've got four to the nut flush). Four callers.

Pot: $113

Third round bet (the turn) is ten dollars. Four checks to you. You've hit the nut flush. You bet. Three people fold and . . . there sits Clarence. Okay, so Clarence still shouldn't be in there with his 5-3 off-suit even in a limit game, but he is. And now he has a ten-to-one draw at simple pot odds of eleven-to-one. Even Clarence can't be faulted for calling that bet at that point.

If you think that (1) all poker players read poker books and/or (2) those who read them pay attention and heed the advice in those books, you are dead wrong. So, if you are saying, "Clarence wouldn't have called with a 5-3 off-suit, and, even if he had, he wouldn't have called on the flop with a pair of threes," oh yes he—representing all the Clarences of the world— would, and does, all the time. He may even have *raised* that pair of threes. Remember who Clarence is? Fact, often overlooked: Even though Clarence has lost a hundred thousand a year for twenty years (that, my friends, is two million dollars) and is a total poker putz, he could easily bust you in any given hand. Not because he is any good, but simply because even a con- gested pig can stumble upon a truffle. And if you've shown up at that game with the mortgage money when it happens . . . You'll call it bad luck.

Probability—odds—defines what should happen over the long haul, the *infinitely* long haul. Appendix 1 reports and ana- lyzes statistics from million-hand runs of cards. A million hands is a lot. If you played poker in a fast-paced casino game ten hours a day, seven days a week for about seven years, you would have seen around a million hands. But even a million hands doesn't approach infinity, and more importantly, inherent in the waxing and waning of large numbers are streaks. In one million-hand Hold'em run in which I pitted AA against random hands, there was one streak of thirty-four hands during which the pocket rockets didn't win a thing. Now, you should hold AA in Hold'em about once in 220 hands, and even in a casino game it would take you about six hours of play to get that many hands. So let's say you sit down feeling tight, you're going to sit there and wait to get AA and you'll fold everything else. (I know, sitting down only to play pocket rockets is a little far fetched, but bear with me.) First of all, statistically you're only going to play one hand about every twenty-five rounds (in a nine-handed game), which in a $10-$20 game is going to cost you $375 in blinds. Second, you could conceivably win zilch with your pocket rockets over thirty-four attempts, or 850 rounds, which is about eight days of twenty-four hour play. Would this be bad luck? You're damn right it would be, given what we define as luck. On the other hand, it's just numbers, lots and lots of numbers.

I just read a book by a man who says he gave up his career as a professional poker player, stumbled away from the table in an incredulous stupor never to return, when he was busted out of a tournament on a four-to-one shot. Firstly, he hadn't been; he'd been busted out on less than a *two*-to-one shot, which are precisely the odds his opponent got when he called the author's bet. Secondly, even were his calculation correct, you're *going to lose* to a four-to-one shot, well, *one out of five times,* for Pete's sake! If you're going to get all twitterpated when you lose against the odds, you're in the wrong game.

Let's put it in nonpoker terms: If your great-uncle Albert borrows the car once a week to go to church and totals it one out of every five weeks (4 to 1 he won't total it), you're going to think this is a pretty high-frequency event. How about if he only totals the car one out of every twelve weeks (11 to 1 he won't total it)? You're still going to look for any excuse not to lend Uncle Albert the car. So why would you think that losing a poker hand that you should win four out of five times, or eleven out of twelve times, is practically impossible? But most poker players think that way: some lucky, low-down, amateur, scum-sucking, yellow-bellied, know-nothing took my God-given, 11-to-1 pot away by beating me on a gutshot; that's why I'm broke this month. I've heard so many of these "bad beat" stories that perhaps I should compile them into a "Poker Whiner's Anthology." The reply to the whining gambler is: you're not broke because the scum-sucking know-nothing got lucky; you're broke because you got stupid and put all your money on the table.

Here's a little chart to make this clearer. We'll stipulate that you have $100 to your name. There are twelve people standing in line in front of you, each one willing to give you even-money on a bet with the odds 11 to 1 in your favor, provided that *every time* you must bet *all* your money. Here's what happens:

First time:	You bet $100.	You win.	You have $200.
Second time:	You bet $200.	You win.	You have $400.
Third time:	You bet $400.	You win.	You have $800.
Fourth time:	You bet $800.	You win.	You have $1,600.
Fifth time:	You bet $1,600.	You win.	You have $3,200.
Sixth time:	You bet $3,200.	You win.	You have $6,400.
Seventh time:	You bet $6,400.	You win.	You have $12,800.
Eighth time:	You bet $12,800.	You win.	You have $25,600.
Ninth time:	You bet $25,600.	You win.	You have $51,200.
Tenth time:	You bet $51,200.	You win.	You have $102,400.
Eleventh time:	You bet $102,400.	You win.	You have $204,800.
Twelfth time:	You bet $204,800.	You lose.	You have zip.
			You're broke.

Now, clearly, this is over simplified. You could lose on the first bet, or you could play a hundred times without losing (although this isn't very likely). But you *will* lose all your money eventually. Just remember Uncle Albert: When he takes your car, it's a write-off for sure. Maybe not this week or next, but in the long run it is a certainty.

Now let's see what happens if, each time, you bet only 84 percent[19] of your capital (starting with $100 to your name).

First time:	You bet $84.	You win.	You have $184.
Second time:	You bet $154.56.	You win.	You have $338.56.
Third time:	You bet $284.39.	You win.	You have $622.95.
Fourth time:	You bet $523.28.	You win.	You have $1,146.23.
Fifth time:	You bet $962.83.	You win.	You have $2,109.06.
Sixth time:	You bet $1771.61.	You win.	You have $3,880.67.
Seventh time:	You bet $3,259.76.	You win.	You have $7,104.44.
Eighth time:	You bet $5,997.97.	You win.	You have $13,138.40.
Ninth time:	You bet $11,036.26.	You win.	You have $24,174.66.
Tenth time:	You bet $20,306.72.	You win.	You have $44,481.38.
Eleventh time:	You bet $37,364.36.	You win.	You have $81,845.73.
Twelfth time:	You bet $68,750.42.	You lose.	You have $13,095.32.

See? You don't have to be a miser, betting only, say, 10 percent of your money each time. As long as you don't bet it *all,* you will end up with a profit. (By the way, in either chart—bet all or bet 84 percent—it doesn't matter at which stage you lose, the results will be the same: Zero in your pocket, or $13,095.32 in your pocket.) A further oversimplification of the chart is that after the eleventh bet, you had eighty-one grand in your pocket and your wife thought you were a hero. After the twelfth bet, it's going to be tough to explain to her that because you've been so smart and careful you now have only thirteen grand in your pocket. If she's as smart as you are (in fact, she's probably smarter because *you're* the gambler) she'll understand.

In this vein, the other night we were playing seven stud high

---

[19] In this scenario, 84 percent gives optimum results.

low. My first four cards are A♥ 2♥ 4♥ 6♥—a dream come true! There are two low cards showing around the table and one heart, leaving me 19 cards to hit one way (to a 7 or better) or the other (ace-high flush), or both, with three cards to come. I'm sitting there taking that pot to the bank, just plotting and scheming to build it to maximum greed-assuaging levels. To make a sad story short, my next three cards are two black jacks and a king of diamonds—a total bust. Makes you want to cry, but—chin up! stiff upper lip!—there's more to come.

In a string beginning a few minutes later, I was rivered in four consecutive hands (God's truth). I had the nuts, big nuts—straights and flushes—through the penultimate card. The last card got me four times in a row. I experienced some inner turmoil. In other words, now I was pissed. (If there are any Brits reading this, pissed in the U.S. means angry, not drunk.) I don't care who you are, unless you are John Finn, who doesn't exist any more than any other cartoon superheroes exist, getting rivered four hands in a row is upsetting. I know—because I've just been preaching to you—I could theoretically get rivered *hundreds* of times in a row, but combined with the four-low-hearts disappointment, this was more than my frail human constitution could bear and—I did let off a little steam. But, it was a limit game, and these things happen. I took stock and calmed down. I was still winning, a lot, and within half an hour or so, I had won back all the damage done in those four hands. Had I been playing with the mortgage money, I may not have been able to calm down sufficiently to resume winning play. Had I been playing with the mortgage money and *losing,* those four hands may have rattled my judgment so much that I would have lost the rest. In the biz, this is called "going on tilt," and it happens to the best. (Get yourself in a game with a big-time poker player on tilt, and you can reap and reap till the silo is overflowing.)

This is one of the problems of trying to make a living exclusively at poker: you are *always* playing with the mortgage money, or the car-payment money, or the milk money, or all three. If you lose you're up a creek, constantly at risk of getting nervous and upset and going on tilt. (My Dad put it more simply, he said, "A scared man can't win," and that's the truth.) You need to have, relative to each person's requirements, a *lot* of money behind you in order to withstand a bad night, or a bad week, or a bad month, just as if you were going into business for yourself, which, in fact, you are. If you supply widgets to Ford Motor Company and they shut down for a month due to a strike, you'd better have the reserves to withstand it. In poker, if Texas Tom, or Lady Luck, comes into town and beats your socks off for a month, you'd better have the reserves to withstand it. But, in widgets or poker, if you have to get into the reserves too long or too often, you may be in the wrong business.

Anyone who is going to count on poker as his sole or major source of income, had better have two years' reserves behind him, plus the capital he's going to invest in poker. You need one year's reserves to withstand a losing year at poker and a second year's reserves to see you through the process of finding something else to do. (Remember, this doesn't apply to those who have a job or other income that provides enough extra to invest in poker. This applies to those who plan to make poker their "sole or major source of income." Even so, you need to feel assured that your income can both support you and absorb your poker losses. If you start dipping into the family budget to cover poker, you'll be at risk just as if poker were your only source of income.)

Two years' reserves, plus poker capital? Impossible, you say. Damn near, I say. Which is fine with me. Just about every pro or aspiring pro out there is going to sit down and play without anything like the reserves, the intellectual and emotional comfort, he should have. When he wins, he'll pay the bills. When he loses, he'll borrow money. Then, when he wins he'll have to pay his debts and still won't be able to pay the bills, or vice versa, and so on. When he gets rivered four hands in a row he won't know what planet he's on. Why is this fine with me? Because one day I'll be sitting at his table, he'll be on full tilt, and shortly thereafter I'll take the family to the Caribbean on his money. And if it's not me, it will be someone else. Count on it.

Johnny Moss, one of the most famous poker players of all time, has said that he never touches his wife's money—money that, of course, he had won and, by virtue of which made her a millionaire.[20] He himself, he says, is broke as often as not and that's the way he wants it. No matter what his misadventures at poker, his family won't suffer. Whenever he sits down to play, he is tranquil in that knowledge. Are you a much better player than Johnny Moss? Are you one of those who doesn't need that kind of intellectual tranquillity to play good poker? How nice; I, or someone else, will send you a postcard from the Caribbean.

Just because you're a rotten poker player today, doesn't mean you can't improve. The Clarences and Harrys of this world make it seem that there is no way out, that winning at poker is some sort of knack that one must be born with. Not so. The Clarences and Harrys, for reasons of their own, either don't try or are interpersonally challenged, which is politically correct lingo meaning "assholes." A number of years ago a good friend of mine decided he wanted to be a poker player. He was hopeless, couldn't poker his way out of a wet box of cards. After he had lost his shirt week after week for a number of weeks, I said, "Tim, you're hopeless." He said, "Dave, why don't you help me?"

Whoa! Existential crisis! He had just asked me to commit the number one serious-poker-player's no-no, which is to help anyone else on the planet become a better poker player. Well, he was a good friend, was playing for serious money, which meant he could get hurt, and, in the end, I confess, I'm not always so Machiavellian as I let on. I took him under my wing. That was a number of years ago, and now I sometimes regret it, although not really. Old Tim became a competent, winning poker player, and when I say, "I sometimes regret it," I mean that he has become a decent opponent who, on occasion, can be a pain in the neck. When I say, "although not really," I mean that I have a hidden little spot of teacher's pride that comes through even though he's winning money from the game that I could be winning,

[20] In *Fast Company.*

and even when, occasionally, he beats me out of a pot.

I might feel worse (or better?) about this but for two factors: although Tim is far better than he used to be, he appears to have reached a plateau and to have abandoned the effort to get any better, and he doesn't have the killer instinct required to be a really good player. Had Tim become my nemesis, it would have served me right for having committed the ultimate no-no. As it is, I can take satisfaction in that, through my tutelage, he is holding his own—and not causing me any great difficulty. The point here is that Tim was at one time one of the worst poker players imaginable—a potential Clarence or Harry—and he got better because he wanted to and worked at it.

Killer instinct. Now there's a phrase to cause shivers. It's used about boxers all the time and simply means that you must want to win no matter who or how much you have to hurt. But even this concept is not as terrible as it seems. For me, it only applies while sitting at the poker table and justly so: the other players at the table are trying to take *my* money just as much as I'm trying to take theirs. When an adult sits down at a poker table, there is but one basic, common understanding: no holds barred, except cheating of course. Away from the table it is sometimes a different matter. I have been known, as in Tim's case, to try to discourage hopeless cases from playing if I know they're getting hurt. What?

My dear reader, this is a book about how to be a winner at poker—*realistically*—as a happy, healthy and whole human being, and not in the fashion of some cartoon poker superhero. We are not machines; we don't need to pretend to be machines to make lots of money playing poker, and to aspire to be a machine is not only ridiculous, it is unachievable. Most of us, as human beings, need to feel good about ourselves, and I, for one, in certain limited circumstances, will trade the potential winnings I could realize from a person for the clear conscience of knowing that I've done the right thing by at least trying to discourage him from playing. I have a set of rules about this, and there's no point in going into them here. You need your own set of rules to fit your own personality. I will mention one rule, just so you don't think I'm a wimp: Although I may try to dissuade someone from playing, if he does end up sitting down to play, then it's no holds barred, and, worse, I will use what I know about that person as a friend against him. After all, if he sat down, he's trying to take my money. As for Clarence and Harry, no mercy; they are not my friends, they apparently can afford it, and if they want to throw away money every week, I'm there with welcoming wallet. I'm sure you've heard, "Don't play poker with strangers." Hell, I *love* playing poker with strangers. It's lucrative and impersonal. My advice would be: "Don't play poker with friends." Unless you're playing for very low stakes or all your friends are rich, then don't try to make money playing poker with friends. Friends are worth more—a lot more—than money, and, besides, trying to win money off them will muddy up your conscience and keep you from playing your best game. David Spanier, a renowned journalist, author, and poker player has said that there is one thing worse than winning money from friends and that is *losing* money to friends! I agree. It's better just to avoid the issue all together.

Now, how do you justify this and keep winning week after week in that private, "friendly" game? This is not as nebulous as it seems. Many or most people who play poker regularly in private games, myself included, have been playing with the same guys for years or even decades. You know them; you know what they do for a living; you know about how much money they make; you may even know their families. You like them, or you don't like them; you exchange war stories from the work and family fronts, and you talk politics, economics, and world affairs. But—if the stakes of the game are of the "someone can lose more than he would really like to" variety—you probably don't socialize much outside the game.

There's kind of a code, an understood agreement here, that develops among the players in a regular game. Part of this comes from within the person who considers himself to be a "poker player for serious stakes," and who, in turn, recognizes that the others in the poker group consider themselves as such. Therefore, a mutual understanding develops that the players are "poker friends." Occasionally, an outside-the-game friendship will develop, but this is rare, and usually there is still the understanding that "we're poker players so, at the table, bet 'em up."

Every once in a while, a friend—a regular, nonpoker friend—who knows my penchant for poker will try to talk me into playing. I don't do it. I would either have to throw the game or bust him, and I wouldn't want to do either. If you read fifty poker books or talk to a thousand serious players, you will be told, in one form or another, that you can play poker for entertainment or you can play poker for money, but you can't do both. Imagine, say, Steffi Graf runs into a childhood friend who says "Come on, let's play some tennis!" Well, she's either going to have to humiliate her friend or condescend and throw the game, and she will probably just decline. Once you start doing something seriously, you are really no longer in a position to do it frivolously. *You are no longer in a position to do it at all, except with others who are doing it seriously.* In the old days, sure, I played "friendly games of poker" with the boys. But not any more. There are a thousand "buts," "ifs," and "well, under these circumstanceses" that I could talk about, but you get the point. There are friends that you play serious poker with and friends you don't. There are friends I would play poker with and to whom I would then suggest we stop if they were getting hurt. There are others—not friends—who I would play poker with and bust into a homeless shelter with no mercy. Why? Because I know they feel the same way about me. One of the fairest-minded (at least by reputation; I never knew him) and most highly skilled card players and card writers of all times was the late John Scarne, and he said repeatedly that if you want to play a friendly game of cards, don't play poker, certainly not for serious stakes. Poker is about money and always has been, and it is not friendly by nature.

One of the primary virtues of the good poker player is patience. Sometimes this need for patience—and the self discipline necessary to maintain it—is positively monumental. My all time record during the five-draw days in Gardena was *four hours* of throwing in hand after hand of junk. God's truth: four interminable, mind- and butt-numbing, boring hours of pure drudgery. My all time record playing Hold'em (or better, *not* playing Hold'em) at the Bicycle is an hour and forty-five minutes. In private games, this varies. Even in private limit games with lots of high-low action, periods of a half-hour to an hour of throwing in hands are still not uncommon.

In private pot-limit or no limit games, well, this requires some more extensive explanation and depends on the nature of the game, the relative looseness or tightness of the players, the average size of the pots, the pace of the game, and the relative ease or difficulty with which some of the players can be manipulated. If you're in a game with a lot of rocks, you may be involved in a lot of hands, stealing antes and bullying and pushing this way and that. But, if you're playing in a pot-limit or no-limit game against fairly loose players in which the pots regularly reach thousands of dollars, the correct strategy in, say, an eight-hour session, is to try to win three, maybe four, big hands. The implications of this are that over an eight-hour period, you may be involved in only a dozen hands total, with only four or five hands seen through to their conclusion. What you are looking for is not just cards, but opportunity. You are, in fact, stalking your prey.

Some years ago, there was an occasional player in the pot-limit game named Andy. Andy was very rich, and money meant absolutely nothing to him except that he was used to bullying people with it. He would regularly throw thousands of dollars in the pot, chasing higher pairs, trying to hit inside straights, drawing to straights and flushes against short odds, trying to fill two little pair; and he considered it an affront to his manhood to fold when someone bet at him. He was, in short, everything one wants in an opponent. But, remember the Clarence two-pair story cited earlier, you (I at least) had to be very, very careful because, although a guy like that is a tremendous asset, he can also bust you down to pre-evolutionary amoeba status when he hits a hand.

Stalking Andy was fun and a real challenge. Since I wasn't anywhere near his financial league, I simply had to wait for the dead-cert, five-star, solid gold, number 10, undisputed, mortal-lock nuts (how's that for qualifiers?)—which had to happen simultaneously with Andy's being on a throw-all-his-money-in-the-pot hand. This took a lot of patience and would pay off about once every two sessions, which was plenty given the size of the pots Andy always created. Had I been on a more level financial footing with him—able simply to play the odds at thousands of dollars each time—I could have challenged him far more often and won more money. Alas, a man's got to know his limitations—and behave accordingly.

Do you have the killer instinct? Do you have your own rules of conduct? Can you be patient, throwing in hands hour after hour? What do you want to be, poker-wise? Do you want to be Clarence or Harry? Do you want to be my Dad? Do you want to be Johnny Moss? Do you want to be Tim? Do you want to be me?

Who am I? I'm a guy who does business consulting and who writes textbooks for major publishers for a living. I also produce audio and video educational programs. I also have been playing poker for about thirty years, seriously playing for about twenty and, of those last twenty, have never had a losing year. Yes, I got into trouble one time when, a long time ago, I decided I was the best there was and was going to be a pro—and didn't have the reserves to back me up. Oh, I won all right. I played in high-stakes private games and raked it in. I sat down at Gardena (in the old days, before the Bicycle, Commerce, etc.) and Las Vegas and Reno and walloped the best of them, the toughest of the tough, regularly. My ego soared. (To this day, some fifteen years later, when I show up once or twice a year at California card clubs, some of the old guard who are still around go scurrying off for their notes on me.)

But, without sufficient reserves, the strain was too much. Two or three losing sessions in a row and you start to wonder if you're going to turn it around in time for end-of-the-month bills. You start to ask yourself if you've lost it. And, finally, you begin to realize that poker as a sideline, as a lucrative hobby, is wonderful; poker as a living is not very satisfying, especially when you have other talents. Former World Champion Puggy Pearson has said, in effect, that being a gambler isn't much, but it's the only thing he can do.[21] Good for him. He has found his niche and provides for his family in a manner that would otherwise be impossible for him. If that's your situation, then go for it, as long as you realize that Puggy Pearsons are, literally, one in a million.

In recent years, one of the best-selling (and, I must say, surprisingly influential) books about poker was, *Big Deal: A Year as a Professional Poker Player,* by Anthony Holden. His book chronicles his attempt to leave the world of the working—in his case, the writing—and become, solely, a professional poker player. In the end, he retreats fairly crestfallen back to his literary ways. I may be wrong, but I believe that in the end Mr. Holden's true discovery—and disappointment?—was that he didn't really want to be a professional poker player; he wanted to be what he was: a successful author who also loved and made money from playing poker. This was my conclusion about myself: poker is a sideline. After all, being a successful poker pro does little to benefit humanity. At least professional athletes entertain the masses. Poker players don't even do that. (Neither do a lot of other purely egocentric financial activities, like playing the stock market.)

Now, perhaps, you understand what I mean when I ask what you want out of poker. If you thought that "Know Thyself" meant the usual platitudes you get from poker books (don't play when you're tired; don't drink and play; stay disciplined) that's not it at all. It means: if you want to make money from playing poker, it's not going to be an evening's relaxation with the boys any more; it's going to be business. And—although, if you're like

---

[21.] Interviews in *Total Poker* by David Spanier (Penguin, 1977) and *Fast Company* by Jon Bradshaw (Random House, 1975).

me, it'll be fun, magic, challenging, and rewarding—it's going to change the way you approach poker (I wonder if Steffi Graf wishes on occasion that she could just go back to playing friendly, sweaty tennis with her childhood friend?) forever.

What do you want from poker? If you want to make money at it, read on.

Chapter 5

Know Your Opponents

or those who don't know it already, this may come as a shock: poker is not a card game. Poker is a people game. Well, then, what are those little, flat, rectangular things with numbers and pictures that we play with? Poker is only a card game in the sense that, for example, painting is a colored goo and canvas game. Most people (me, for example) can go out and acquire the best art supplies money can buy and still end up with a painting that would be rejected for hanging on a kindergarten wall. On the other hand, a very few people can take an old piece of charcoal out of the barbecue and create a masterpiece on the sidewalk. Art is not in the supplies; it is in the artist. Winning and losing at poker is not in the cards, it is in the player.

This doesn't mean you can't lose any one particular hand because of cards; of course you can. You could also be a great artist, painting some bucolic scene, and have a tree fall on your canvas, although for Picasso this wouldn't have made much difference. Nor does it mean you don't have to know the basic mechanics of how cards work, simple odds, and so forth. An artist must have enough technical knowledge to know, for example, which colors to mix to get the desired shade.

You need to know the basic technical aspect of cards, for these are the tools you use. The point is, in poker, these are very easy and can be learned in a day or so by most people. (My six-year-old daughter is taking a little longer, but she is getting it. Oh, Lord, am I leading her into a misspent youth?) This is probably another of the factors that make poker such a popular game: superficially, it is a very easy game. There are a few simple rules to learn, and, if one *wants* to delve deeper, there are some very simple, basic odds (probabilities) to learn and, voilá, you can play poker. It's sort of like painting with stencils or by the numbers: it's easy and amusing and you can say you're painting. If you are playing poker for buttons, then just read the little paper inside a pack of playing cards and deal!

But if you are a serious player-for-money, then you should know that serious poker is a people game, and people, not cards, are what you really have to know and study in order to play it well. This is the reason that most mathematicians and many technically oriented people are not good poker players: their faith and attention are all in the numbers, which is not where they should be. Following are two simple examples starring Matt, the mathematician.

Matt is playing five card draw, pot limit. After the draw, he has three aces. Fred drew one card and now bets the pot, $200. Three players fold leaving only Matt to "keep Fred honest." Matt's 200-megahertz brain takes less than a nanosecond to decide to call. For those of us with 16-megahertz brains, here's why: There's $400 in the pot and Matt has to call $200: simple pot odds of two to one. Matt knows that if Fred was drawing for a flush the probability is only 0.191 that he has it; if he was drawing for a straight, .170. He also figures that if Fred was drawing to two pair, the probability is .085 that he has improved to a full house, and Matt's trips will beat two pair. Therefore, Matt's worst-case scenario, the flush, still gives him 1 to 4.24 odds-on to win. Simplifying, Matt figures that if he makes this call 1,000 times he will win no fewer than 809 times and lose no more than 191 times. Matt happily calls. Fred shows down an ace-high spade flush and rakes in the pot. Oh, well, says Matt, it's a great investment. Under exactly those circumstances, for every $200 I lose I will make no less than $1,688.

The truth is that, *au contraire*, Matt is soon going to be broke. He will *never* win in that situation with Fred because he doesn't pay attention to people. The three players that folded before Mat know that Fred never, ever bluffs, doesn't believe in it, considers it immoral. They also know that the last time Fred bet two pair after the draw was in the winter of 1936. He lost that hand and has checked two pair after the draw ever since. Therefore, the true probability that Matt was going to win that hand is essentially zero. At zero probability to win Matt would need infinity-to-one odds in the pot just to break even, that is, if he could keep playing for an infinite amount of time. Of course, Fred is so damn tight and readable that he loses all the time, too, except when Matt is playing.

The table on the next page illustrates the situation showing Matt's worst case, the flush.

About the table:

Column 1: See how boring and easy that is? In every case, the *card* probabilities are the same. If you can remember a simple ratio of $4^{1}/_{4}$ to 1, you've got it. You know as much about the *card* probabilities in drawing one card to a flush as Amarillo Slim does.

Column 2: Now here it starts to get interesting because the *only* variable in the equation is the human factor. Whether or not a person is inclined never to bluff, or bluff occasionally, or bluff frequently, or bluff all the time, it is up to you to observe, figure out, and know. The variables here are the player's personality and the situation. Some players will almost always bluff in some situations and almost never bluff in others. Once you have analyzed the player, then you need to analyze the situation, but more about situations later. Anyway, only in the case of some stupid, drunk, emotionally disturbed, or interpersonally challenged player who bluffs 100 percent of the time do the strict card odds solely apply. But, you may say, figuring the percentage of time a player will bluff and multiplying it by the card odds, why, that's math! Sure it's math, but it's *people* math, not card math. And people math is the only kind that really counts because it's the only one that's variable. Besides, as I keep repeating, the math itself is simple, it's judging the person—finding his "percentage"—which is difficult.

Column 3: Your chances of winning decrease to zero as your opponent's inclination to bluff decreases. Therefore, the less inclined he is to bluff, the higher pot odds you need to make a

Column 1		Column 2	Column 3	
Probability of making a flush drawing one card	Odds Against making flush drawing one card	Percentage of times player will bluff after drawing 1 card to a flush	Percentage of times you will win if you call with less than a flush	Odds of (Leading number less than 1 indicates odds-in-favor)
0.191	4.236 to 1	100%	80.9%	0.236 to 1
0.191	4.236 to 1	95%	76.9%	0.301 to 1
0.191	4.236 to 1	90%	72.8%	0.373 to 1
0.191	4.236 to 1	85%	68.8%	0.454 to 1
0.191	4.236 to 1	80%	64.7%	0.545 to 1
0.191	4.236 to 1	75%	60.7%	0.648 to 1
0.191	4.236 to 1	70%	56.6%	0.766 to 1
0.191	4.236 to 1	65%	52.6%	0.902 to 1
0.191	4.236 to 1	60%	48.5%	1.060 to 1
0.191	4.236 to 1	55%	44.5%	1.247 to 1
0.191	4.236 to 1	50%	40.5%	1.472 to 1
0.191	4.236 to 1	45%	36.4%	1.747 to 1
0.191	4.236 to 1	40%	32.4%	2.090 to 1
0.191	4.236 to 1	35%	28.3%	2.532 to 1
0.191	4.236 to 1	30%	24.3%	3.120 to 1
0.191	4.236 to 1	25%	20.2%	3.944 to 1
0.191	4.236 to 1	20%	16.2%	5.180 to 1
0.191	4.236 to 1	15%	12.1%	7.241 to 1
0.191	4.236 to 1	10%	8.1%	11.361 to 1
0.191	4.236 to 1	9%	7.3%	12.734 to 1
0.191	4.236 to 1	8%	6.5%	14.451 to 1
0.191	4.236 to 1	7%	5.7%	16.658 to 1
0.191	4.236 to 1	6%	4.9%	19.602 to 1
0.191	4.236 to 1	5%	4.0%	23.722 to 1
0.191	4.236 to 1	4%	3.2%	29.902 to 1
0.191	4.236 to 1	3%	2.4%	40.203 to 1
0.191	4.236 to 1	2%	1.6%	60.805 to 1
0.191	4.236 to 1	1%	0.8%	122.609 to 1
0.191	4.236 to 1	0%	0.0%	infinity to 1

profitable call. Most poker books will tell you never to call for "the size of the pot," which is a phrase often heard in poker. This is usually true—if your *only* criterion is the size of the pot. If, however, you have made a calculation based on the one (card) constant and the assorted (people) variables that the size of the pot makes it worthwhile, then call. An example of carrying "don't call for the size of pot" to the absurd follows:

One night in the limit game the game was seven stud, buy the deck. There are four people in the hand (I was out), and Bill and Jack declare low with the two others going high. Now, remember, Jack thinks he is a hell of a poker player. There's $281 in the pot. The first high hand bets a token one dollar, the other high hand calls, and Bill, Jack's competition for low, calls. Jack folds—a one-dollar bet! Now, had Jack had a total clinker that he was just hoping to back into low with, this might have been understandable, but he didn't. He had a playable hand.

Should he have called? Of course he should but not *solely* for the size of the pot. Jack had just been offered a one dollar bet at odds of 142 to 1 ($281 + the three one-dollar bets, divided by two). In folding, Jack forgot to calculate two variable "people" factors: (1) At 142 to 1, I'd call in case Bill had misread his hand! (2) Himself.—Jack just flat out isn't good enough to turn down odds of 142 to 1. What he is saying by doing so is that his judgment is so good that he will *never* make one mistake in 143 decisions. Nobody on the planet is that smart. (If there *is* somebody that smart out there, then let's make him or her ruler of the world, because the rulers that we have now tend to have a mistake-to-decision ratio of about one to one.)

A last word about the table on page 102: there *are* in fact some variables in calculating card odds; some are subtle, but most are not complicated. For example, there is the matter of flashed or exposed cards. Let's say you're deciding whether or not to draw one card to a spade flush. If, for one reason or another, you have seen six flashed cards, none of which was a spade, your odds against catching go down from 4.24 to 1, to 3.5 to 1—much more favorable. If, on the other hand, you saw six flashed cards and they were all spades, your odds against catching go up to 13 to 1—less likely than hitting an inside straight. Appendix 1 gives more information on card odds, but remember: don't get wrapped up in mathematics; it's a simple, secondary issue. Your knowledge of people is far more important. (The *really* complicated mathematical stuff is that any chaos theorist, theoretical physicist, or mathematician will tell you that you can't calculate these odds with any certainty at all but only as a range of probabilities with some outcomes being more likely than others. For the modest uses these calculations are put to in a poker game, however, lowly, standard, pedestrian, layman's calculations will do.)

Really, really the last word about the chart: To be safe, you should always add a little more margin to your odds whether drawing for flushes, straights, or whatever. If you *always* call, say, $100 against $425 to draw to your flush, you're playing a break-even proposition at best, which is not why we play poker. At worst, you're playing a losing proposition because you're not leaving room for the times you will hit your flush and lose! As a general rule of thumb, I use 5 to 1 to draw to flushes and add similar margins to the odds of drawing to other hands.

Our second example finds Matt in the same game, pot limit. The dealer has chosen five card stud, high-low split, with a twist. It is the betting round just before the twist, four players remaining. Two players are showing high with Matt and John showing low. Matt is showing 7-6-4-2 and has a seven in the hole, a pair of sevens that won't win high and is certainly a clinker for low. John is showing 8-5-4-3, hole card unknown to Matt, of course. There's $2,000 in the pot. The high hands check and John bets $1000. Matt folds.

Again, dissecting Matt's thought process: $3,000 in the pot gives him 1.5 to 1 simple pot odds at the moment, 2 to 1 potential pot odds if one of the high hands calls, and 2.5 to 1 if both of the high hands call. Remember, since Matt has no chance of hitting a straight to win both ways, only half the pot is available for him to win. He'll have to dump his hole card and twist to beat John's eight low. Of the cards remaining (at least that he hasn't seen) that can help, there are one ace, two fives and two threes, making a total of five cards. He can see seventeen cards. Eight cards were folded the first round. Twenty-seven unknown cards out there, twenty-four of which are left in the deck. One of the high hands may have an ace in the hole, the other a queen, which leaves Matt with as few as four cards out of twenty-four, or 5 to 1. Since his maximum potential pot odds for this round are 2.5 to 1, he folds.

Were Matt a people-player instead of a card-player, he would have known that, not only should he not have folded, he should have raised. I'll bet a lot of you noticed that John bet a thousand dollars into the nuts—and you thought that either John is a total jerk or that I had goofed in creating the example. In fact, neither is the case; this actually happened to me the other night—different names, of course, as we all know that my name isn't Matt. When it happened, what I knew about "John" was: (1) John is good enough to know not to bet into the nuts unless he is trying a maneuver; (2) He is not good enough to realize that he shouldn't try this maneuver on me, nor is he good enough for this to be a double fake; (3) If John really had an eight he would *check* into the possible nuts and then perhaps call if I bet. (4) Ergo, John has a big clinker in the hole and is hoping to drive me out if I don't really have a seven low. In other words, John doesn't know if I have a seven low or not, but he knows he'll have to twist to make his eight. Since he will call if I bet, he tries to take the initiative by betting first and hoping that I will fold if I don't have it.

This is not card knowledge, this is people knowledge. If the "John" in my game knew people, he would not have tried something so lame on me. I just raised him back and put the pressure on him, where it should be. *I'm* the one showing the nuts. *He's* the one who has to worry. The "John" in the Matt story was different, however. He knows people and knew that Matt would fold if he didn't have an eight low beat. That sort of thing works with "Matts" every time.

If you are showing the nuts, have a clinker in the hole, and "John" bets into you, the possible reasons are:

1. John is an idiot.

2. John thinks you are an idiot.

3. You have a tell, which has given away your clinker (and John thinks you will call or raise if he bets, but check if he checks).

4. You have flashed your clinker (and ditto).

5. You are being cheated, which means John knows you have a clinker in the hole (and ditto).

6. For some reason John made a mistake.

In (3), (4), and (5), if John thinks you will bet showing the nuts then he won't give away his advantage by betting first, unless (1), (2), or (6). Whichever of these possibilities is applicable at any given time is up to you to decide based upon your knowledge of "John."

Our next example of putting too much faith in numbers stars—me! This time I got to play the fool. The game is Spit-buy and I'm dealt A45K, which is an excellent starting hand with two draws—one free, and one paid-for twist—to hit. The guy on my right, Carl, bets. I raise. Five people call around to Carl, who reraises. I reraise, and everybody calls. The common card is turned up: a 3, giving me A345K. Great! Carl checks. I bet, and four people call around to Carl, who just calls as well.

Carl draws one card. (By this time I'm assuming that he has four goodish low cards, and that the board, the 3, had paired him, which would be the reason he hadn't raised on the second round.) I draw one card and get a six. I'm happy: A3456. Carl bets. I raise. There is a raise behind me and a raise-killing one dollar raise behind that. We all call, and there are still six people in the pot. Now comes the twist. Carl stays pat. I stay pat, and the four others buy one card each. After the draw, Carl checks.

I bet. There are two raises back around to Carl, and he raises. I call as do two other players.

When our hands come up for the chip declare, I'm low, and the two others are high—and Carl is high-low. Everybody except me is thinking, uh oh. Why am I not worried?

A while back, I went through a period that had begun with my thinking that I didn't have a sufficiently thorough knowledge of the mathematics of poker. So I had decided to study up on it and spent hour after hour at the computer doing all manner of calculations and tests of probability. I was right, of course: I didn't know this aspect of poker as well as I should and had a lot to learn. Where I went wrong was that all this study managed to tip the scales of my judgment, influencing me to put more weight on math than I should. The result was that, while I learned a lot, I began to go through a period in which I won much less and much less often than normal. I actually lost *twice in a row* at the limit game. This had never happened before. It took me a few weeks to realize what was going on, shake those nasty mathematical devils off my shoulder, and return them to servant, rather than master, status where they belonged.

The hand I'm describing with Carl took place on the darkest day of that dark season and is one of the main factors that brought back the light. To continue:

Why am I not worried? David the mathematician figures: well, so Carl has a low straight. Using, as he must, the 3 on the board, Carl could have a wheel, a straight to the six, or a straight to the seven. The chances of holding each individually are equal; therefore, the odds are 2 to 1 in favor of his having a straight six or straight seven, both of which I will beat.

Carl bets and I raise: I have it all figured out. Because I raise—thus making it look as though Carl will lose low and, therefore, also have a dead high hand—the two high players get their enthusiasm back and raise as well. That's it for the raises. Carl calls, I call—and Carl turns over a wheel, taking the whole pot and making me look very interpersonally challenged.

Now, we discussed earlier about not getting excited about

losing against the odds. The problem was I had *not* lost against the odds. I had simply neglected, in my mathematics-induced stupor, to figure the odds properly; I had completely ignored the people factor, ignored Carl as a person and a poker player. This is poker death, every time. I *know* Carl, and had I been paying attention, I would have known from his behavior and betting pattern that he had the hammer. I've folded a lot of big hands, certainly rough six-lows, against him and other players because the people factor told me I was beat, irrespective of the card odds. Just as with Mat's calling Fred's flush draw, the true probability that I was going to win that hand was essentially zero. No wonder I lost: the odds were infinity to one against me. The good news was that I learned my lesson.

You don't have to be Freud to read people. You just have to be observant. An individual who is going about his life normally, that is, not actively trying to mislead or deceive you, has behavior patterns that seldom vary. In response to given stimuli, that individual will react the same way most of the time. If you punch Harvey, he will almost always punch you back. If you punch Ted, he will almost always run away. If you punch Charlie, he will almost always punch you back unless you are bigger than he, in which case he will almost always pull a gun and shoot you. And so on and so on. The trick is to know Harvey, Ted, and Charlie well enough to predict their behavior.

In most of life's encounters, this is hard to do. If Dan works for the competition and you want to see what he will do if you undercut his prices, it may take you years to establish a pattern. What he does one time may or may not be the same thing he does the next time. A nice thing about poker is that it gives you a very high number of events, examples of behavior, over a relatively short period of time, and it does so in a repetitive, limited context.

If you play in a regular, say weekly, private game with an average of 100 hands played per game, in one year you will have about 5,000 opportunities to observe the players' behavior, all relative and relevant to poker. How does Ziggy play when he's tired, when he's fresh, when he's winning, when he's losing? Under which circumstances will he check, bet, raise, fold? He's tired and losing; is it more, or less, likely that he will bluff? He's tired and winning; is it more, or less, likely that he will call/fold/raise/check/bluff/play loose/play tight? About once a month, Russ has a big fight with his wife before the game. When that happens, he plays looser/plays tighter/bluffs more/bluffs less/calls more/folds more. If you make a nasty remark to Bill, he will get nervous and play worse/calm down and play better/get aggressive/withdraw and be more/less likely to come after you with a bluff. If you bluff Rick out of a pot, the next time you bet against him he will always/never/sometimes call, which means never/always/sometimes bluff him twice in a row. And then, of course, there are the classics: Frank puffs faster on his cigarette when he's bluffing; Juan sits back in his chair if he's got it, sits forward if he hasn't; Larry fingers his chips if he's going to call, looks left if he's going to raise. Etc., etc., etc. All of this would never occur to Matt; he thinks poker is a card game.

This stuff is easy. All you have to do is pay attention—and keep notes. I said before that behavior is habitual unless someone is trying to mislead or deceive you. *All* poker players, of course, think they are deceptive, and *all* poker players can be grouped into two categories: (1) those who think they are deceptive but are not, and (2) those who are deceptive. The ratio of Category 1 to Category 2 is about 1,000 to 1, although membership does fluctuate somewhat. For example, Don may not be deceptive to me, but he may be to someone else. I may be a Category 2 to many people, but a mere Category 1 to some others. (Remember what I said about, no matter who you are, there is always somebody better? Never, ever forget that.) In fact, even with the same group, I may be a Category 2 some nights and a Category 1 other nights when I'm off my game. If you are playing in a game with a bona fide Category 2, forget it, find another game; you are going to get your butt kicked.

Human behavior—personalities, quirks, strengths, weaknesses—and observance of same are what win and lose at poker, not cards. The other night, we were playing five card stud, high-low split with a twist. I was playing low and showing 8-6-3-A, with a five in the hole. Jack was playing high, showing 10-3-Q-K, and had a pair of either kings or queens. My low opponent, Bill, showed 7-K-6-2 and was going to have to twist his king to make a seven. I bet the max. Bill called and Jack called. One of the players who was out of the hand said, "Jack, you're all alone for high, you should have raised." Jack said, "I don't think Dave is low. I think he has a pair of aces." Now, Jack was right to be careful of my ace showing. He was wrong to have told me and everyone else what he was thinking. Comes the twist and Jack didn't improve, I played pat, and Bill drew a five. Because I know Bill, I knew he had made his 7-low.

I'm screwed, right? Wrong. Jack has given me the out. It's my bet and I check. Bill bets the max. Jack calls, and I raise. One of the other players said, "Dave is crazy. He's raising into the nuts." Jack said, "No he's not. He's got the aces." Another player said, "No he doesn't. He just doesn't think that Bill has a seven." All of this is music to my ears. Bill, of course, raises back. Jack, influenced by the last comment, calls. I make the third and final raise, Bill and Jack call. We declare. Bill goes low, all alone, and Jack and I go high. Jack doesn't even wait for Bill to bet. Saying, "Goddamn it, I knew he had aces," he folds his cards in disgust. Jack had talked himself right out of that pot.[22]

Now some other player may have thought, "He's doing this because I gave him the idea when Bill drew out on him. He has a busted low." That's the point. I didn't do this randomly hoping it would work. I did it because I know that one of Jack's weaknesses is that he has a very high opinion of his own opinion. When I went high, I *knew* that Jack would start kicking himself for having been so stupid as to listen to the other players, should have known he had been right all along and, the clincher, prides

---

[22.] This is a good example of the added potential for moves and bluffs that a betting round after the declare provides. Had there been no betting round after the declare in this game, my busted low and I would have had to pack up and go home when Bill hit his 7-low.

himself on not calling final bets when he "knows" he's losing (he of the 142-to-1 fold). Against another player, Harry, for example, this wouldn't have worked. Like most very poor players Harry lives in mortal fear of being bluffed and is a regular calling station if he has anything remotely similar to a possible winner. Another of Jack's weaknesses is that he likes to explain his thought processes to the rest of the table. Once he has done so, he has to stick by it to show how confident he is that he is right. Jack, to all intents, flat out *told* me how he would behave if I turned out to be going high.

After Jack had folded, I showed my five in the hole. Again, I know Jack. I knew that showing him he had screwed up would not cause him to reevaluate and improve his play. I knew it would simply upset him and start him on the road to Tiltland. It did.

Am I right 100 percent of the time in these evaluations, predictions of behavior? Of course not. Concerning the people I play with regularly, I am right between 76 percent and 93 percent of the time—I keep track of such things—depending on the readability of the player and the situation. Jack, for example, is very easy to read in some situations, as above, and more difficult in others. If I drop below 70 percent in these evaluations concerning an individual or a situation, however, I stop and try to take a close look at why—hit the books; it's time for a refresher course. Is it me? Is it he? Am I slipping or is Nick, for example, improving, inching closer to that Category 2? Although I've played against a number of people who, over the course of time, have improved their play, I've never actually played against anyone who started out worse than I am then improved to be better than I am.[23] But I am certainly open to the possibility that it could happen; remember my advice about being humble.

There are too many variables of human nature for anyone, or even a machine, to be right 100 percent of the time. This excess of variables is known to physicists and mathematicians as chaos

---

[23.] Although, as I have mentioned, I have played against folks who were *already* better than I.

theory. Chaos theory applies to everything from predicting the position and speed of a particle, to predicting the weather. The analogy most often heard is that a butterfly flaps its wings in Tokyo and the weather changes in New York. In other words, little, tiny, teeny factors that are too numerous to know can influence the outcome of an event. If, theoretically, one could have all the information concerning all possible variables, then one could predict, not just human behavior, but the future with 100 percent accuracy. Chaos theory recognizes this as impossible, however, and makes predictions based on probability.

Although poker, and its related human behavior, is a much less complicated matter than the weather or the future, it is still simply impossible for anyone to know and calculate all the possible variables of human behavior all the time. A player who has been following certain patterns for years may suddenly behave differently. What happened? His dog died? His daughter was just accepted at Harvard? His uncle left him a fortune? He stubbed his toe? The IRS is after him? He had a spiritual vision? He lost his cuff links? This sort of thing can happen to anyone. A while back I signed a massive (for me, at least) consulting contract; no financial worries for a long, long time. My poker went straight to hell and stayed there for a month. Just couldn't concentrate.

Had Jack not behaved as predicted in the example above, I would have thought, "Uh oh," and done two things: (1) tried to find out why, and (2) monitored his future behavior to see if the change was permanent. It could have been just a fluke: he twisted his ankle and the pain is distracting him and altering his behavior. It could be permanent: he has had a revelation and this is the new Jack.

Another axiom of physics and quantum mechanics is that the very act of observing a particle may change its behavior. Is that particle there because it was going to be there anyway, or is it there as a result of (the energy transferred to it by) observing it? The same applies to people, especially the more astute ones. If people feel or know they are being observed, they may change their behavior accordingly. In most poker cases, comprising

Category 1 players who are the vast majority, this change will be ineffectual.

One night I saw that Harry had begun scratching his nose ostentatiously whenever he had a winner. Harry doesn't know that he has about eighty-seven other tells which have nothing to do with scratching his nose. It had obviously finally occurred to Harry that people were watching him for tells and, by God, he was going to fool them. So, sure enough, later in the game, we were playing English Stud. Harry is showing four to a wheel after both twists, which he has taken down. I had started out well, but had ended up with a 9-6 low, a clinker—except that Harry was broadcasting at 50,000 kilowatts that he didn't have it. When Harry started ferociously trying to scratch the nose off his face, I almost—almost—felt sorry for him. How pathetic. Now I knew that not only did he not have a good hand, it was really terrible: probably both hole cards paired him. The pot was very big or I might have let him get away with it. Sure, why waste such knowledge on a tiny pot? Let Harry think his nose-scratching act was working until it really counted to wax him for a big pot. As it happened, this pot was very big, and I was going to have to disillusion Harry.

The high hand ahead of me bet, and I just called. (Since this game has a three-raise limit, I didn't want to kill a raise by raising one dollar, which is the normal way to look weak, nor did I want to warn Harry by raising. Another player might have noticed that I hadn't killed a raise and been warned. But I knew Harry didn't notice stuff like that.) Two high hands behind me each raised and, of course, Harry raised. By this time I was afraid we would have to call a doctor to see to his nose. The high hand ahead of me folded. I called, and the two high hands behind me called. Really nice pot. We declared, and in the final betting round Harry tried the same thing again. Poor Harry. A full house won high, and everyone was shocked that I had won such a big pot low with only a nine. "How could you stay in there with a nine?" "Oh, I just got stubborn. I was really lucky that Harry didn't have it."

Harry either gave up or forgot about continuing to scratch. Perhaps he decided we weren't astute enough to notice tells. This was too bad, but it was much easier on his nose. Now I'll have to rely solely on his eighty-seven other tells.

You *can* fake tells and make it work. Category 2 players do it all the time. In fact, the better the player, the more likely he is to be fooled by a fake tell *if* it's done believably. Harry just wasn't subtle enough, and if something so crude is tried against a good player, it will certainly backfire. But if you do it well, that's another story. In fact, here comes one.

In the days when I was often playing in Gardena, there was a good, solid, regular pro named Chuck. As are many card-club pros, he was very tight; if he was in a hand, you knew he was in there with good cards and had a good shot at winning it. Once, playing five card draw, which was all they played in those days, I caught a big hand, kings full. There were three other players still in, plus Chuck. I bet out. Just after I bet, a woman sitting on my right who was out of the hand said something to me. I don't remember what it was, but no one else heard it, only me. I said something in reply that the others did hear. In other words, they heard me speak but didn't know it was in response to a question. The three other players appeared not to notice, but Chuck looked up and stared at me.

As you will see throughout this book, I'm not in favor of employing *generalities* of behavior to make poker decisions. If, however, you don't know a player well enough to have contradictory information, then you can use this as a rule of thumb: if a person bets out and starts talking, he is bluffing or is at least very weak. This will work in a very high percentage of all cases, although that percentage will decrease with the increasing skill level of your opponents. I had not intended to "set Chuck up" in this case. It was a coincidence. But as soon as he looked at me, I knew what he was thinking. He was trying to size me up as either a run-of-the-mill talking bluffer—or not. The three others folded, leaving Chuck. He looked resigned and called. It was clear that he was calling more educationally than anything else.

I showed down my boat, and he trashed his hand. He didn't nod or smile or look satisfied. He was a pro. I thought, "Well, Chuck, is this the beginning of a new relationship?"

A while later, I had another big hand. Chuck was not in the pot. I bet out and started babbling. I got a call and two over-calls, no doubt on the talkers-are-bluffers principle. As I showed down my winning Ace-King flush, I could see Chuck out of the corner of my eye and, this time, I detected a slight nod as of con-firmation. From then on, whenever the opportunity arose and Chuck was around I reinforced my "tell."

I then went back to a saner life and didn't see Chuck for about five years, until one day I wandered into the Bike in Bell Gardens. By then they were playing Hold'em, and as I stood at the rail looking around—there sat Chuck playing in a $10–$20 game. I got on the list for that game and eventually sat down. We went through the long-time-no-sees, whatcha-been-doins and a few minutes later, he got up and walked off. In Chapter 4, you thought I was kidding about people running off to look at their notes. Chuck came back, and a while later, I'm on the big blind with king-rag. There are six calls around the table, including Chuck, but no raises, so my king-rag and I are in the hand. (To be more specific, my hand was K♥ 3♣.) The flop comes up 5♠ K♣ 2♥. How about that? I'm feeling expansive, decide to see if there's any strength around the table, and bet out on my (weak, no kicker) pair of kings. Two people fold, four callers, including Chuck. Now, I don't know these other people, but nobody raised, and it doesn't *feel* like stiff competition or sandbagging out there. A couple of them are probably holding aces and want to hang around for the turn. I'm pretty sure one guy has hit a pair of fives because he's got that look that people get (a sort of resigned optimism) when they are calling on the underpair.

The one that bothers me is Chuck. If Chuck is in there and calling, he has hit a pair of kings like me, with one difference: he wouldn't be in there with king-rag (which at least tells me he has-n't hit two pair). Furthermore, since he hadn't raised, he doesn't have king-ace. I put him on king-jack or king-queen. Uh-oh . . .

Up comes the turn: 7♥. I decide to keep pushing and bet. Two callers, including Chuck. At this point I'm fairly certain the other caller has a pair of 5s and is hanging in there hoping to catch two pair or trips. Then there's Chuck . . . On the river we get a 10♦, a real Hold'em card. I bet out. The other guy folds and its down to Chuck, who is reaching for his chips to call. I say, "Looks like you're gonna get me, Chuck." He hesitates about half a second, puts down his chips, smiles, waves his finger at me, and says (using the nickname the old Gardena players had given me), "Brazil, whenever you talk . . ."

That was all he said. He didn't finish the sentence, but as he trashed his cards he flashed the king-jack of diamonds. Chuck was slipping. In the old days he wouldn't have started to tell me why he was folding. But, boy, did I feel good! And I certainly did not show him my hand.

The other night Edgar was playing in the limit game. Edgar is a good card-player but a mediocre people-player and, there-fore, is only so-so overall. As do most "card" players, he prefers to play stud games to be able to see many exposed cards. (Herein lies a hint for you: If you are playing with "card" players who are better at that aspect of the game than you are, try to play games with few exposed cards like draw, Hold'em, Omaha, etc. The fewer cards that are exposed to the table, the more a player has to rely on his people-playing skills.) Edgar tends to be too tight, a nut player who rarely bluffs. So, if Edgar is in in the late rounds of a hand, you'd better have a hammer to beat him with. Of course, this means that he suffers the fate of all too-tight players: when he gets a hand either everybody drops, which means he wins little, or if someone stays, it's usually with a good enough hand to beat him.

Another of Edgar's weaknesses is that, like Jack and 98 per-cent of all poker players, he likes to spout about his poker prowess, telling the table what he knows or thinks he knows. I had two chances to take advantage of these weaknesses the other night. The first was a hand of English Stud. Left in the hand at twist time were Edgar and Jack and me. I had made a full-house on my fifth card but had been slow-playing it to encourage Jack to keep trying for his flush. Edgar was going low and by twist time was showing 3,4,5,6 off-suit. Now I not only wanted Jack to throw more money in the pot to keep trying for his flush, but I also wanted Edgar to hit a straight and declare both ways, in which case I would win the whole thing. With Edgar raising his low against two obvious highs, it would mean an extra $40 for me from Jack if I could keep him in to the end and an extra $50 from Edgar if he twisted and hit and decided to go both ways.

As I said, I had been slow-playing my full house, and I just kept it up. I had [77] 8,7,8,3, so I paid $5 for a twist, dumped my 3, and got an ace. We had a betting round, then I paid another $5 for the second twist, dumped the ace and got a 2. These were good cards to hit, as they made it look like I was twisting to hit a full house and probably hadn't hit. Nines, tens, or jacks might have looked like a straight and scared Edgar off. Jack had not hit his flush but had paired on kings, showing. Edgar had clearly been twisting to improve his low to a straight. I had been look-ing so meek and hopeful about my twists that, sure enough, at the declare Jack went high, hoping I might just have the pair of eights and Edgar went high-low. Edgar bet $5, I raised to $10, and Jack, seeing that even if he could beat me, he couldn't beat Edgar, folded. Edgar called my raise and said, "Straight to the seven." I turned over my hole cards and raked in the whole pot.

Here's the point of the story. Edgar, very disgusted and very pissed-off, said, "Oh, I see. Dave only bets them up if he hasn't got them. If he's got them, he sucks you in." Now, any time someone tells you something like that you have to decide: is that what he *really* thinks or is that what he wants me to *think* he thinks? In Edgar's case, my built-in people analyzer told me that he was saying what he really thought, and I filed it away for future use.

"Future use" came about ten hands later. We were playing seven stud, and my first three cards were three 8s, wired. There were five other players including Edgar who was showing an

Ace and bet first. I raised, and from then on, I kept betting and raising every chance I got. If central casting wanted a guy who looked just like he had a big hand and was betting his brains out, I was that guy. On the fifth card, I got the fourth 8, showing 8,2,8. There were three other players, including Edgar who was showing ace, king, king. Edgar bet his kings, and I raised (one king and one ace were out, so I was safe), two players called. Edgar raised. I raised. Two players called. Edgar raised the last raise . . . and so on through the seventh card at which time there were just Edgar, Nick and myself left in the hand. (What Nick was doing in there, who knows? He was trying to hit a flush and was drawing dead, but I didn't complain.)

After the final bets and raises, Edgar, a sure winner and acting smug said, "I've got you, Dave." He was actually sounding condescending. I said, "Oh? Whatcha got?" and he said, "Kings full," turning his cards with a flourish. In true poker tradition I said, "Gee, Edgar, that's no good" and turned over my four 8s. Edgar's chin almost hit the table as a look of utter disbelief washed over his face. The disbelief then turned to slack-jawed confusion, and Edgar was in Tiltland the rest of the night.

This last story reveals the wages of ego, the fall from pride, and you've got to try not to let it happen to you. Edgar's ego and pride, like Jack's and so many other people's, are so wrapped up in his poker playing that he is unable to be analytical when something adverse happens. Being humble doesn't mean being self-effacing or timid. It is simply a practical matter in that—I know I've said it before and will certainly say it again—sometimes you will be outsmarted or outplayed no matter who you are. If the effect on you of being outplayed or outsmarted (or out drawn) is to send your ego crashing through the floor, then you are in serious trouble. You will not leave yourself the analytical ability to remedy the situation.

Sometimes that analysis will mean that you can think things through, discover where you went wrong or what factors changed to make your judgment erroneous. Sometimes that analysis will mean that you should get up and leave the table or quit the game. Whatever the conclusion, you have to be able to think clearly and you can't do that if you're feeling like an overused doormat or if your ego rather than your reason is making decisions for you. If you get beat, even a bad beat, so what; it happens to everybody. Edgar's bad beat was not only in the cards—losing with kings full to four 8s is a bad beat in anybody's book—but it was psychological: he had *read* me as having a weak hand and had been wrong, and *that* is what put him on tilt. By chance, he had ended up with kings full to reinforce his position, but he had thought he hadn't even needed the full house. He had read my hand as weak and would have played the same way with three kings or maybe even two-pair aces. Of course, he had set himself up for this by telling me his analysis of my play.

While we're on the subject, the above examples are classics in the "vary your play" category. When should you slow-play? When should you bet them up? This all depends on who you are playing with, the circumstances, the cards, etc. But the basic principle is: keep them guessing, vary your play in such a way as not to establish patterns of behavior, or, better, in such a way as to establish false patterns of behavior. If the opportunity to exploit Edgar's misconception of my behavior had not come up so soon, I may have repeated the slow-play of a big hand just to reinforce his ideas. Then, once I figured I had him hooked on the idea that "Dave always slow-plays big hands," I'd hammer him with contrary behavior. Once, quite a long time ago, about eleven years, I bet a big hand into Jack. He sat there and thought, looked at me, thought, looked at me, and finally said, "Nope. Poker face. I'm out." Obviously, he had read somewhere that one way to read if an opponent has them or not is the "poker face," that classic, stony, frowning, staring, quiet, don't-move-a-muscle face. And, in fact, as a rule of thumb it's true: if an unknown opponent bets into you and gives you that look, he's usually got them. Again—they never learn!—Jack's mistake at the time was not to have applied the principle, it was to tell me what he was thinking. Jack's on-going mistake is to continue to apply that rule of thumb universally, irrespective of what he should have learned from individual observation. So, whenever I have a good bluffing opportunity against Jack, I bluff into him and adopt that look. I swear—God's truth—it hasn't failed once in eleven years. However, should it fail one day, I won't go to pieces over it; I'll try to analyze why it didn't work and, if necessary, simply junk that strategy and find something new.

Many examples given above and elsewhere in this book point to one thing: For your own sake, if you don't learn anything else about poker, please at least learn this: KEEP YOUR MOUTH SHUT. Perhaps this should even be a chapter heading. If you must talk, talk about the weather, chat about sports, brag—or lament—about the last time you got laid, but don't ever, ever, ever talk about your strategies, your insights, your thoughts, your plans, your feelings—anything about your game. Unless you are very experienced and very good, it is not even a good idea to try to mislead or trap people by giving them wrong information concerning, for example, a strategy. A good player will see through what you are doing, and you might as well have told him your strategy straight out.

If you think you've had a revelation—"Dave always slow-plays big hands"—KEEP IT TO YOURSELF. If you must tell someone, tell your wife, your mother, your dog, but only after swearing them to secrecy. It is best not to tell even nonpoker-playing friends as they especially can come back to haunt you. (You sit down at the poker table, and Rudy says, "I ran into a guy named Fred the other day. Your name came up; said he was a good friend of yours. We had a really great chat.") It's a smaller world than we think sometimes. Poker is a tough enough game to beat without giving your opponents instructions about how you play or how to play you. Yet players do exactly this all the time, over and over again, bless their silly hearts. Very, very few times have I ever sat down at a poker game where the players, especially those who have just lost a hand, don't analyze the play after each hand: "Well, I did that because . . ." "You shouldn't have done . . ." "I wouldn't have played it like that, I'd have . . ." on and on.

We all want to be well seen and respected. We all want to justify our mistakes, so we don't look stupid, and brag about our victories to get some credit and respect. It's human nature. Just—please!—don't do it at the poker table. Remember Miranda: Anything you say can and will be used against you in poker court.

There *are*, however, many opportunities for misleading patter and chat in a poker game that don't carry the risk of giving away your secrets. If someone asks me a strategy question, "How would you have played that?" for example, I always give a nonanswer, something like, "Lessons are extra," or "I wasn't paying attention." However, if I'm asked a specific, easy question, "How many cards did you draw?" or "What did you have?" I *always* lie (which is perfectly legal in poker, by the way). Now, you might think that after a while folks would cotton on, especially in a regular game. Well, (1) they often don't, and (2) it doesn't matter if they do. Example: I say, "I drew three," and some jerk, as often happens, says, "No you didn't, you drew two." The result is that now I know who's paying attention and who isn't, and (don't laugh now, I'm serious) it adds a bit to the mystery and danger of playing cards against good old Dave. "That Dave, what's he up to?" Now, why is the guy who told on me a jerk? Obviously because he should have KEPT IT TO HIMSELF. If I catch someone lying like that, believe me, I KEEP IT TO MYSELF. Why share my information with the rest of the table? If I fold and someone asks, "What did you have?" I lie. If someone who dropped out in stud wants to know what my last card was—the card that would have been his—I lie. Always lie. Those people asking you those questions are trying to take your money away from you—why make it any easier?

There are some types of question that you have to be prepared for and watch out for—and *ask* when it's appropriate. After you have bet, a good player will often ask you, straight out, "Are you bluffing?" or "Can you beat trip 6s?" or something of the sort. The reason this is done, and the reason you should do it too, is that people answer! Much of the time, you get the truth, as incredible as that may seem. And the players who aren't prepared for the question but are "smart" enough to lie or not answer, give the truth away to the astute player anyway. What you need to do to prepare for this is to practice—really practice, like in front of a mirror—giving some kind of pat answer or developing a truly blank stare, but that is more difficult. My pat answer is: "Gee, I don't remember." I combine this with a look of surprise, as if I'm taken aback, not only at being asked but at not remembering. I say and do the same thing, every time, whatever the truth is. If I'm strong or weak, if I'm bluffing or not, I always use the same pat answer and expression. It's not very inventive, perhaps, but it works. The trouble with deciding to use more than one pat answer is that you run the risk of falling unconsciously into the habit of using one answer for some situations and another for others. That will be picked up on right away.

It is not a good idea for even the good player to try to second-guess the questioner and give a directly misleading answer. As any cop or insurance investigator will tell you, when taken by surprise, it's really very difficult to lie convincingly in reply to a direct question with someone looking you right in the eye; very few people can do it and not be detected. The best strategy is simply to be prepared and then deflect the issue.

Okay, okay. If you really think you're good enough to pull it off and have sufficient information about your opponent, then you can give misleading or manipulative answers to this type of question. I hesitate to talk about this because, truly, the best thing to do in most cases is to give the pat answer as outlined above. But opportunities do arise. I used to play regularly with a guy named Ted. He would ask this type of question and, depending on the answer, would either always call or always fold. If he asked, "Are you bluffing?" and you said yes, he would always call. If you said no, he would always fold. The trick here, aside from knowing your opponent, is still in the preparation. Knowing that this or that opponent has a tendency to ask these questions, you can analyze and prepare your answer before hand. Another guy I used to play with would always ask "Can you beat . . .?" No matter what you said, if you hesitated and fumbled a bit before saying it he would read you as weak and call or raise. Most people who play this poorly, however, and are, therefore, so easy to manipulate, are either not astute enough to realize that asking questions works, or are such obvious candidates for manipulation that you don't need a book to tell you how to do it. Harry, for example, has never tried to ask this type of question, neither has Clarence, although Harry, in particular, is ridiculously susceptible to questioning. If you ask, "Does an 8-low scare you," and he says no, it really doesn't; he can beat an 8-low. If he fumbles and hems and haws, trying desperately not to say anything, he can't beat it.

Furthermore, most people associate the breaking of eye contact as indicating deception. Therefore, if someone looks you in the eye and asks, "Can you beat two pair?" the easiest way to make him think you're about to lie is to look away. This does not call for dramatic movements of the head and shoulders. Just flick your eyes quickly to the right or left, blink once and . . . say whatever you're going to say. Remember, your opponent will tend to think you are lying, so you may want to tell the truth. The problem with this, as in so many aspects of poker, is that it depends on how astute your opponent is. If he's only sufficiently astute to have read a book or two and know that "most people will tell the truth in these situations," then you will have outsmarted yourself. He won't notice the eye flickering and will take your answer to be the truth. Whether or not an opponent will take the bait you give him depends primarily on whether or not he notices there is bait to be taken.

A case in point came up the other night. Jack made a very convoluted play in an English stud game against Harry. This had to do with leaving certain cards at the twist, dumping other cards that appeared not to make sense and setting an entire scenario to make it look like he might be going high instead of low. Well, all he accomplished was ruining his hand and ending up with a mishmash that was no good either way. The fool-Harry strategy had gone right over, way over, Harry's head; he hadn't paid the slightest attention to what Jack was doing with his cards. After the hand, Jack thoroughly explained what his strategy had been (of course), while Harry just sat there in happy oblivion, not even understanding what Jack was talking about. So, if you're going to try any very tricky stuff with your eyes or whatever, make sure your opponent is the type who will pay attention to that kind of thing. Usually, it's better just to keep things simple.

Human nature is like the Mississippi River. Superficially, it is always the same, rolling inexorably south to the Gulf. You can count on it, predict it, bet on it. But if you're going to spend a lot of time on the river, you have to know it more intimately. You have to know not only where the snags and bars are but where they might have sprung up today when they weren't there yesterday. The more closely you pay attention to it, the more variables and potential for variety you find. As we discussed before regarding chaos theory, the more information you have the better you can predict behavior—of a river, a galaxy, or a person. Take a rule of thumb like the "poker face" rule mentioned above. People like Jack will put their boat on it and always figure it will take them south in a smooth ride. They don't respect the river enough to consider that it might have developed a sandbar or two, and they don't know the river well enough to know where to look for potential snags. Sure, you can use rules of thumb, that's what they're for. But you have to maintain a constant vigil, on the lookout for exceptions. If someone gives you the poker face, or if someone bets-and-talks, is he obeying the rule, or is he using it as a ploy? If you can't make that determination and be right a majority of the time you can't win at poker.

The player, the person, is all important in poker. Have you ever played against a machine? I have. Many people have: those who have poker games in their computers. I have one poker program in particular that is pretty good as poker programs go, but I've never met a computer poker game I couldn't bust. Even in the machine, however, the nature of the "player" is all important.

A few minutes ago, I was taking a break from my daily chores (writing this book being one of them) and I switched my computer over to the poker game. Within a few hands, I had two pair, QQ88, and "Betty" had just bet into me. I knew what I would do, but much of the time I go to "Ask" to see what the programmer, the machine, would do. The machine informed me that, in an eight-handed game, the odds of two-pair queens-up winning at the showdown are .67 to 1 (this is odds-on). The machine told me I should bet the ranch. What the machine had neglected to take into account is that "Betty" had raised before the draw and then drawn two cards. In some 20,000 hands with Betty, *every* time she has drawn two cards she has had trips, no exceptions; therefore, my probability of winning if I called was zero, or so near zero that there would have to be a trillion dollars in the pot to call. There are other mechanical players in the program who bluff and screw around, but not "Betty." The mathematics of poker apply *only if you know absolutely nothing* about your opponent. If that is your case, you shouldn't be playing poker in the first place. The very, very first thing you need to do when playing, especially with strangers, is to size up your opponents. (End of the story: I folded. One of the other mechanical players called, and "Betty" won with trip tens.)

A word about computer poker games: Some recent books recommend playing computer poker to get in hundreds or thousands of hands of "free" practice. Yes, I agree, sort of. If you need to learn the very basics of poker then computer games can be a big help; however, I believe this is their maximum utility as a teaching tool. As entertainment, hell yes, some of these games are great to blow off a couple hours and relax. No game I have encountered to date, however, has been able to come up with truly challenging players, which could mislead a relative novice into thinking, "Hey! This is easy!" That relative novice might then decide to head on down to his local casino, where he would then be stampeded right back home again, broke. So, my advice is: if you need or want to practice the very basics, or if you just want some entertainment, then play computer poker. But it ain't the real world, so don't let it get you overconfident. (About a month ago I acquired the *World Series of Poker "Adventure"* from Masque Publishing, which is structured just like the real WSOP at Binion's Horseshoe. I am already the fifteen-time "world champion"—and bored with the program. Would that it *were* the real world!) [24]

Now, what *is* handy to have on your computer (and here comes a bald-faced plug) is a program like The PokerWiz which I developed with my friend Ricardo Pessanha. As I mentioned, it is a study program that allows you to set up any sort of poker situation you like in an assortment of different games and then run off a hundred thousand or a million hands—or however many you like—and see the results. Do you want to know the odds of your four-flush outdrawing a pair in seven card stud with three cards to come? Just set it up and run it. How did I know, back on page 83, that pocket rockets could have a losing streak of as many as thirty-four hands in a row? The PokerWiz told me so. It's great, and at this writing there's nothing else on the market that I know of that gives you the wealth of information The PokerWiz does. You can even set up a game like, say, Hold 'em with ten players, and "deal" hand after hand, one at a time to get a feel for the random distribution of the cards. How often does someone have a pair? How often does that pair improve? How often does it win or lose? *Here's* where you can spend a couple hours at the computer and acquire a feel for how cards work. you can discover odds and probabilities that would require complex and tricky mathematical calculations—or memorizing eye-glazing charts in books. One thing you'll find is that the theoretical probablilities one finds published in poker books are often off by several percent from what actually happens when the cards are dealt! Remember, though, you're learning how to use your tools, the cards. When it comes to using those tools other factors take over and the cards take second place to

---

[24.] If you're as dissatisfied with computer poker as I am, just wait: there's hope! By late 1997 my computer partner and I will be coming out with what we hope is a truly challenging computer poker game.

people. Now that we've had a word from our sponsor, back to our program . . .

Once you know how cards work, and especially, once you know people, you can play without even looking at your cards.

Hold on a minute. What I'm going to tell you now is so unbelievable that, well, you may not believe it. In any case, it is God's truth—and it works. I'll start over.

I often—*often*, mind you—play all or most of a hand without looking at my cards. Sometimes, I even announce that I'm not looking at my cards. The fun part of doing that is that players rarely believe you; they think you've looked surreptitiously and are just showboating, or if they do believe you they think you are nuts. The main reasons for not looking at your cards are: (1) to have fun and test your theories; (2) to build your wild and loose image; (3) to completely confound your opponents and set them up. Of course, the overriding reason for doing *anything* in serious poker is to win money, and this is just another ploy that helps to do that. The frequency with which I do this depends on the frequency of favorable situations encountered. Occasionally, an entire poker session will go by without presenting a favorable situation, but this is rare. The average frequency is one or two times a session and is best applied in fixed-limit games rather than in pot limit or table stake games, for obvious reasons. How does this work? Let me illustrate.

The other night I was out of a hand and got up to get a sandwich. (Let me sidetrack here to make another point. I avoid eating a big meal before or while playing poker. Something I suppose in my metabolism, makes me a bit fuzzy-headed if my tummy's full. I have heard others mention this and, thus, I apparently am not alone. On the other hand, abject hunger is distracting too. What to do? What I usually do is just snack in bits and pieces over the course of the poker session, making perhaps a light sandwich and nibbling on it over the course of a couple hours—yuck! This keeps the energy up and keeps stomach pangs down while not inhibiting my play. It is worthwhile for you to examine this in terms of yourself as it is a true, though silly-sounding, phenomenon.) Anyway, while I was puttering around the food table, trying to find a couple pieces of bread that had not yet turned to bricks, the hand ended, and the new deal was begun for seven stud high-low. The dealer, immediately to my right, (actually to the right of my chair since I wasn't in it) shouted, "Are you in, Dave?" I decided to see what would happen and said, "Sure." I kept appearing to putter as I watched the deal and saw that I had A♥ as my first up card. I didn't say anything, however, until the dealer said, "You're first with an ace, what do you want to do?" "Bet two dollars," I said, from ten feet away. My neighbor to the left reached over and took two dollars from my stack and put it in the pot. Of the seven other players, two dropped and five called.

The next card was dealt and the dealer said, "You got a king. What do you do?" Now, this wasn't great, as I would have much preferred to be showing a card to a low, say a three or a four, but, what the hell. "Bet two dollars." Of the five other players, four called and the dealer, sitting just before me, raised. He had what I call the "I'll show *you*" look on his face, which meant he probably didn't have much, he was just pissed off that I was playing from ten feet away. Pissing off other players with your play is a very useful thing to do. If you *really* piss them off, you can often put them off their games for the rest of the night. "I raise," I said. Everyone called the extra four dollars and the dealer, showing signs of major upset, meekly called the extra two. Now I knew the dealer had only raised in irritation. Had he reraised, I may have had to return to the table. "Are you gonna come back and look at your cards, or what?" he said. "Just a minute," I said. "I'm trying to find a piece of meat that doesn't look like it's been here since last week."

Now, of course, my tactic had acquired a subtactic: upset the dealer as much as possible. He was losing. I was winning, and my cavalier attitude about throwing money in the pot was really getting to him. This reinforced my assessment that he didn't have much. If he had had a big hand, he would have been keeping quiet, happy for the extra money. His thinking probably went something like this: "I'm sitting here with a lousy hand, but I'm not going to let that SOB beat me or make me fold when he doesn't even know what he has." There was one other player, however, who I thought deserved some analysis. He, in fact, *was* sitting there quietly looking pleased that I was stupidly building a pot for him, and he had that alert, watchful look that people get when they see a big hand coming their way. The dealer's and my having raised had kept him from having to raise and showing his strength, which was even better for him.

My next card up was a nine, and I was still the leader. "When the dealer growled that it was still my bet, I said, "Three dollars." One player called, and the strong-looking hand raised. He apparently had come to the conclusion that the dealer would not raise for him again. The man after him dropped, the next guy called, and the dealer sat and looked alternately befuddled and irritated for a few seconds before finally calling. I called. I figured again that the dealer did not have a calling hand, and that my ploy from the food table had made him stubborn. His hesitation was, therefore, a sign of a heated debate going on in his brain. The left side knew he should be out, but the right side didn't want to surrender to my sandwich. Had I been sitting there playing normally, he could have assuaged his ego by "reading" me for having a stronger hand, thus allowing him to drop with his pride intact. But, how could he fold playing against a sandwich?

The strong-looking guy was showing 2, 5, 7, off suit and was, therefore, almost certainly low, but his behavior was indicating such strength that he probably had four to a wheel. If he hit, he could swing. The situation from my point of view was mixed. He probably had an ace in the hole, which would only leave him eight cards to make a straight, of which four were exposed. (If he had four to a wheel without an ace that would leave him twelve cards because the sixes would make him a straight to the seven, but I was quite sure he had an ace.) This was good because it meant he would have a tough time hitting a wheel. It was also bad, however, in that his having an ace meant that it was less likely that *I* had one or would get one.

Of the other three players, two looked low but weak, and the dealer showed a mishmash. This was really getting interesting, but I was running out of excuses to stay away from the table, so I went back and sat down. The dealer said, "Well, are you going to look at your hole cards now?" I said, "Nah, that would just confuse me. Besides, I've got mustard all over my fingers. Deal!" My last card up was a 9, so I was showing A-K-9-9. The strong low hand got a 10. Good: one less shot at a wheel. I bet $4, the next hand, one of the weak-looking lows called and the strong low raised to $8. The weak-looking low before the dealer folded, and the dealer, looking disgusted, called. I raised to $12. "How can you keep raising if you haven't even looked at your cards?" he half-shouted. "Just stupid, I guess." The weak-looking low behind me muttered, "Jesus Christ," and raised to $13, killing the last raise. The strong low called, and the dealer practically threw the $5 into the pot. I called the $1 raise.

The last card was dealt down, and when finished with the deal, the dealer grumbled, "Are you going to look, *now*?" "That would be cheating," I said.

I bet out, $5. The weak low folded, the strong low raised to $10. The dealer raised to $11, and I raised to $16. They both called. Hands went under the table with chips. Saying "Just a minute," the dealer sat and sat, thinking and thinking. His ears were smoking from so much thinking. Finally, he looked disgusted and brought his hand up on the table. We opened our hands and . . . he had gone low! I was all alone for high. Such a triumph! I bet $5 and the strong low raised to $10. The dealer, looking utterly confounded, raised to $11 and I raised to $16. The strong low and the dealer called. They turned over their cards, and the strong low had 7-5-3-2-A. The last card had given the dealer a bad 8 low—but he also had a pair of jacks. I said, "Let's see what I've got," and turned over my cards. Nothing. The pair of nines was it. The dealer went nuts for the rest of the session and played solely with the intent of wreaking revenge on me. From my point of view, this is an excellent frame of mind for an opponent to be in, especially that guy. I waited till now to tell you, but the dealer was Carl, button pusher extraordinaire. I *really* enjoyed pushing his buttons back at him.

With $221 in the pot, $111 of which was mine since I had won high, I had managed to have fun, reinforce my "wild" and lucky image, confuse the other players, introduce a "loose" atmosphere to the game, put one player off his game for the rest of the night, and make $56 while doing it. Had the situation been different, that is, had it not developed in such a way that I thought I could pull it off by hammering my psychological advantage over Carl, I would have sat back down at the second up-card, analyzed the possibilities and either played on or folded as required, without fanfare. Remember, I do this sort of thing quite often, but *only* when a favorable situation presents itself. If I start off with a ploy like this and the situation deteriorates, I just quietly fold up. I don't know the people you play with, so I can't tell you when and when not to do it, or even *if* you should try it. You will have to analyze that for yourself, remembering first that you must know your opponents and their behavior, and second that the situation must "prime" the other players to be susceptible to it. If you try this and make a lot of noise about it too early, and it flops, the only thing that will happen is that the other players will think you are interpersonally challenged.

Another good opportunity for not looking at your cards comes when you have a strict percentage advantage. In both the limit and pot-limit games, 5-card stud, high-low, with a reversible twist, chip declare is very popular. This is a great opportunity to run a percentage blind bet by ostentatiously not looking at your new hole card. The other night we were playing this, and Tim and I were going low. I was showing 8,6,4,2 and had a 2 in the hole. Tim was showing 10,9,8,3, hole unknown. The best Tim could draw to would be a 9 low, I would be drawing, twisting, to an 8-low. Comes time to dump for the twist. Tim dumps his 10 and turns up an ace. I dump my hole card, the paired 2. Tim and I both get a card down, and I take mine, stick it under the up cards and say, "I'm not even going to look. I've got him beat going in." Now, this is dumb, right? Not if you know Tim and monitor his behavior.

The high hand to my right bets and I raise. "How can you raise when you haven't looked?" he squawked. "Confidence," I said. A high hand behind me raised again and Tim, looking upset and uncertain, called and killed the final raise. The high hand before me called, I called and the high hand behind me called. Now, had Tim shown some confidence in calling, I would have read him as having hit his 9-low and I would have said "Oops, I'd better look now." Since he had looked uncertain, I still had the percentages on my side. (Remember—I can't emphasize enough—this was working in direct ratio to my knowledge of Tim as a player. Against another player, a player for instance who might know how to look worried when he wasn't, I wouldn't even have tried it. For even a good player having hit his 9-low could only call when looking at my possible 8-low.) With the betting, declaring, and final betting over, Tim turned up a king. With a flourish I said, "Well, let's see what I've got," and turned up a 10. Lucky? No. Just not unlucky, and there's a big difference. A player said, "Tim! How could you stay in on a king?" and Tim said, "How was I supposed to know what he had when even *he* didn't know?" And therein lies the point of the whole episode: people will stay in with really bad cards when they otherwise—if I had looked at my card and bet out—may have folded. More money in the pot.

Is this dangerous? Well, you are going to lose some of those blind bets, but if you figure your percentages—and do it against the right people—you will win more than you lose and your wild and loose image will skyrocket. A good player, of course, will know what you are doing and figure his own percentages, so don't pull it against someone you think knows what's going on. Also, I personally would only do this in limit games, not pot limit or table stakes, for this reason: The object of this ploy is to get your opponent to call with lousy cards. In pot limit or table stakes, it would be much more likely that he would only call with a decent hand and, therefore, much more likely that you will lose if he calls. Here again, though, this depends on your opponent. In the example above, I figured at the time that I had odds-on of 1 to 1.25. This is fairly slim, but in a limit game will pay off in the long run. For a pot limit or no limit bet, however, I would look first. By the way, it was pretty silly of Tim to call with a king. His king meant I needed a pair for him to win, and, at the time, there were only four cards out that could have paired me. With twenty-four unknown cards, that was 5 to 1 against my pairing, while Tim was only getting pot odds of about 2 to 1. Bad move, but that's exactly what I wanted: a bad move inspired by my wild and loose" play.

There is yet one more opportunity to bet "blind." It happens a lot in the limit game, and it's a function of where I sit. Position is extremely important at the poker table. This applies to your betting position within a particular hand, as well as to your seating position at the table. In any case, one of the positioning strategies is to sit next to players who are sloppy with their cards. But, so many of the players in the limit game are so careless with their cards that it's often a true toss-up as to where to sit for the best "view." I usually sit right across from Nick, who has the apparently incorrigible habit of flashing cards right at that seat when he deals. When he deals stud and the twists at the end, I often see many of the down cards, including my own as they sail their way to me. This then, is my other "blind" bet opportunity. I know, you're going to say it isn't blind, and of course it isn't. But it sure looks like it and does get the boys in a dither when my "blind" bets turn out to be winners. Seeing cards, however, can be a false blessing sometimes in that it can make you overconfident. For one thing, Nick only deals once in eight times, and very often what I see means I have to get out. Although this may seem to save me a lot of money, chances are that without seeing the cards I would have gotten out anyway. You can't make a profitable night based on seeing flashed cards one out of eight times. Nor can you make a profitable night out of seeing your neighbor's cards, even every hand. Again, he's only one of many at the table. It can also be a trap.

One time I was playing $10–$20 Hold'em in California, and the guy to my right would flash me his cards, a real show, almost every hand. He would flash, get out, flash, get out, flash, play, whatever. In many ways this was very helpful! But then I learned my lesson. Comes a hand, he flashes pocket nines. I have pocket tens. He raises the blind, I raise, leaving only the two of us in the pot raising each other. The flop comes all low cards, he hits nothing. He bets, I raise, he raises, etc. The turn, he hits nothing. He bets, I raise, he raises, etc. Then, on the river, he hits his third nine. I think, "Well, that's the breaks." The second time it happened, he flashed pocket jacks, I had pocket queens. When he hit his third jack on the river, I thought, "Oh ho!" The third time it happened, he flashed pocket queens, and I had pocket aces. He raised the blind—and I folded. I then looked around the table and said, "Anyone want to make a side bet there's a queen on the river?" Everyone folded except the big blind, who folded after the flop, so I didn't get to see the river, which could have been manipulated away from the queen in any case. The guy to my right packed up his chips and left, and a couple hands later, the dealer changed.

I should have caught on the first time when he kept raising on his pocket nines. Only a tenderfoot or a jerk would do that. But I was caught up in the exhilaration of "knowing" the guy's hand and fell right in. This was classic dealer-player collusion, one of the two most common kinds of cheating these days in public poker, the other being player-player teams. What? A dealer at one of those fancy, plush, secure, safe California card rooms cheating? Come on. They say you can buy a United States senator for the price of a weekend in the Caribbean. If a casino dealer is for sale, how much do you think he or she would cost?[25] The California card rooms and Nevada casinos do all they can to

---

[25.] People who reviewed this book before it went to press told me I was committing a vicious calumny against casino dealers by comparing them to United States senators. I realize they were right, and I apologize. I only wanted to point out that slimy behavior is a possibility—although a teeny, tiny one—even among dealers. It is, of course, a given among senators.

keep cheaters out, but some forms, like dealer-player collusion, are too easy to get away with, at least for a while. Let my lesson be your lesson: if it seems too good to be true, it probably is.

The problem is, how do you know when someone is "innocently" flashing cards? If you're in a big game and you're about to go all in on the basis of having seen someone's cards, beware; certainly take caution if there are more cards to come and the guy has been flashing his cards regularly at you. In fact, just a few days before this happened, I had been playing where the guy on my *left* was flashing his cards. That was legit, apparently, because I took him to the cleaners, which is one reason I may have fallen for the trap so easily (here I am defending myself, giving excuses why I was such a putz in that trap). What you have to look for is illogical play. As I said, that first time, only a real jerk would keep raising on pocket nines, or even kings or queens. Long about the second raise, any experienced player will back off, figuring he might be beat, and that's what I should have seen. If you're in a big game with strangers and some guy on either side of you starts flashing his cards, if I were you, I'd leave because the chances are that anyone experienced enough to play in a big public game would be experienced enough to be able to keep his cards down. In a limit game it might be worth your while to see what's going on, at least once, but even so, don't get overconfident. They might let you win one or two, then wallop you for a big one later on. We'll talk more about this later.

There's another issue here, that of ethics. Is it ethical to look at flashed cards? Well, it depends. In English, as in most languages, we differentiate between "looking at" and "seeing." (We also have a third distinction: "watching," which is not exactly unique to English but is a much rarer, or somewhat more convoluted, concept in many other languages.) "Looking" is active, and "seeing" is passive. And therein lie my own, personal, ethical boundaries.

To me, if you're craning your neck and assuming assorted acrobatic positions in order to see an opponent's cards, then that's "looking", and that's cheating. It's also stupid because others are going to notice what you're doing. On the other hand, if you're sitting there in a normal playing position, minding your own business, and someone is flashing cards at you, this is the totally passive activity of "seeing" and is simply part of the complete poker player's overall strategy of being observant of all factors. This has many variations. For example, if you're dealing, i.e., shuffling, and you shuffle or deal in such a way as to expose cards to yourself, that's cheating. If someone else is dealing or shuffling and, by being generally maladroit, lets you see cards, that's being observant. If it's your turn to cut the cards and you do it in such a way as to be able to look at the bottom card, that's cheating. If someone else is cutting the cards and exposes the bottom card to you, seeing it is simply being observant. You get the idea.

There is also a major distinction between the "friendly," or "semifriendly," game and the "pure business" game. When playing poker for long stretches, because I seem to require more legroom than that provided by the average chair, I often tilt my chair back as a matter of comfort. (I also try to get away with this at protracted dinners, but the success of the maneuver depends entirely on the relative formality of the dinner and the relative proximity of my wife.) In a friendly, or semifriendly, game I'll usually say something like, "Watch how you hold your cards 'cause I'm sitting back." In a business game, like in a casino—the hell with them: let my opponents on my right and left notice for themselves that I've changed position and take their own evasive action.

The same principle applies to "marked" cards, by the way. If a card has acquired a nick or a scratch or a bend that enables me to identify it—then I would apply the friendly/business criteria. If, on the other hand, a player is nicking, scratching, or bending cards for purposes of identification, that player is a cheater.

Be warned: as we have discussed before, to me, and to any serious poker player, there is no such thing as a friendly game of poker.

Chapter 6

Bluffing

here is so much to say about bluffing that one really can only talk about the most important aspects or poker books would run to thousands of pages. Bluffing is what makes poker poker; it is the ultimate people game. It is also what makes poker American. Card games of all sorts are played all over the world, but some 80 percent of the world's poker players are Americans. This is no accident, nor is it an accident that poker has become America's most popular card game. In American culture, bluffing is a part of life. You'll quit your job if you don't get a raise. You'll buy from the competition if you don't get a better price. You'll leave your husband if he does that one more time. You'll sue if the invoice isn't paid today. You'll start a nuclear war if they don't pull their missiles out of Cuba. On and on and on. Whatever the threat, one of your American interlocutor's first reactions is almost sure to be, "Is he/she bluffing?" It adds a dimension to interpersonal relations that is not available in many cultures.

In those cultures, you will simply be taken at your word, face value. To ask "Is he bluffing?" will just not occur to them. If you go to your Belgian boss and threaten to quit if you don't get a raise, your boss will think: "He's going to quit, I'd better decide on that raise." An American boss in a similar situation may well come to the same conclusion but only after he has considered whether or not he thinks you're bluffing. This is a problem for Americans when dealing with the world in politics or in business. On one hand, we tend to bluff into calling stations:

- **American:** Look, your price for this land is too high, we're going to have to build on the other side of town. *(Other side of town is the pits. American really wants this guy's land but wants to force price negotiations.)*

- **Japanese:** Okay. Sorry we couldn't do business.

Your bluff was called, because your "opponent" doesn't know what a bluff is. Or,

- **Russian:** We can't buy your widgets unless you can improve your quality up to your competitor's standards.
- **American:** *(Thinks: quality schmality, he's bluffing, hoping for a better price.)* Well, what we can do is knock 5 percent off the price on orders of 100,000 units.
- **Russian:** Sorry, I said quality was the problem. Didn't I make myself clear? *(And he orders from the competition.)*

Both parties to a bluff, the bluffer and the bluffee, must have an inbred, cultural recognition of what's going on. Americans tend to think everybody bluffs, and it isn't so. Others tend to think Americans are extremely brash, quick with a deal-ending threat, when of course it was just a bluff. Thus, poker. We Americans all know the game because its roots are in our culture. This is why, as a general rule, non-Americans are not good poker players. I've known a lot of non-American poker players, Brits especially, who are sharp as a tack with card odds and have the patience of Job to sit there and wait for good hands. But when they bet, God bless them, they have it, every time. A good player will catch on soon enough, but Americans who have no experience playing with them, or who are mediocre poker players, lose because they just don't want to believe that a person exists who doesn't bluff.

A while back, one of the guys brought along a visiting British friend to the game. This fellow had obviously played poker before, but he was not what one would call experienced in that he seemed to be having a hardish time understanding high-low wheel, high-low six, twists, buys, widows; in other words, the vagaries of a dealer's choice game. He pretty much sat and watched for a while, occasionally seeing a bet to get another card but then folding. By and by he finally played a hand all the way through—and won. There were some comments around the table on the order of, "You don't play many hands, but you seem to win when you do." Our plummy friend said, "Well, that seems about right, doesn't it?"

Well, he hadn't won any of *my* money. And he wouldn't for the rest of the evening. Like so many of his compatriots he was a nut player; a patient, intelligent, worldly nut player who knew Americans would call him like lemmings when he bet. Unfortunately for him, there were a couple of people in that game who had seen him coming and, on several occasions, very successfully sucked him into hands in which he thought he had the nuts but didn't.

When you discover a non-American who does bluff, well, he just can't seem to get it quite right. He knows about "bluffing", knows what it's supposed to accomplish, but it's usually at the wrong time, in the wrong situation, or in a thoroughly typical situation, whatever, but it doesn't wash. You know he's bluffing as if he were holding a neon sign stating the fact. This happens with many non-American cultures, but it seems to be disproportionate among Brits and Germans.

Asians and some Hispanics who have learned the game will bluff but, in most cases, it is not exactly, precisely a bluff. (Remember, we are talking about *foreigners* here, not about Asian- or Hispanic-Americans, to whom this definitely does not apply.) Asian and Hispanic societies are extremely class conscious. They are used to the way money and power force certain predictable behavior from those of lower status. When, especially, an Asian throws a lot of money at you in a poker game, you are not exactly supposed to consider whether or not he is bluffing and act accordingly; you're supposed to sort of bow low and back slowly out of the room muttering soft compliments to his obvious superiority. Poker is very democratic if nothing else, and, needless to say, this doesn't work.

Now, don't all you folks start buying plane tickets and heading east and west. If you do, I don't want any letters from a bunch of poker players who found the exceptions, because there are many of them. There are excellent, complete poker players all over the world who, for one reason or another, have jumped cultural fences and are the equal or the better of any Yank. There also are other cultures for whom bluffing is as natural as it is for us: Brazilians are good bluffers, as are Australians and some Arabs, although very rich Arabs seem to have no idea of the value of money and will tend to call and bet on anything and everything. Besides, if you go to England to play poker, that doesn't mean you're going to be playing with Brits. Whenever I play in England, the poker players all seem to be Greeks, but they don't usually bluff very well either.[26]

There are several kinds of bluff.

First is the classic: you missed your hand and want to try for the pot anyway.

Second is the defensive: You have a weak hand and would rather try to run them out than to check or call and, perhaps, lose.

Third is the advertisement: You want to let the other players know that you do bluff so they will call you when you aren't bluffing.

[26.] Actually, here's an interesting point: In English casinos, virtually all the games are pot-limit. Your being American, the players will start sniffing around for information about your poker background, invariably asking where you play in the "States." Depending on your own level of confidence, here's what you should tell them: If you say you play pot-limit and no-limit in Vegas and private games, they will back off and be wary. If you tell them you play mostly in the California card rooms, they will give you lots of opportunities to make a bundle. Why? Because they know that most of the games in California are limit games and they think you will be unused to big, pot-size bets and will start throwing them at you. That's a fact, and they get all flustered when you take it in stride and start winning all their money. So, if you want a vulnerable image: you play limit poker in California. If you want a defensive image: you play pot-limit and no-limit in Las Vegas.

Fourth is the counterbluff: You think a player is bluffing, so you counterbluff by raising him back.

Fifth is the test of strength bluff: You bet or raise back to see how your opponent reacts.

Sixth is the percentage bluff: Your opposition may well think you are bluffing, but will decide it's going to be too expensive to find out.

Seventh is the come bluff: You have a come hand, say a four flush or a four straight, will probably win if you hit, but would rather win the pot *right now* without having to hit (because you might miss!).

There is yet an eighth type of bluff, but we'll get to it a bit later.

Let me say right off the bat that rare is the occasion when number three, the advertisement, is required. In general, you don't have to go trying to get caught bluffing; if you bluff, you will get caught occasionally anyway. But let's take them one at a time.

The Classic Bluff: This is what most novices think of when they think of bluffing. You miss your flush or your 6-low and throw as much money as possible in the pot hoping your competition will think you have it and fold. Since this is the most common sort, it is also the most highly suspect and the most likely to be called if not done properly. Whether or not this works depends on, primarily, external factors. What do your opponents think of you? Do they think you're tight and rarely bluff? Do they think you bluff a lot? Are they really weak, or is someone sandbagging? If you have the reputation of being a frequent bluffer, it is very likely you are being sandbagged. If you have the reputation of being very tight, there could still be some medium-strong hands out there waiting to see what you will do. In order to increase your chances of bluffing successfully, you can't just throw your money in the pot; you must analyze the situation first. To wit:

Some years ago we were playing lowball draw. My night had been only so so with a run of lousy cards and some bad beats in which players had last-carded me a number of times, and I was feeling kind of discouraged. So when we're playing lowball and

I pick up my five cards and see four jacks looking back at me, I know the poker gods are trying to tell me something, namely: "You don't need cards to win, you lazy bum! Get out there and play!"

The pot is opened four hands to my right. Three people call and—I raise. Two players after me fold. The dealer calls. The opener calls. The next two hands call, and the player on my right reraises. I don't hesitate—I reraise. That is the end of the raises, and they all call back around. Now the guy on my right who had reraised me is Jack, whom I know like the back of my hand. I know that I have walked into him sandbagging a pat hand by just calling the opener. The only way I am going to pull this off is to make him think that I have a better pat hand and, thus, make him draw. Part of this has already been accomplished by my raises. I can see he is beginning to wonder if he should draw. The problem is that he is sitting ahead of me and will have to decide to draw or not before knowing what I am going to do. So, when the dealer picks up the deck and says, "Cards?" I immediately say, "I'm pat," apparently too excited to contain myself. They all grumble at me that I am speaking out of turn, but apparently it works.

When it comes Jack's turn to draw, he hems and haws and thinks and thinks, and finally says, "Well if Dave's so excited, I guess I better draw." He takes one card. Now, my move was a pretty obvious one, but, I keep repeating, you have to know who you're playing against. I knew that Jack would think I had made a mistake in blurting out that I was pat rather than think I was trying to pull off a ploy. I, of course, stay pat. Two of the other players draw one card, and the dealer takes two. (He called one raise cold and then two subsequent reraises to draw two cards? It happens all the time, especially in home games. There are some really bad players out there, bless their little hearts.) So here's what happened, God's truth. The player under the gun bets out! The player next to him calls, and the next player raises! Then Jack raises! I know what is happening and can't believe my luck: the first and third players and Jack are *all* trying bluffs!

After Jack raises, there is one raise left, and again I don't hesitate, I raise.

To my astonishment (yes, astonishment—even though I "knew" what was what, this was still astonishing), the dealer drops. The opener drops. The second player drops. The third player drops—and Jack drops! I win! This was one of those occasions when it is worthwhile, almost compulsory, to show the others what you have done. A bluff like that will go down in the lore of your game and become a permanent part of your reputation. (Besides, I confess, I was just too damn proud of myself to keep it quiet). I say, "Don't feel bad, guys, I had you nutted," and show down the four jacks for all to see. The only sound to be heard is jaws hitting the table and finally a squeaked "Oh, my God!" Then Jack: "Damn it! You son of a bitch! I broke up a pat eight and paired!"

Now, you may have a question or two, but most obvious is this one: "How did you know they were all bluffing after the draw?" Because I knew the players, and I knew that they were sandbaggers all. If any one of them had had a real hand, he would have waited for me to bet and then raised. The only one I was really worried about was the second guy who had just called the opener. In the aftermath, they all talked about it, of course. The second player said he had called with an 8-low thinking that the opener was bluffing and maybe my pat hand was a worse 8. When three raises came behind him, he didn't know who he was going to lose to, but he knew he was going to lose to somebody, so he got out. And, sure enough, the opener, the third man, and Jack had all paired on the draw. I was lucky to have had two raises ahead of me, as that had cemented number two's decision to get out. If number three and Jack had folded, or, worse, if they had just called, my goose would have been cooked. If number two (I don't know why I got into this number thing, his name was Sam) had called the opener with an 8 knowing that I was behind him with a pat hand, he must have had an inkling that something suspicious was up, and, especially if the dealer had folded, he probably would have called me just to see. The fact that number three (Louis) and Jack had decided to run their own bluffs helped me immensely: the only guy at the table with anything like a real hand dropped as much because of them as because of me. I knew that, or I should say I "knew" that. In other words, that had been my analysis of what would happen, but you never know—I could have been wrong. As it was, that hand was the turning point for me that night. For the rest of the game I couldn't do anything wrong, partly because of the boost to my morale and partly because that play had put all the others off balance.

The Defensive Bluff: One illustration of this is the Dave-bets-and-talks-Chuck-out-of-the-pot example seen earlier, beginning on page 115. As you may recall, I was in first betting position with king-rag, a king had come on the flop, and I was betting into Chuck, who I read as having king-queen or king-jack. Now, it's not that I don't have a hand—I have top pair! So this isn't a true type-1 bluff. Because Chuck is sticking around, I'm pretty sure I'm beat, and I sure as hell can't check into a showdown if I want to have a shot at the pot. If I don't bet, I'm dead (I may be dead anyway, but I want to go down fighting). I have to use the combination of the betting initiative and what I know about Chuck to convince him he's beat, which is what happens in the end. This is one instance when it is better to be betting from the front rather than from the rear. Ninety-nine times out of a hundred, you want late position so all the other folks have to act first. But to pull off this type of defensive bluff you have to be first, or you have to count on the other players checking around to you, which is shaky at best. Even if they oblige you by checking, bluffing from last or late position is often just too suspicious and you're likely to be called.

Another instance happened the other night in a hand of Spit Buy. Since this game is played with a twist at the end, there are two chances to draw—once for as many cards as you need, and once for one card. Then high-low is declared with chips in hand. We had declared, and one guy was alone for low, Tim and I declaring high. The low-man bet and Tim just called. Now, here's what had happened and what I figured: We had all been trying for low. All three of us had taken one card at the draw, and Tim and I had each taken one card at the twist, Bill, the low man, had been pat at the twist. My first draw card was a dud, and my second draw card paired me on 5s. Since I had figured Tim and Bill for low, I thought maybe I could back in for high with my pair of 5s. When Tim declared high along with me, I figured he must have done the same thing. Now, calling a bet in high-low with a player behind him is one of Tim's favorite bluffs, and it's not a bad move—I've adopted it myself for occasional use (never too old or too good to learn a new trick!). The end bets in this game can get pretty big, and by just calling, Tim is forcing me to call a big bet while not risking extra money by raising. This is sometimes even more believable than a raise. The problem is that Tim does it too often. So I have to figure the same thing happened to him that happened to me: when drawing for low, he had paired and had tried to back into high. Now, paired on what? was the question. I really can't call with a pair of 5s. I have to raise or get out. I make rather a show of thinking about it and raise the maximum. The lone low hand, Bill, raises again, so Tim is stuck staring two raises in the face with, I hope, just a low pair. Sure enough, he folds. Tim then shows his cards to the table to justify folding, and he has a pair of 7s.

This was a clear example of a defensive bluff. My 5s *could* have been a winner under the circumstances: Tim, drawing for low, could have paired on 4s, 3s, or 2s—or just hit a high card— but the risk that he had paired on 6s, 7s, or 8s was too great for me to take a chance on letting the cards win by themselves. My pair of 5s needed help, and I gave it in the form of a defensive bluff. This, then, is the distinction of a defensive bluff: your cards *might* win on their own, but you'd rather not have to find out. In the Chuck example, my kings with no kicker *might* have won had I been wrong about what Chuck was holding. He could, for example, have been hanging in there with a lower pair, perhaps queens or jacks in the pocket, but I didn't think so, and I didn't want to find out by checking into a showdown. It was better to help my weak kings along with a defensive bluff. (In the Tim example above, you might think that he could have figured out about me what I figured out about him: that I was probably holding a low pair in a busted low hand. Well, remember that I said Tim had reached a plateau. As always, whether or not a particular maneuver should be tried depends entirely upon who you are playing against.)

The Advertisement: I don't really have much to say in favor of this since I think that 99.9 percent of the time it is wrong to bluff just for the sake of advertising. Unless there is a particular reason, such as a truly spectacular bluff that you want remembered and talked about, like my four jacks, you should just keep your bluffs to yourself. Another reason to show that you have bluffed is if you think it will upset another player sufficiently to help put him on tilt as I do with Jack and others from time to time. But in both these cases, the bluffs are carried out *for their own purpose;* in other words, I was bluffing to *win the pot,* which is the whole point. After the bluff works, then occasionally it is a very good move to show what you have done. But just to bluff, for the sake of getting caught is almost always a waste of time and money. As I said, if you bluff you will get caught often enough without trying to make it happen.

I am hesitant to say anything in favor of this for fear of giving the wrong impression, but, as with all things, there are a couple of limited, specific exceptions in which an advertising bluff *might* be called for. One day I was having a particularly good run of cards at a California card room. I didn't need to bluff or maneuver in the classic sense because I was getting so many good hands. Whenever I bet I had it. This created the "tight player's" problem: after a while I wasn't getting any callers. From the evidence the other players had seen, I was just another nut player who happened to be getting a lot of nuts, so they all started folding when I was in the hand. Well, I thought, I'd better run a bluff or two to loosen them up. I didn't want a run of cards like that to be wasted on peanut-sized pots. So I started bluffing on trash. Because I was also getting a lot of good cards, this meant I was playing *many* hands, and sure enough, I eventually got caught. That was worthwhile. When I finally got caught, remarks like "He's been bluffing all this time" (short memories), started going around the table, and I started getting callers and cleaned up.

Two points: First, okay, I started bluffing with the intention of eventually getting caught, but before I was caught *I won money on the bluffs*. In other words, I didn't do something really stupid and obvious to insure that I would get caught right off the bat. Second, and here's the real point, in twenty-some years of serious poker playing I can think of perhaps two or three occasions in which this situation came up. This is hardly a high-frequency event. So, keep advertisement bluffs in your arsenal, but remember that your next occasion to use it might be in ten years or so.

There is one other circumstance when the advertisement applies, but, again, to do it *just* for the sake of advertisement is a waste. There are certain types of people—modern political correctness prohibits me from saying which types—who, once they have caught you bluffing them, will call every last bet you make for the rest of eternity. Yes, you should bluff against these people and hope to get caught. But that still doesn't mean you should *only* bluff to get caught. Rather, bluff well to try to make some money with the idea being that when you eventually get caught you will use that fact to full advantage. Or, if, for some overriding strategic reason, you *really* want these people to catch you out right away, bluff—win the money, and then show what you have done. That actually works even better, and you haven't had to waste money while doing it.

I hope I have been clear on this point. Many people think that to establish themselves as wild and loose, they have to sit down to a game and get caught making outlandish bluffs right off the bat. This isn't so, and those who do this deprive themselves of the bluff later on since, as was the plan, nobody believes them anymore. They don't get no respect. There are ways to do this without throwing money away and without depriving yourself of any of your strategic armaments for use later in the game, as we shall see in the image section, in Chapter 8.

The Counterbluff: Elements of this were present in my four-jacks example above. When two guys raised ahead of me after the draw and I reraised, convinced they were bluffing, this was a type of counterbluff. It wasn't *entirely* a counterbluff because I needed to get the number two man, Sam, and the dealer out as well.

An honest-to-goodness counterbluff happened just the other night. The game was seven stud high, and after the sixth card there were four of us in. I'm showing a mishmash that includes two clubs, one of which is an Ace. In fact, my first four cards had been clubs, with only one other club showing, and I'd been trying for the fifth one ever since. Nick is showing a pair of kings and trying to make it look like two pair or trips by betting the hell out of it. Well, I know it isn't trips because I have one king in the hole and have seen the other one flashed. But if he has two pair, he's the leader of the pack. I certainly can't beat it yet, and the other two hands are showing a nice assortment of trash, so they probably can't beat it either. Nick, of course, realizes this, and this is why he's trying so hard to make those kings look better than just a pair (he's actually doing a defensive bluff). Because of the obvious bluffing situation, because I know he doesn't have trips, because several of his potential two-pair cards are out, I put Nick on just the pair of kings and a lot of hope. That means that my Ace must be worrying him, and I'm beginning to lose faith that I'll get the fifth club. So, I start thinking counterbluff; time to start setting it up. When he bets out after the sixth card, the two trash hands fold—finally; they should have been out three cards ago—and I raise. Nick says, "What the hell've *you* got? "Better than kings," I say. He calls, and we get the last card down. Sure enough, I have managed to miss my flush. Three cards to pull, hardly a club in sight, and I miss. Imagine that. Good thing I had started working on Plan B.

Nick is squeezing out his last hole card, which for me is another indication that all he has are the kings. He finally looks up and says, "Can you still beat kings?" "Gee, I don't remember!" I say. Trying to look very confident, he bets out. I don't wait even a nanosecond to raise him. "You finally got that last club, hey?" "Gee, I don't remember!" Looking disgusted with his cards and the world, he trashes his hand. "You're a lucky SOB to hit on the last card like that." "No doubt about it," I say, and rake in the pot.

Now, Nick didn't really put me on a flush. He put me on aces, maybe aces up, but he didn't want to admit that all he had had were the kings. Figuring I had aces, there was nothing he could do. His kings were beat and he had to fold.

Well, there was *something* he could have done. He could have counterbluffed my counterbluff, but he hadn't read me properly. In an almost mirror-image situation with Carl the other night, that's exactly what I did. Same game: seven stud high. On the fifth card I hit three diamonds showing. This doesn't do squat for me, since I have a pair of kings in the hole, neither of which is a diamond. But it looks good on the "front porch" as they say. Carl, unfortunately, has just hit a pair of aces. There's only one other player in the pot not showing anything interesting. Carl bets, the other guy gets out, and I raise. "Hit a flush, huh?" "Gee, I don't remember!" "Yeah, yeah, you never remember." Carl calls. The next card up gives me four diamonds showing. How about that! I might hit a flush after all, and, meanwhile, it's looking scarier and scarier. Carl checks. I bet, and Carl raises! "Carl!" I say, "You hit a full house?" Carl hasn't prepared himself to answer questions and he just sort of looks down at his lap. To me, that means "No." I raise. "You can't raise. I could have a house here." "You're a daisy if you do," I said (I had just seen *Tombstone* the night before). Carl called. Now, Carl's calling is silly. He's admitting he doesn't have it. He should have either raised or folded. But clearly he thought he had one more draw to hit something, and he was going for it. The other possibility is that he hadn't decided yet whether or not I really had a flush, so he just called to get one more card and think about it. The last card brings me zilch: no flush, no king, not even two pair, and there's Carl, inspecting his last card. Now this is one of Carl's tells. Most people, if they hit something big, certainly a flush or a full house, will see it right away, put down their cards, and start thinking about what to do. Only a novice or very bad player will look six times to make sure he's hit his hand, and Carl is definitely not the former and usually not the latter. What Carl did, however, was to look at his last hole card and then keep looking up and down between his hole cards and his up cards. This tells me that Carl hasn't hit anything and is looking around trying to find something that he may have overlooked. He eventually puts his cards down and looks at me. He checks. I bet, and Carl raises. I raise back. He looks down at his cards, studies a few seconds, and folds. When he picks up his cards to trash them, I see a 6♥ on the bottom, which is where he had placed his last card. This was a real dud, no help at all. "At least I have sense enough to fold when I know I'm beat," he says. "Good play, Carl. I had you."

In case you lost the story line, what happened there was:

Me: Classic bluff, Classic bluff
Carl: Counterbluff,
Me: Counterbluff, Classic bluff
Carl: Counterbluff,
Me: Counterbluff.

That's a lot of bluffing! Well, that's poker. Those who think that bluffing is missing your hand and betting out are very mistaken. Very often, as I think I've said before, the cards are incidental. Poker is a test of wills in which players jockey for position and psychological advantage.

The Maneuver Bluff: If you go back to the example of "John" betting into "Matt's" seven-low on page 104, this is an exact case of the maneuver bluff, and, as seen in that example and the following discussion, you have to be very careful and know your opponent very well to pull it off. Recapping, John, showing an 8-low, bet $1,000 into Matt's possible 7-low. The point of the maneuver was to drive Matt out if he didn't really have a 7-low. Matt didn't have it, nor did he think it odd that John was betting into the nuts, and he got out.

Another example of a maneuver bluff is found in the raise I made and the subsequent "I'm pat" statement, spoken out of turn, in the four-jacks example above. With the bet and the coffeehousing, I wanted Jack to break up his pat hand. Had Jack stopped to think about it, he should have realized what I was trying to do. But he didn't. In a classic bluff, your opponent's reaction should be: "He has a better hand, I fold." In a maneuver bluff, your opponent's reaction should be: "He may have a better hand, I'd better do something about it."

I don't know how many people play straight draw poker, jacks or better, anymore, but for those who do the maneuver bluff comes up frequently. If you've ever opened or raised on two pair, stood pat, and bet out after the draw, that's a maneuver bluff. You're bluffing as to the value of your hand, but you are actually inviting a call! You are also trying to force players after you to break up hands and draw for miracles to beat your pat hand. This used to happen all the time in the old days in Gardena. I did it, we all did it, until one day I read *Education of a Poker Player* by Herbert O. Yardley. He describes a hand in which Monty stays pat on three 10s. Staying pat on trips? Who ever heard of that? Well . . .

The next time I was playing in Gardena I had two pat hands in rapid succession, say within a half hour. A few hands later I get—three 10s! The pot is opened. I raise, get three callers, and stand pat. Chris, a weight-lifter and denizen of the old Rainbow, as was I at the time (denizen, that is, not weight-lifter), is sitting on my left and had lost to both my earlier pat hands. When I stand pat he says "Again?" and draws three cards. The pot is checked to me, and I bet out. Chris says, "You can't be pat *all* the time" and calls. The other players fold. I show down my three 10s and Chris shows his two pair aces and trashes his hand. "Standing pat on trips? Who ever heard of that?" says Chris. I think: chalk one up for Herbert and Monty. (The truth is, a lot of my poker winnings can be traced back to Herbert and Monty. If you've been playing poker seriously for more than two weeks and haven't read that book, you are remiss.)

The Test of Strength Bluff: This occurs in any poker variation, but it is especially prevalent in Hold'em. In Hold'em, it is imperative to try to read your opponents' cards as closely as possible, and sometimes a raise is the quickest way to do that.

Imagine that someone in early position raises the blind. Is it a pocket pair? Is it Big Slick? Is it ace-queen suited? Is it a 7-2? What is it? The bet comes around to you. You have a pocket pair of jacks, and you want more information. Your opponent has been playing solid, tight Hold'em for three hours. You raise. The guy raises back. You raise. He raises back. That's all you need—he has a pair of aces. (If he doesn't, don't blame me. You've misjudged his character and/or ability.) If he hadn't reraised the second time, you would probably put him on QQ, KK or, just maybe, Big Slick suited. In that case, he probably thinks *you* have the aces, which could be handy if one comes up on the board.

Using this as a model, you can apply it to any poker variation. The other night, playing seven stud, I get [QA]A and Jack is showing a jack. I bet. He raises. I raise. He raises. Jack has got three jacks wired, no doubt about it. On the next card, an ace falls elsewhere on the table, and when the bet comes around to me, I fold. Those raises in the cheap first betting round told me all I need to know: there's no need to spend any more money on this hand.

The Percentage Bluff: This happens a lot in high-low stud, especially if there is a twist, and your opponents are relatively loose. There are those who say it isn't really a bluff but just a percentage bet. In any case, this is what I described on page 131. Recapping, Tim and I were going low. I could twist to an 8-low, while the best Tim could twist to was a 9-low. We both take our cards down, and I take mine, stick it under the up cards, and say that I'm not going to look at it. We have equal chances of hitting good cards or bad cards, and I have the "percentages" in my favor since I'm drawing to the better hand. The whole point of this is either to get Tim to come in with a bad card or to get him to fold when he might have me beat. As it happens in that example, Tim stays in with a king, losing to my ten because "How was I supposed to know what he had when even *he* didn't know?"

I did this twice the other night against Edgar. Both times I was twisting to the better low, so I stuck my twist card under the up cards, announced I wasn't looking, and bet out. The first time, Edgar had caught a queen and folded. When I turned up my twist card, it had paired my 5s. The second time, Edgar had caught a king, and folded. My twist card had paired my 6s. Had I looked at my card, Edgar may well have convinced himself that he "smelled something" and stayed in with his bust. Since he could think of no excuse to call, he folded.

Does this work against anybody? Well, yes, if you play it properly and remember that sometimes you are going to lose. A "percentage" bluff or bet is exactly that: you figure you will win more often than you will lose. People react differently: Tim called with his king, while Edgar folded his king.

What about the "Harrys" of the world? The other night I was low against Harry, and my percentage bluff wasn't precisely that: I had seen my twist card flash as it came in, and I knew it had paired me. But I played it the same way, sticking it under the up cards and announcing "blind." I bet out, and it comes around to Harry. Harry has obviously hit a clinker because he's looking very unhappy and undecided. "Undecided" is really moot in regard to Harry because he would have to hit a pair of kings not to call. He just likes to look as if he's thinking about it first. He says, "I wish Dave wouldn't do that blind thing." I say, "The only reason I do it is to get you to come in on bad cards." Offended, he says, "Well it didn't work this time" and folds. Had he thought about it, Harry could have figured out that I was trying to talk him out of calling, but Harry is Harry.

Now, when I bluffed against Harry, your 5-star calling station, I was fully prepared to lose but, I confess, every once in a while "getting Harry to fold" becomes a challenge, and I take it upon myself to bear this cross for humanity. And I don't do it very often. When I *do* get him to fold, I consider it a moral victory and allow myself to feel quite smug about it. There's also an ulterior motive, which we'll see in a minute.

The more serious point is that—what!?—I told my strategy

to the table! It doesn't matter. The other players had already discussed fifty-seven varieties of theory explaining why I do it. Although they've come up with the right reasons, not one of them has ever come up with the appropriate counter measure, and they still get all confused and off balance and don't know what to do. What is the appropriate counter measure? Raise me back. Raise into the possible nuts? Sure. If you've hit anywhere near your hand, and I'm blind, then *you* have a percentage bet. The odds will be greatly in your favor that you've hit better than I have, so you should raise. But what if you get a bad card? Then it's a toss-up and you'll have to figure your chances of winning against the money in the pot. But you should still raise and test the "percentage" bettor. Then if he raises you back, you can revert to a classic "Does-he-have-it-or-doesn't-he?" situation. What you should not do is let me manipulate you like a puppet. Whatever you decide, you should at least grab the initiative—and do it!

Another type of percentage bluff occurs in high-low when you're holding a low hand that is a potential swinger. The other night we were playing pot-limit five stud, high-low with a twist. I'm low, showing 4568, and Juan is high showing a pair of queens. I have a two in the hole, a lock on the low and the twist coming. It had come down to the two of us. Juan checks his queens and I bet the pot, $150. Now, Juan doesn't know if I have the straight now or am going to have to twist for it. If I do twist for it, he still won't know whether I hit it or not. He does know that, whatever happens, my next bet is going to be $450 if he calls this one. It's just not worth it, and he folds. This is clearly a percentage bluff in which *all* the numbers were on my side. It doesn't matter to juan whether I have the straight or not, by calling he has everything to lose and practically nothing to gain. This is one reason I virtually never play for high in a pot limit or no limit game as we'll see in more detail in Chapter 7, Betting & Money: you often get trapped into putting lots and lots of money in the pot in the hopes of getting just a little bit back.

The Come Bluff: Say you're playing Hold'em. The flop comes two clubs, and you have two clubs in the pocket: flush draw. You take the initiative and bet, or if someone else bets first, you raise. The turn comes up a diamond: no help. Same thing: you either bet out or raise if someone bets first. You're hoping to accomplish two things: (1) get more money in the pot if you do hit your flush, and (2) more importantly since you're about a 4 to 1 dog to hit at this point, you're trying to win the pot *right now*. You're trying to show that you *already* have a hand and are hoping that your opposition will fold. You're also disguising the fact that your hand is a come hand, so that if you decide to continue the bluff after having missed on the river, it won't be so easy to read as a missed-flush classic bluff. The big advantage to a come bluff is that you have a big out if it doesn't work: you may actually hit your hand and win anyway! If you wait till the last card to try your bluff, you have no outs; it either works or it doesn't.[27]

In the end, a bluff is a bluff. These seven categories describe different ways to use it, different ways to set it up, different manifestations of the same thing. Many of them work together: if you're planning on a classic bluff, if you miss your flush, then you should begin setting it up early with a come bluff.

You may have noticed, however, that in many of the cases described above, the bluff involves a raise rather than an original bet. A bluff *bet* is often just too suspicious—and cheap—whereas a bluff *raise* packs more wallop. This is especially true in a limit game, where, given the size of the pot, a player might call a relatively cheap end bet just to "keep you honest" or "for the size of the pot," and it works even better in high-low split declare games. In those games, you have the added advantage of having

---

[27.] In fact, in any game but especially in stud and widow games, if you're on the come you should often be betting and raising. ("Often" be betting and raising? Well, remember: "always" and "never" almost never [!] apply to poker.) If you disagree with this, there's a discussion of the point in the chapter on betting and money. When you've read that, if you *still* disagree, let me know and we'll set up a televised debate.

someone who's going the other way (and is therefore no competition for you) do your raising for you.

This is what happened in the example with Tim under "defensive bluffs." Since Tim and I were high and there was a low man between us, I could count on the low player for an extra raise. When it came back around to Tim, he was looking at the prospect of calling two raises with his lousy hand, rather than just calling mine. He was then doubly inclined to fold. (Note: That low player, Bill, shouldn't have raised unless he was sure that Tim was going to call. Bill was guaranteed half the pot, and his duty to himself was to get as much high-hand money in the pot as possible. His raise helped me to run Tim out, thus making the pot shorter for himself. Had he just called my raise, it would have been much easier for Tim to decide to call one raise instead of two.)

If bluff-by-raise is more effective that just bluff, then bluff-by-check-raise is the most effective of all. There have been thousands of times when I have checked a worthless hand to try to get someone with a weak hand to bet, only to raise him back. Had I just bet out, the other player may well have convinced himself of something fishy and called. But by check-raising I make that player feel foolish, as if he has walked into a trap with a weak hand and now has no option but to fold. To illustrate:

The other day I was playing $20–$40 Hold'em at the Mirage in Las Vegas. I'm on the big blind and a guy four seats down from me raises; the three players in the interval having folded. One guy by the dealer called, and the rest folded to me. I look at my hand and find a J-4 off-suit looking back at me. It may be worth mentioning here that, in Hold'em especially, I don't usually look at my hand until just before it's my turn to play. The advantages of this are that I can't give away anything about my hand if I haven't seen it yet, and I can use the time, while the cards are being dealt, to watch other players as they look at *their* hands. There are those who will tell you that you should look at your cards right away in order to begin strategizing. I'm more comfortable doing it my way and, I suppose, have enough experience and acumen to look at my cards and make an instantaneous decision as to strategy. You, however, should do whatever works best for you. In this case, my J-4 off-suit and I made the instantaneous strategic decision to call the raise.

Now let's see . . . my cards were total rags and I was in terrible position—under the gun—so why on earth would I call a raise? I believe I have mentioned before that cards in poker are only part of the story, and a small part at that. At that moment, in that game, I *owned* that table and everyone sitting at it. I had been winning consistently for about three hours, to the point that the local pros had been asking for table changes. I had them flummoxed. So I knew that if I called the raise, the raiser and the other caller would be thinking "Uh oh, he called the raise." Just my being in the pot would put the other two players on the defensive.

Another factor: The raiser hadn't seemed all that confident in raising. He definitely did not have the air of a man with a big pair in the pocket, more like A-J or A-Q suited. Reinforcing this opinion was the fact that he was a local pro or semipro. Typical of his type, he had been sitting there stony silent, with his beard and dark glasses masking his face, the ubiquitous baseball cap pulled down low, and the requisite Discman plugs in his ears. Why so many denizens of casino poker rooms have plugs and wires sprouting from their ears is a mystery. (There was a bit of a stir in California some years back when it turned out that some of these plug/wire arrangements were actually receivers, and the players were getting helpful hints from sharp-eyed colleagues over the airwaves. I don't know for sure, mind you, but I sincerely doubt that this still goes on.) So, why did the fact of his being a local pro reinforce my analysis of his hand? Because they've all read the same damn books and 97 percent of them all play alike.

If a drunk, a "tourist," or a truly superior player, raises in sixth position with two callers ahead of him and pot odds of 3.67924 to 1, you don't have a clue what he's got. If one of the "97 percenters" raises in sixth position with two callers ahead of him and pot odds of 3.67924 to 1, you can bet the ranch that he's got exactly what Sklansky, Malmuth, et al., have told him he should have in that situation. That is why you, I, all God's chillun need to read Sklansky, Malmuth, Brunson, Baldwin, et al.: *to find out how everyone else is playing!*[28] We'll discuss this in greater detail later, but, meanwhile, back to the check-raise bluffing story . . .

So there are three of us in the pot: me, "Wires", and the third guy. Because I have "Wires" pegged as a 97-percenter I am sure he, having raised before the flop, will bet out after the flop and keep betting, no matter what the board shows. The flop comes 2♠ 3♠ 8♥. I, with zilch, check. "Wires" bets as predicted. The third guy folds. I call. (Call with nothing? Wait.) The turn comes up 10♦. I check, "Wires" bets, I call. (Wait.) The river comes up 7♠. I check, "Wires" bets—Now!—I raise. "Wires" tears up his cards and throws them at the dealer. My J-4 off-suit was the nuts.

On the flop, with two spades showing, I had decided to play as if I were hoping to hit the flush. Of course, I had to hope that "Wires" didn't have spades, but the odds were in my favor that he didn't. So, when he bet out on the river, that clinched it; he either had spades or nothing at all, and the odds were in favor of nothing at all. Had he had any kind of a real hand, like a pocket pair, he would probably have checked when the flush showed on the river. If you go back to the Matt chart on page 102 you will see that here we had a situation in which the player "Wires" was in the 100 percent bluffing category; he would always bet in that situation whether he had it or not. In that case, the strict card odds apply, and the card odds said he didn't have it. Once again, predictability-as-poker-death has been shown.

What we have here before the check-raise is the *eighth* category of bluff, but I needed to tell you the "Wires" story before discussing it. The first seven categories involve bluff-by-bet

---

[28.] There's another reason to read these books: these guys all know how to play poker! My point here is not the value of their advice; it is the unimaginative mis-application of that advice by the "97 percenters."

or bluff-by-raise; here we see—are you ready for this?—bluff-by-*call!* Calling a bet with nothing is a bluff—you're bluffing that you have a calling hand!—and can be incredibly effective when you think your opponent is weak or may be bluffing *you*.

When "Wires" was betting and I was calling, he could have been thinking a number of things, including: he's calling on a come hand; he's calling on a big hand (like a set) to trap me; he's calling on a pocket pair; he's calling on top pair on the board but is worried I have a bigger pair in the pocket; he's calling on an underpair. I absolutely guarantee you, however, that it never occurred to him that "he's calling on absolutely nothing." Pay attention: Players *bet* with nothing; players *raise* with nothing; nobody but nobody *calls* with nothing. Except me, and now you if you want to.[29] Bluff-by-call is, obviously, a set up for a final bluff on the end. With one very rare exception, you're not going to get very far by calling with nothing on the last bet. You're going to have to revert to a more common or garden-type bluff by betting out or raising after your bluff-by-call has made your opponent think you have "something." Say you're playing Hold'em and the flop comes

$$A\heartsuit 9\heartsuit 2\heartsuit$$

You have J♣10♣. Zip. Because of the action before the flop, you're pretty sure your opponent has an ace and a good kicker, probably a queen or king. Now, this is good news for you because if he has an ace, he doesn't have a flush. If his ace and kicker are suited, he doesn't even have a flush draw. Now your strategy depends on your read of your opponent, as always. He may bet his ace to "test the waters" and see what you will do. He may check. Whichever, if he bets, you should raise, and if he checks, you should bet. This would be a classic bluff: you're representing having the flush. Now, if he just calls you, you need to

---

[29.] This is a completely different situation from the one described earlier in which Tim, as my low opponent, calls the bet from the high bettor ahead of me. Although he is just calling, since he is ahead of me it is actually a bet.

be very careful, because in order to pull off the classic flush bluff you'll have to keep pushing all the way to the river. And if he's decided to call you now, he may be digging in, having decided to call all the way.

Many players, however, will raise you back with a pair of aces in this situation, again, to see if you really mean it. If that happens, then you are in business. Your opponent will be expecting you to (a) fold or bluff back if you don't have it or, (b) raise back if you do. By just *calling* the raise, you'll set off an avalanche of questions in your opponent's mind: "Does he have the flush and he's just lying low waiting to trap me? Does he have four to the flush? Does he have a pair of 9's? Does he have a set? Does he have a pocket pair?" On and on. By raising or betting and then just calling when your opponent raises you, however, you're making it look very much like a trap or a flush draw. Again, he *won't* be thinking: "He's calling me on absolutely nothing."

Okay, Okay. Here's the caveat: Unless you're playing against me, of course, or someone who plays like I do. Then, one thing that definitely will occur to your opponent is: "He's calling on nothing to set me up for a bluff down the road." "Jeez," you say, "this guy gives me all this advice about moves to make and then backs off and says it won't always work!" That's right—and it's the only responsible thing I can do. Always, always, always (see, I said "always" *almost* never applies) whether or not a move, a tell, a reverse tell, a bluff—whatever—will work depends *entirely* on who your opponents are. A move that works brilliantly with one guy may totally backfire with another. And anyone who tells you differently will be setting you up for a big fall.

A final word about "Wires" and how he let himself be led down the path: In that same game, a guy who was sitting next to me eventually turned to me and with frustration evident in his voice said, "Every time I get ready to check-raise you, you check too." Well, folks, you gotta smell them traps—and it ain't that hard. It's a simple matter of having respect for your adversary. If someone is checking and calling, or just calling—in any case you're betting your brains out and he hangs in there with you—

it behooves you to wonder why. He's either got some cards, some hopes, or—most dangerous of all—a plan. If you have the dead-cert nuts, then no worries. But if you don't—which is about 99 percent of the time—just to keep betting and assuming that your opponent is a dunderhead who is calling all your bets because he has nothing better to do, will lead you right into trap after trap. "Wires" could have saved himself a lot of money—and even won the pot!—had he thought "Well, that guy is going to hang around, I'd better just check." If he had checked on that last bet his AQ or AJ would have won the pot. Unfortunately for him he was in a rut—and I knew it.

To bluff or not to bluff, to call or not to call. When do you bluff, when do you know you're being bluffed? Far and away, as always, your primary criterion in deciding whether or not you're being bluffed is: who bet? Let's say it was Arnie.

1. **Does Arnie bluff?**

2. **Is this a situation in which Arnie often, usually or always bluffs?**

3. **Is Arnie winning or losing?**
   Does he bluff more/less when he's either winning or losing?

4. **Has he just lost a big hand?**
   Yes? What does that mean? More/less likely to bluff?

5. **Has he just won a couple big hands in a row?**
   Yes? What does that mean? More/less likely to bluff?

6. **What's he saying he has?**
   He's saying he has a flush.
   Is that possible? How many of his flush cards are left?

7. **Does his betting pattern make sense?**
   Has he looked throughout the hand like he's been trying for a flush?
   Is Arnie a sandbagger?
   Any evidence of Arnie's sandbagging during the hand?

8. **Does he look confident/worried?**
   If he looks confident/worried, is he a good deceiver?

9. **What did he say when you asked him, "Are you bluffing?"**
    You didn't ask? Tut tut.
    You did ask, and he said, "No/Yes." What does that mean?

10. **Does Arnie think you're a strong/weak player?**
    Do you have a reputation for being tight or being a
    calling station?

11. **Is there a strong/weak player behind you whom Arnie
    would/wouldn't try to bluff?**

12. **What does Arnie think you have?**

13. **Arnie knows you are winning/losing, does he think that
    makes you more/less likely to call/fold?**

14. **Does Arnie have any tells?**
    If so, what are they telling?

15. **(In pot-limit or no limit) Is it a big bet?**
    Is Arnie afraid of making a big-bet bluff?
    Does Arnie think *you're* afraid of big bets?

16. **(In a limit game) Is it a big pot?**
    Does Arnie pay attention to pot size?

17. **How is Arnie playing tonight?**
    He's playing his normal game. What does that mean?
    He's playing better/worse than usual. What does that
    mean?

18. **Is Arnie after you for some reason?**
    In a previous hand or game, did you anger or humiliate
    him?
    Is there someone behind you who Arnie might be after?

There are more criteria, but these are the main ones. Let's examine
them one at a time.

1. Does Arnie bluff? This may seem like a silly question.
Everybody bluffs, you say. No they don't, either. Most people
do, but some people don't. Some bluff so infrequently that it is
usually in your best interest to consider that they never bluff.

I've played with many people like that: they sit there with the patience of an Indian hunter and once every decade or so they pop up, play a hand aggressively, and bet out. These are nut players and the only reason they ever win anything is that the world, and, thus, its microcosm, the poker table, is so full of suckers that they get calls. There is a guy, for example, Dick, in the pot-limit game who I figure has bluffed six, maybe seven times in the last twenty years (there's one time I'm not sure about). The only reason he wins money is that Clarence and, frequently, some Clarence look-alikes are in that game. If he's in the pot, I'm out—unless I've got a hammer, which, of course, is the downfall of all too-tight players. So, "Does Arnie bluff?" is not a silly question, it's the first thing you've got to know about your man.

2. Is this a situation in which Arnie often, usually, or always bluffs? Back in the old days at the Rainbow in Gardena there was this guy. He used to wander in just about every day, sit down, get his first hand, raise, and rap pat. Every time, every day. I used to love to see him coming toward my table because I knew there was at least one guaranteed pot coming my way. At first I tried to finagle the hands: I had to try to get those pots without letting him know what I knew. In other words, if I started calling his raises and calling his bets after the draw with a pair of twos, he would figure that I was on to him and would stop his daily routine. So, I would raise his bets to make him fold. I would reraise him before the draw and rap pat myself. I would do anything I could think of to call his bluff without letting him know I knew he was bluffing. Then one day, I had run out of ideas, and I just flat out called him with—a pair of twos. He showed no pair, and I won the pot. And you know what? It didn't make any difference. He kept right on bluffing that first hand into me, and I kept right on calling him with nothing and winning. Now, maybe this was just his (inefficient) way of setting up his wild and loose image, right? Well, if it was it didn't help. He would start out his game that way and then get worse, losing and losing.

Another odd thing: as soon as he came into the building, why weren't players yelling invitations from thirty tables for him to come and sit with them? Why did it appear that only I and perhaps two or three other regulars noticed this guy's peculiar habits and took advantage of them? I don't know, but I can guess. This guy had a name. Even twenty years ago he was known among poker players as a guru of sorts, a writer of poker advice, a researcher, perhaps a pioneer in computer analysis of poker hands. The guy couldn't play poker for beans, but he had obviously done some great marketing and self-promotion. The innocent masses were intimidated, which, I figure, is why they didn't invite him to play at their tables.

Presently, he is an even bigger name; his face and products are ubiquitous in the poker world. I would be interested to know if his poker has improved in the years since I, and others, used to take all his money on a daily basis. I suspect not. I suspect that he has always been and still is like the truly successful gold prospectors of the '49er era: he realized early on that there was a lot more money to be made selling shovels and whiskey to the prospectors than in the actual prospecting. Smart. (By the way, regarding his first-hand pat bluff: the next time he would rap pat he had it, every time. This guy had a reputation of taking copious notes; he was a researcher and guru, after all. Well, if he was taking notes about the efficacy of his plays, I hope he wrote something like, "If I try the same move on the same player day after day, after about the first day it seems not to work anymore. Unfortunately, it has taken me 984 days to notice this.")

In any case, the point here is: there are some people who will usually or even always bluff in a given situation. Is Arnie one of them?

3. Is Arnie winning or losing? All good poker players, theoretically, play the same game whether winning or losing. That is the rule, the advice, the dictum: Don't let your winning or losing affect the way you play. In practice, it just ain't so. Most players will play looser or tighter, will be more or less inclined to bluff depending on whether they are winning or losing, and it is

your obligation as a serious poker player to have observed and recorded who does what. Generally speaking, *very* generally speaking, a big loser is more inclined than not to bluff (classically, this is a desperate attempt to get his money back) especially if the end of the game is nigh, and a big winner is more inclined to sit on his money and not risk his winnings on a bluff, especially if there is a lot more game-time remaining.

Now, here's why the generality "big losers tend to bluff more" is misleading. On the one hand, it is fairly typical of the gambler to throw more money away in a continuing, losing effort to get his money back until he is totally out of time, out of money, or out of credit. Many gamblers can't afford to lose a hundred dollars, so if they're losing five hundred they think, well, hell, might as well lose a thousand. I'll never forget—not because it was unique but because it was so typically common—one time some years ago I was playing $20–$40 Hold'em in Las Vegas and a guy sat down across from me with about $2,000. He was obviously a regular of some sort, either a pro or a local resident, as several people at the table and most of the dealers knew him. He started off bad and then got worse. Down, down, down. When he had about $800 in front of him, he started getting really silly, and this very quickly led to his having $200 in front of him. One of the players who knew him said, "Hey, Mark, you're not doing so well today. Why don't you take what you've got left and give it a rest." He said, "Look, I got $200. What'm I gonna do with $200? Might as well lose it." And he did. Well, all sorts of ideas of what could be done with $200 went through my mind—a couple weeks' food for the family being one of them. Gamblers tend to lose sight of the value of money, and many will throw away significant quantities of it, good money after bad.

So the generality applies, right? Only generally. How do I know there are exceptions? Because I, for one, am an exception. I play much tighter than usual if I'm losing a lot, and I have a damn good reason for doing so. I have bad days just like everyone else, and if I'm losing a lot, I figure this must be one of them. In other words, the fact that I'm losing means something is wrong; for some reason my judgment may be off and I'd better not trust it, better just play the nuts for a while till I get it figured out. No more wild and woolly Dave, because wild and woolly Dave is losing his ass. Even if my brain or my ego attributes my losses to bad cards, tough breaks, bad beats, I trust neither at that moment and, anyway, the bottom line is the same: I'm losing, and that isn't normal. It's time to retreat to high ground, minimize the casualties, get out the binoculars, and have another close look at the battlefield, the enemy positions, and our strengths and weaknesses. How do I know when I'm back on track? Obvious: I start winning again.

So if you're playing against *me,* analyzing *me,* your analysis should run something like this: Dave's way down with no signs of having started a comeback. He's gonna be playing tight, tighter than a . . . (fill in your own metaphor). So, if he's betting he's got 'em.

Why doesn't this make me vulnerable to the people I play with? After hundreds of weekly games, haven't they noticed that I'm tight when I'm down? No, they haven't. And the reason they haven't is that I've spent a *lot,* I repeat, a *lot* of time, energy, and effort building up my wild and loose reputation: Bet-'em-from-the-food-table-Dave; bet-'em-up-blind-Dave; raise-'em-with-nothing-Dave; yell- "I call"-from-the-bathroom-Dave (I haven't told you about *that* one yet). No one at my regular games has any inkling of what I do or why I do it. The other night one guy said, "What the hell's he betting on?" Another replied, "It's Dave. You never know *what* he's betting on." That is music to a poker player's ears. There are three truths here: (1) in reality, I am one of the tightest players I know—I never make an uncalculated move (which is certainly *not* to say I never make mistakes; sometimes I make them by the boatload); (2) the people I play with think I am the loosest player they have ever seen which means (3) I can switch tactics when I need or want to play tight, and no one notices.[30]

[30.] I've been caught! My wife, who read this manuscript many times as my principal

The questions to ask are: "Is Arnie winning or losing?" and "Does he bluff more/less when he's either winning or losing?" If you don't know, you'd better find out.

4. Has he just lost a big hand? Is Arnie the type of player who gets upset when he loses a close one? Will he try to recoup his losses from the last hand by bluffing this one? Jack, for one, has read that this is typical behavior; therefore, the best thing that can happen when playing against him is to get a really good hand right after having lost a big or a close one. The other night, playing seven stud high-low, my 6-low, which I had had from the fifth card, was last-carded and beat by a wheel. The only effect this had on my behavior was to make me hope that I would get a hammer in the next hand to play into Jack's belief in rules of thumb. Sure enough, the next hand is Spit Buy, and the common card makes me a pat straight to the six. I bet and raise like crazy, stay pat for the draw, of course, and bet and raise like crazy some more. As we have seen before, I really don't have to spend much mental effort analyzing Jack because he tells me everything he's thinking. This time he says, "Dave's just trying to get his money back from that last hand." He convinces

---

editor and overall helpmate, finally broke down and told me that I have a big-time tell. She says that when I've switched gears and have tightened up because I'm losing, I sit up very straight, tend to keep my arms and elbows drawn close in to my body, and seem to "withdraw" to another plane. Why was it a major decision for her to tell me? Because she plays in the weekend-dishes games too, which are the most blood-thirsty and no-holds-barred of all games—and was loathe to give away an edge like that. Good thing I wrote this book—and that she decided to help me by taking my ego down a notch. Otherwise I may *never* have known, and gone to my grave with dishpan hands. (Actually, some years ago I was advised of this when I overheard two regular opponents gossiping about me. One said: "Dave can be losing for hours, then he gets some kind of look in his eye that he's just not going to lose any more, and before you know it he's winning again." You know something? I have only now realized that my ego—which was feeling pretty stroked by this comment—prevented me from recognizing this as a tell!) It is also lucky that my current opponents show no evidence of having noticed. How do I know? After my wife told me the above, I decided to test this at the limit game. I played the next two sessions tight and didn't run a single bluff in either session. Well, my bets were called 100 percent to choruses of "Dave's really hitting cards tonight." It never occurred to them that I had switched gears on a semipermanent basis. Q.E.D.

himself and everyone else at the table, so when I declare high-low and rake in the whole pot, it's a big one.

5.   Has Arnie just won a couple big hands in a row? Is Arnie the type of player who will get overconfident after winning a couple big ones and try to bluff his way through the next? I do this sometimes, but it's not overconfidence. Most poker players believe in "rushes" or streaks of good hands and, in fact, rushes do occur. If I see that my having won two or three hands puts the table on "rush alert", then sometimes I'll take advantage of it and run a bluff. On the other hand, I don't do this very often and whether or not I do depends on who I'm playing with, because bluffing after a few winners is one of those textbook-typical cases. What does Arnie do? I don't know; I don't know Arnie.

6.   What's Arnie saying he has? Anytime a player bets at you, whether you suspect a bluff or not, the first thing you should be doing is analyzing his hand regardless of whether it's the first betting round or the last. What's he betting on? The readability of the player and the cards out, in stud, combine to help you to your conclusion. If Arnie is saying he has a club flush, is it possible? How many clubs are out? If there are a lot of clubs out, would Arnie have noticed this? Does Arnie think *you* would have noticed this? Would he try to run a bluff when he knows that you know he would have to have hit one of two remaining clubs in the deck?

The other night, in seven stud, I hit a heart flush on the fifth card. Happily, by that fifth card there are hearts all over the table, and my principal opponent is Bill the card player. I know that Bill will have counted and filed away the number of hearts out and that he will be thinking (a) no way do I have a flush, and (b) no way am I going to get a flush. Now, as much as Bill knows about cards, he knows zilch about people. He should have known that I knew that he knew that I knew that he knew, etc., and that I would never try to bluff into him when it's so obviously difficult for me to have the hand I'm claiming. But he doesn't think in those terms and, thanks in part to my wild and loose image, I can start raising without fear of his folding. Bill sits there quietly calling my raises along with three other players. At the showdown he voices disgust at seeing my flush: "Jesus, Dave, only you could hit the case heart on the last card." Ho, ho. He had had a straight from the sixth card and had thought he was trapping me, but good.

Conversely, if you're showing a possible hand and virtually none of your cards are showing around the table, it could be a good time to bluff into a "card player" who will consider you have good chances of having the hand. How does Arnie feel about it?

7. Does Arnie's betting pattern make sense? This is applicable to all games, but it is especially important in games like Hold'em, Omaha, Draw, and the like, where you don't have the luxury of seeing a lot of cards exposed. Let's say you're playing Hold'em. There are three raises before the flop, and Arnie's in. The flop comes up 3,4,5 off-suit, and Arnie starts betting like he's got the nuts. Now, is Arnie the type of player who would call three raises before the flop on a 6-7, or on a pair of 3s, 4s, or 5s in the pocket? Has he done that before? (You should know.) Or do you think that Arnie was calling on, say, a pocket pair of jacks and, when the flop didn't show any queens, kings, or aces, decided he could take the initiative? Or did Arnie start out with two unpaired high cards, say Big Slick, and figures nobody has the little stuff on the board and, therefore, he can safely run a bluff? Was Arnie one of the raisers before the flop, or did he come trailing in? If he was one of the raisers, does that mean he had big cards in the pocket, or was he perhaps setting up a double-bluff on little cards?

I do this fairly often, and when it works it really pays off. With something truly lousy, like a 7-2 off-suit in the pocket, I'll start raising and reraising before the flop as if it were pocket rockets. If 7s and 2s come up on the board, nobody believes you have that junk. If the board offers you no assistance, you can either continue trying to convince the table you've got the aces or just quietly fold, mumbling something about that not being your suit.

The question of sandbagging is also especially relevant to Hold'em and similar games when analyzing betting patterns. Is Arnie a sandbagger? Does he regularly sit there quietly before the flop with big cards in the pocket, appearing to trail in as everyone else raises and gets excited? Does he check-raise big hands? Did he check-raise this time? Does he check-raise to bluff? (As you know, check-raise is one of my favorite bluffing patterns.)

8. Does Arnie look confident/worried? Here you really have to know Arnie. Is he a Category 1 or Category 2 deceiver? Arnie looks confident. Does that mean he's really confident, or being deceptive. Confident of what? Is he confident that his cards will win or that his bluff will work? Arnie looks worried. Here's a little generality you're invited to use with caution: Almost always (almost!) if a player bets at you and sits there looking worried, he's got it. The chances are he is either (a) a very bad player to use such an obvious ploy or (b) thinks you are a very bad player to potentially fall for it. In either case, he'll have the hand. Only very, very rarely will this worried look be a double bluff because nobody wants to look worried when he's actually bluffing. If, however, you're playing against an extreme novice who hasn't got the slightest clue about poker, that worried look may be genuine.

Sometimes, an especially haughty or overconfident look is also a sign of a bluff. Again, it's up to you to size up Arnie.

9. What did he say when you asked him, "Are you bluffing?" Did he answer? Did he look at his lap or the ceiling? Is Arnie prepared with nonanswers? The last thirty-seven times you asked him that question, what did he say and how did it relate to the truth? "We've already gone over the efficacy of asking for information".

10. Does Arnie think you're a strong/weak player? Are you a calling station? Now here's a big problem: Most players will recognize a calling station when they see one and simply not bluff into him. Edgar arrived at our game one night and said, "Oh, Harry isn't here. That means there's bluffing tonight." Now that was funny; it was also to the point. The problem is

that I've never met a calling station who thinks he's one. This sets up a paradox of galactic proportions: Calling stations call because they always think they're being bluffed when in fact they are almost never being bluffed because they are calling stations. Furthermore, how can this bit of advice help a calling station recognize that Arnie is not bluffing into him (because he's a calling station) when the calling station can't possibly recognize himself as a calling station because he *is* one, and if he *did* recognize himself, then he wouldn't *be* one? Well, all I can do is try, and here goes: Think about it. Do you have a reputation of calling on anything? If you do, then Arnie is probably *not* bluffing into you because he knows you're going to call. Don't you get that? If you are a calling station and if I were there with you now in body rather than just in written-word spirit, I would have you by the collar and be slapping you around: Can't you understand? Whack! Don't you see? Whack, whack! Shape up. Whack! Get a grip. Whack! Pay attention!

11. Is there a strong/weak player behind you who Arnie would/wouldn't try to bluff? Now, here's a question for the rest of us to consider. Arnie bets, and you're first to decide to call or not, but there are others behind you. You have to turn around mentally and look at them. (What the hell: turn around physically and look at them if you want to.) Is one of them a calling station and does Arnie know that? If yes to the former and yes to the latter, then Arnie is probably not bluffing. He might try to bluff *you* out, but not that calling station behind you. Here we arrive at the point at which I promised to discuss my ulterior motive when I occasionally bluff into Harry, or other calling stations for that matter, and, once again, it's the exception, which means you have to be careful of the generality. We'll go through it carefully.

First, there *are* some situations in which even an inveterate calling station will not call. This varies from one individual to another, but in Harry's case he will not call if he thinks he's being tricked or made to look stupid. He *is* being tricked, poor guy—he's being tricked into folding. If I see such a potential situation developing, then I will use Harry's presence behind you as added incentive for *you* to get out. You, as a reasonable, thoughtful person, will figure that I'm not bluffing because Harry is sitting there waiting to call, and most of the time you will be right. Second, and this almost smacks of advertising, I will bluff into Harry and get caught *just to reinforce Harry's paranoia that he's always being bluffed*. In this book, I have done my Christian duty and tried to get the calling stations to look themselves over and reform. At the table, it's no holds barred, and if Harry is paranoid about being bluffed, I will give him occasional opportunities to reinforce that paranoia. For those who think I'm contradicting myself about the value of advertising, I'm not. I *still* only bluff Harry when I think he might, just might, fold. In other words, my intent is to win the pot, not advertise. If, however, I do get caught then it hasn't all been wasted; it has reinforced Harry's paranoia. Clarence, another calling station, isn't worried about being tricked or made to look stupid. Clarence's break in standard behavior comes if he's losing a lot, the end of the game is nigh, and the bet will bust him. Sometimes, in that specific situation, he will fold, and I will use that information when the opportunity arises. Bluffing into Harry or Clarence and getting caught isn't just for their benefit, either. I want to confuse the other players, as well, by letting them know I will bluff into a calling station. Keep 'em guessing!

12. What does Arnie think *you* have? You have to analyze Arnie's hand, and Arnie has to analyze your hand. Then you have to analyze what you think Arnie thinks you've got. Why is he betting into you with such gay abandon? How good is he at reading other players' hands? There's one guy in the limit game, Carl, who is one of the best card readers I've ever seen anywhere in the world. He will look at you and say, "You've got queens and nines," or "You've got trip 6s" and, by golly, that's just what you've got. Dangerous fellow, what? Well, the first time I played with him I sure thought so. Then, about half an hour later I realized, to my utter astonishment, that not only is this guy amazing, there's also something wrong with him. First of all, he

shouldn't be showing off his prowess to the table. If *I* could read cards like that, believe me, I'd KEEP IT TO MYSELF (I think we've been over this). Second, incredibly, he doesn't follow his own advice! He'll look at you and say, "You've got a full house, fours over kings," which is *exactly* right, then he'll call with his flush! Over and over and over again Carl will tell you exactly what you have and then call with a loser. The point of this is not to probe the mysteries of Carl's psyche, but to let you know there are people out there who have an uncanny ability to read your hand. If Arnie's one of them—and he doesn't have Carl's problems—then you've got to figure out why he's betting into your possible straight and act accordingly.

13. Arnie knows you are winning/losing; does he think that makes you more/less likely to call/fold? In poker, as in life, you not only have to know who and what you are, you have to know who and what other people *think* you are. If you're good at projecting an image, then the other players should be thinking what you want them to think. Meanwhile, Arnie knows you are losing or winning, and you have to decide if his interpretation of what that means will make him more or less likely to bluff you at that moment. I can't help you. I don't know Arnie, and I don't know you.

14. Does Arnie have any tells? Most players do. Back in the very early days I used to have a doozy. I used to get kind of a smirk on my face when I was bluffing. How did I find that out? Because some blabbermouth—bless her heart—told me so one time in Gardena. I swear, you can learn everything you need to know about poker, about the other players, and about yourself just by listening to the chatter at the table. Examples of tells (just a couple): When Nick bets and you're deliberating whether or not to call, he will always say, "You'd better get out." If he accompanies that with waving his hand, as if shooing you away, he has them big time. If Harry hits a card in stud and says, "Oh shit," that's the card he wanted, every time. Carl (the cardreader) switches tells over periods of time. For a period of a few months, if he hesitates and deliberates before betting or raising, he's bluffing,

every time. He will then switch, and, over the next few months, hesitation and deliberation means he's got it. Now, that's pretty weird. If Jack, Carl, or Tim bet or raise into the potential nuts, they have nothing and are hoping you don't have what it looks like you have. If Tom or Carl appears to be all alone going one way with the other players apparently all going the other way, their bets and raises are, much more often than not, bluffs. If Carl trails along calling then suddenly gets aggressive on the last round, he has it and has been sandbagging (but, as mentioned above, if his doing this means he's betting into the potential nuts, he doesn't have squat).

I caught Jack the other night in a classic tell, classic in the sense that it's one of those textbook tells that I always warn you to use with caution: being so excited about a big hand that a player will actually get confused and say something inane. Tim was dealing Omaha. The betting before the flop had been pretty lively, led by Jack who's been raising like he's already got the nuts. The flop comes Q♣ 2♣ 2♥. With four titties in my hand, I've got a real hammer: the nut full house. I lead the betting now, getting ready to put that pot in the bank. However, the turn is the K♣. My first thought is, Great! maybe someone hit a flush, until Jack blurts out, "Come on, let's go. It's Tim's bet." Now, Tim is dealing and, obviously would be *last* to bet—and there go my queens full, right down the drain. Wanting to needle Jack, I turn to him and say, "Tim's dealing, Jack. That kings full has really got you rattled." Jack says, "What? No! Waddaya mean? I just said . . ." By then it was his bet, which he did, and I trashed my titties.[31] In the end it's Tim who turns out to have hit the club flush, calls and loses to Jack's kings full.[32]

Last but not least in the tells department: Harry—poor Harry again—actually bounces and squirms around on his chair,

[31] Memo to Matt, the Mathematician: Matt, what happened? I'm supposed to win that hand over 91 percent of the time! Would you have called Jack's bet? Of course you would have; poker is a game of math and cards, right?

[32] Memo to readers: Remember I said Tim had hit a plateau? Well, Tim is an accountant, a numbers man, which is part of his problem.

like a kid who needs to go pee, when he's got a really big hand. (Jeez, Harry is *really* bad. I lied before: sometimes I do feel guilty—but I get over it.) In any case, the list of tells is as endless and varied as the human race. It's your job to observe Arnie and see what his tells are telling.

15. (In pot-limit or no limit) Is it a big bet? Is Arnie comfortable in a game with big bets? Would he bet the pot at you, or tap, on a bluff? Many people won't, many people will. Some people will give their bluffs away by being scared to bet the max. But they could also be fishing for a call. Say it's a pot-limit game, there's $1,000 in the pot, and Arnie, with plenty of money in front of him, only bets $300. Is he making it easy for you to call, or is he afraid to risk $1,000 on a bluff? Say he bets the full $1,000. Is he so confident of his cards, or does he know that you get nervous, afraid of big bets? Obviously, if you're afraid of big bets, you shouldn't be in a big-bet game, but that's not the point right now. A lot of people who are afraid of big bets do, in fact, play in big bet games. Are you one of those? Does Arnie *think* you're one of those? If you've done your job of image-projecting right, he may well think so. When *I* sit down to a big game, as I've mentioned, I often want to look as timid, meek, and worried as possible to encourage players to try to bully me with big bets.

16. (In a limit game) Is it a big pot? Let's say you're playing Hold'em with $20-$40 limits. The first round, six people call three raises, making $480 in the pot. The second round, five players call two raises, making $780 in the pot. The third round, now at $40 limit, three people call one raise making $1,020 in the pot. The last round, two players check to the third, and he bets $40. Now, only an extremely naive—and dreamily optimistic—player is going to try to steal a thousand-dollar pot with a $40 bet. At 26.5 to 1 (for the first potential caller), it's going to be worth a call, with any kind of hand at all, just in case the bettor misread his hand! Is Arnie extremely naive or dreamily optimistic? Would he be oblivious to the size of the pot? If not, he probably has a hand.

17. How is Arnie playing tonight? The mirror image of this

question is: How are *you* playing tonight and how accurately does Arnie perceive your state of play? Is Arnie on tilt? Are you on tilt? Does Arnie *think* you're on tilt? Have you set Arnie up to *make* him think you're on tilt? Has Arnie been playing good poker all night, guessing right more often than wrong? You decide, then decide what that means. Does your analysis mean he's more likely to be bluffing you, or is it more likely that he has them?

18. Is Arnie after you for some reason? Did you irritate Arnie by beating him out of a big hand earlier, or even last week? Is Arnie the type of guy to hold a grudge and come gunning for you (poker-wise)? We have seen in a couple of examples that irritating players to the point of making them want to "get back" at you is a very useful thing to do. It diverts their focus from playing good poker. Now with some people, this will mean that they'll only come after you with the nuts. For others, this means they'll start throwing money at you (especially in a big game) and daring you to call. Which is Arnie?

Okay. We've identified and analyzed eighteen different thought processes you need to go through when deciding if a bet is a bluff or the real thing. All the situations listed will usually have an effect on a player's behavior and, therefore, on the likelihood of his bluffing or not. You're thinking, well, next time somebody bets I'll excuse myself from the table, call the office, and have them put the data on the mainframe to tell me what to do. Well, here's the truth, and you may or may not like hearing it: Once you have trained your brain to pay attention to all the various bluffing/not bluffing factors, and have accumulated sufficient experience, the whole process will develop into a **feel**. You're just going to *know* when you're beat and when you're not. The reason I say you might not like hearing it is that it almost smacks of pure intuition. That is, it may seem that I'm telling you that, if you don't have some kind of innate intuitive power, then you're up a creek as a poker player. This is not what I'm saying.

If you read books by some of the top pros you find that many of them seem to get around to this proposition: "sometimes you just know, like ESP." What these players themselves don't realize is that it is not ESP or "intuition" as we normally think of those phenomena (though it may well be ESP and intuition as they actually are). It is simply the result of the very rapid processing of information gleaned from observation, even if subconscious. In your first week as a serious poker player you probably will not have sufficient experience to process automatically all the information opponents are providing you with; it may be quite an effort to catalogue it and then think about it. But, as you gain more experience, your brain is just going to figure this out for you very quickly without your telling it to. You're going to develop the **feel** for reading hands and players' intentions. When a guy bets, it's just going to pop into your head: pair of queens. How? ESP? No. It's just that, consciously or subconsciously, you've seen ten thousand people who acted just like that guy did and turned out to have a pair of queens. You do, in fact, "just know."[33]

At least much of the time. As I've said before, you're not a machine. You're a squishy, furry, lovable, fallible human being, and as such your brain will occasionally be thinking "Gee, I'd really like some peanut brittle" when it should be concentrating on other matters, like whether Arnie is bluffing you or not. Then, you're either going to blow it by calling or not calling when you should be doing the opposite, or you're going to have to haul your brain back to the table, whip it and slap it around a few times, and get it to remember what's been going on since the beginning of the hand. When you bet into a good player and he sits there thinking, that's what he's doing. Actually he's doing two things: (1) he's waiting for his brain to catch up with the

[33.] In Doyle "Texas Dolly" Brunson's *Super/System* (1978; B&G Publishing Co., Inc.; Las Vegas), which many in the biz consider the "Bible" of professional poker players, he discusses this "feeling" on page 430 and would seem to agree with my analysis, or, actually, I should say that I seem to agree with his analysis since his book came some twenty years before mine. My opinion, as with all my opinions in this book unless otherwise noted, was reached independently, however. I guess great minds think alike!

action, going over your every move from the beginning of the hand and relating that to your overall personality and behavior patterns, *and* (2) he's waiting for you to give him more information. When Nick bets I always give him a good few seconds to see if he's going to "shoo me away" with his hand, for example. If you know what to look for, you can train your brain to look for it. With experience (which is simply repetition), your brain will do it subconsciously. You require much more informational input to drive your car to the supermarket than you do to analyze a poker play, yet, *with experience,* you can do that, fight with the kids, reassure your wife that you really will fix the screen door today, plan your next speech to the Kiwanis Club, and try to remember if the oil needs changing, all at the same time. Our cerebral mainframes are amazing.

How frequently should you bluff? I doubt that by now you'll be surprised if I tell you: it depends. Most novices and bad players (a) bluff too much and (b) think they're being bluffed much more often than they really are. The other day, I got up from a (winning) ten-hour session of $20–$40 Hold'em at the Mirage and, scouring the session in my mind for possible tidbits to include in this book, realized that in ten hours I had only bluffed three times, twice successfully and once unsuccessfully. Not very much, right? On the other hand, my notes from a previous six-hour (winning) session show that I had bluffed nine times, six successfully and three unsuccessfully. Now what kind of pattern is that? Well, it's not a pattern, unless you can say that my usual pattern is to be flexible and adaptable.

There is a bit of irony in bluffing frequency. You can get away with a lot more bluffs against tough, experienced players than you can against average, inexperienced, or loose players. As mentioned above, average or inexperienced players tend to think they're being bluffed all the time anyway, and so are inclined to call. Loose players generally hate to lay down a hand—which defines them as loose—and so are inclined to call as well. It's the tough old rocks out there who are susceptible to being bluffed.

Very often, since they only play premium hands and make solid bets, they think everyone else is like that too. It doesn't occur to them that someone might be in the hand just screwing around with rags. If, therefore, they miss their hands, they are inclined to think you've hit yours when you bet.

So, the answer to the question, How often to bluff? is this: it depends on your opponents. If you're in a loose game in which players are calling you left and right anyway, then you need to bluff hardly at all. If you're in a tight game, you may have to "teach" the rocks that—son of a gun!—this guy bluffs! No, I'm not advocating advertising. Bluff to win the pots. If you eventually get caught, getting caught will lead to loosening up the rocks so that they pay off your legitimate hands.

I, apparently, judging from other poker books, am in a minority who believe that bluffing should be a profitable enterprise. As long as you don't just throw money in the pot willy nilly, if you bluff in a calculated and well thought out fashion, it should be profitable. So, how do you do that?

Do:

1. Only bluff into hands which you have reason to believe are weak or mediocre. There are very few players (the really astute ones) who will lay down a big hand because you've convinced them that you have an even bigger hand. This is difficult enough in a pot limit or no limit game. It's practically impossible in a limit game.

2. Bluff principally against tight players and then only when it seems "realistic" that you could have them beat. What do I mean? The player has to be able to look at your cards, or at the board and say, "Oh! He has a _____." If you go back to the "Wires" story on page 160, the three spades coming up on the board created a context in which "Wires" could look and say, "Oh! He has a flush." In other words, your opponent will want to put you on a hand, so make it easy for him to find a hand to put you on.

3. In limit games, try to wait for situations in which you can bluff with a raise rather than just with a bet. We've discussed this before.

4. Whenever possible, try to bluff with a check-raise rather than with just a bet. Let's say it's the last betting round in a hand of Hold'em. You're heads-up with Fred, and you're first. If you bet out, Fred's first thoughts are going to be, "What's he got? Is he bluffing?" If you check, let Fred bet, and then raise him, Fred's first thoughts are going to be, "Oh, shit, I've been trapped." He may subsequently think, "What's he got? Is he bluffing?" but that first reaction of having been trapped gives you a tremendous edge. This is especially true in a fast-paced game in which decisions must be made in seconds and first impulses can be powerful persuaders.

There are a couple of caveats here. The obvious one is that if Fred doesn't bet, you're cooked. You have to be sure, like I was with "Wires," that he's going to bet. The second one is that you must have established a reputation of being a check-raiser; if you've been sitting there playing for six hours and have never check-raised, it's going to look suspicious to say the least.

One of the very first things I do when I sit down to a new game is start establishing myself as a fiendish, relentless check-raiser, even at the risk of costing myself a few bets in the early hands. (This is not hard for me to do because I *am* a fiendish, relentless check-raiser.) This has myriad benefits. For one, obviously, people get very wary of betting when you check, which is exactly what you want them to be. They no longer know if you've checked because you're weak or if you've checked because you're trapping them. It also confuses the hell out of them when you *don't* check-raise, i.e., when you bet out. In the context of bluffing, you now have your opponents set up to fall for a check-raise bluff. Though they may be reluctant to bet in the first place, when they do and you raise they'll definitely get that "I've been trapped" feeling.

5. Here is one generality you're invited to use at your own

peril. If you see that a player has been severely stuck (stuck means "losing" in poker parlance) and has managed a struggling comeback to even, he is usually bluffable. Usually, a player in that situation will not risk a marginal call that could put him back in negative territory; however, *make sure he's back to even or winning a small amount.* This is important because, often, when a player has been stuck and has come back to *almost* even he will be thinking, "If I call and win this one, I'll be over the top," and he'll be more likely to talk himself into calling.[34]

6. Here is another generality. If you're thinking of bluffing, go for your chips as if to bet. If your opponent makes a grab for his chips as if to say, "If you bet I'll call," go ahead and bluff. That opponent is usually weak and is trying to stop you from betting. Couple of big caveats here: (a) If this doesn't work, then you'll know you're playing against someone like me. Since most people think the chip-grabbing move is used to try to stop bets, I grab my chips when I *want* someone to bet. Get the idea?[35] (b) Sometimes, a defensive chip-grabber will call you, but he definitely would rather not. He's hoping to stop your bet and check into a showdown. Against this type of chip-grabber, the defensive bluff is a good move, i.e., not a pure bluff, but a bet with a medium hand; if he folds, good; if he calls with a weak hand, you still might win.

[34.] That almost-back-to-even is a very vulnerable psychological moment—and you and I need to remember this when *we're* the ones in that situation. There is a certain exhilaration of expectancy that comes with being almost even after having been way down, and it can make us do foolish, overly optimistic things. Beware that moment lest you plunge back into the depths. This is not so true (usually) when you've actually gone over the top. At that moment you are much more inclined to feel a calming relief and to be willing to sit back, take stock and try to make smart plays.

[35.] This is a good move to set up a check-raise when you really have a hammer and want to insure that your victim bets into your check-raise. You check and then make a grab for your chips as if threatening to call if your opponent bets. Your opponent will smugly tell himself he's seen *that* move before and bet right out. When you come back with a raise he may even think, because of your chip-grabbing move, you're counter-bluffing him and raise you back. Believe me, when you take these standard moves and turn them around, that is do the opposite of what everyone thinks the move means, you can really mess with some heads.

Don't:

1. Don't try to bluff into a huge pot in a limit game. We've discussed this before.

2. In general, don't try to bluff a big winner or a big loser (unless, naturally, your knowledge of your opponent is such that you know he—as a big winner or a big loser—is less likely to call).

3. Don't try to bluff a known calling station, except as discussed earlier.

4. Don't bluff from an obvious position. That is, you're last, four players have checked to you, and you bet out. This is just too lame, and someone is likely to call you, which is why, of course, it's great to be last with a big hand.

5. Don't bluff if it's unlikely that you can have the hand you're representing. As we discussed before, in stud, for example, don't try to fake a heart flush if there are hearts all over the table.

6. Generally speaking, don't try to bluff out more than one opponent. With two or three opponents your chances of pulling off the bluff drop dramatically.

7. Don't bluff on the spur of the moment. Analyze the bluffing potential of your hand from the earliest betting rounds, and if you're considering bluffing at all, start setting it up early.

8. Finally, the least understood and yet the most important admonition of all: DON'T BLUFF IF YOU DON'T NEED TO! As in my ten-hour, three-bluff Hold'em session mentioned above, if you're catching hands and the other players are paying you off when you do, why bother to bluff? This is the ultimate, paradoxical beauty of poker: since the bluff is such an integral part of the game, you very often don't need to bluff at all. The mere fact that you are playing poker will lead many to read bluffs into your play when in fact you haven't bluffed since 1942.

Chapter 7

Betting and Money

Well, here's what it's all about in the end. There's just no way around it: poker is about money, that's how you keep score.

I recently read in a poker book that "The best reason to play poker is profit." I won't bother to cite which book here, because *lots* of poker books say virtually the same thing. Well, profit may be the best reason for some, and profit has certainly been a very strong motivation for me in the past, but, for me, now, I play just as much for *pride*. I play poker to *win*, not to win money per se, mind you, just to *win*. Now, ahem (pardon me while I clear my throat, shuffle my feet, and try not to look disingenuous here) when you win at poker you, uh, win money. And the better you play, the more money you win.

Don't go flipping back to earlier chapters looking for the places where I said that it is important to keep your ego (pride) separate from the game. That would be to misunderstand. There, I'm talking about losing a hand, standing a loss for an evening's session, or even being on a losing streak. That happens to the best of the best, and you will recover if you can remain sufficiently analytical, which means not letting your ego and *that kind of pride* get in your way.

A couple weeks ago I built some shelves around the house. Now, I'm not a carpenter, but I worked hard at it. The shelves look pretty sharp, and I am proud of that. Nor am I a car dealer, but the other day I managed to wangle a pretty good deal on a new car, and I am proud of that. I *am* an author of English-teaching textbooks, and when someone comes up to me and says, "I can speak English today because of your course," I am proud of that. Well, I am also a poker player, and when I've

187

played good poker, I'm proud of that as well. I also have a pocket full of money, which, I confess, feels pretty good too. Which brings us back to the original point: How do you know if you've won at Scrabble? You have the highest numbers on the note pad. How do you know if you've won at baseball? You have the highest numbers on the scoreboard. How do you know if you've won a ski slalom? You have the fastest time. How do you know if you've won at poker? You leave with more money than you started with. You acquire that money in poker by either making or calling bets. So let's get to it.

Betting decisions are deceptively simple in poker and come in three flavors:

- Vanilla: If there's no bet to you, you have two choices: bet or check.
- Chocolate: If there is a bet to you, you may have three choices: call, raise, or fold.
- Strawberry: If there is a bet to you, you may still have only two choices: call or fold.

You get strawberry if:

1. the raises have been capped, i.e., the limit to the number of raises has been reached by the time the action gets to you;

2. in a table stakes game,[36] the bet is already for more money than you have on the table, in which case you would only be able to call "all in" or fold;

3. in a table stakes game, you are heads up with an "all in" bettor, in which case you can't raise because he has no more money;

[36.] I'm not referring only to pot-limit or no limit here. Remember: many private games, and all casino and public card room games (that I know of) are played table stakes even in limit games. Even if it's a $1–$2 limit game, when you run out of money on the table, that's it for that hand.

4. similar to (3) above but not heads up, the bet to you was "all in," there are players behind you, but none of them has more money than the bet so you still can't raise.

Not being able to raise a bet *can be a serious handicap to your play* as we will see in a little while.

In all cases, folding is easy. The entire discussion on folding is: fold when you think you have a loser and the pot odds don't justify a call. We'll take the other options one at a time.

Vanilla

When to bet

There are two situations when you have to decide to bet or check: (1) you are first to have to act, under the gun, and (2) you are not first but those ahead of you have checked.[37] Obviously, these are very different situations.

When you are under the gun you may have little information about what the players behind you—the entire rest of the table— are going to do. Let's say you're under the gun before the draw in five card draw, jacks or better to open. You look at your cards and, lo, there's a full house looking back at you. Should you open, i.e., bet? Well, if you do, and the rest of the table is either holding weak hands or reads you as extremely strong, they may all fold leaving you to win the ante with your hammer. If you check, and the rest of the table checks as well, your full house will disappear into the muck for the next deal and won't even win that! What to do?

[37.] There is a third situation, at least it is so designated in poker parlance: that of being on the big blind when there have been no raises to you, whereupon you may put more money in the pot if you wish, thus obliging the other players to do the same. Whereas most people think of this as being an opportunity to raise or call, official poker lingo designates this an "option" to bet or check. Whichever, we will duck the issue here and take it up in Chapter 9.

The standard platitude in most poker books is to check, the argument being that if no one opens you would only have won the ante anyway, and with a hand like yours it is worth the risk of forgoing the ante in the attempt to trap one or more players. Well, this is *card* advice and, as you know, in my opinion this is only a small part of the story.

You'll notice that I said above you "may" have little information about what the other players will do. If you've just sat down with strangers and this is the first hand, that situation is still only marginally acceptable. As I have said before, the very first thing you have to do when playing with strangers is to start sizing them up. Now, if you are playing with your regular gang and don't know what to do with your under-the-gun pat full house, then you have not been studying your lessons. **If you can't look around the table at your regular opponents and decide if one of them is going to open for you or not, then it's time for you either to quit playing in that game or, perhaps, quit poker all together.**

I mean it, too. But I don't mean you have to be right all the time. Nobody is right all the time about anything.

Let's take a moment here to discuss a general principle. Throughout this book I have been yammering that reading your opponents—analyzing their play, predicting their intentions—is the first and foremost component of winning poker. But these guys are strangers! How can I instantly size up strangers? But I just started on "people poker!" How can I start being right about what my opponents are going to do when I'm only now starting to analyze them in that way?

I didn't say you have to be right. Even in my bold-faced admonition above I only said that you have to *decide*. Let's say you look around the table to see if anyone is going to bet your full house for you. Harry is sitting there bouncing around on his chair which, if you remember from Chapter 6, means he has a big hand. You therefore make your decision to check your full house to trap Harry—and you watch in disbelief as Harry checks along, and it's time for a new deal. It turns out that Harry is having a hemorrhoid attack and his bouncing tonight is totally meaningless. You don't know that right now, but you do know that for some reason Harry's bouncing didn't turn out as predicted. And that knowledge was worth the mistake!

Let's say you sit down to a new game with strangers in a casino and have the full-house scenario we've been talking about. The guy in seat four is holding his cards very protectively and apparently studying the other players with great interest. You decide this means he has a good hand and will open for you. You check. He checks. Everyone checks, and, again, your full house goes back in the muck. *It doesn't matter that you were wrong;* what matters is that now you have some information about that player, that is, that when he acts like that it doesn't necessarily mean he's going to open. Again, the knowledge gained from having made a decision, or drawn a conclusion, acting accordingly and being wrong is worth the mistake. Never, never do anything in poker, or in life for that matter, for "no reason" or because you don't think you're sufficiently astute to figure out the situation. Go ahead and try to figure it out. If you're wrong, (1) you can eliminate that particular conclusion from your list of possibilities, or at least keep it in reserve for further study and, (2) you will find out something about yourself.

Again, however, as discussed before, if you're consistently wrong or wrong more than you are right, then maybe you're out of your depth, or maybe you're just off your game for some reason. But you have to have been acting on decisions and conclusions even to know that! If you've made a particular move, ask yourself, "Now why did I do that?" If your answer is "I dunno," you're not even giving yourself the opportunity to learn from your mistakes.

The other day I was playing pot limit Hold'em at the Mirage. I'd been doing okay, not great but okay, and was winning a moderate amount. Then, in a period of about ten minutes, I had two major reversals. The first time, I have top pair on the flop, but there is a possible straight showing, 7-10-J off-suit (I had A♣J♣). From the action before the flop, I can't put either of my two opponents on the straight, so I decide to bet out on the strength of the top pair and to make them pay if they have a draw. Well, that was a big mistake. The first opponent raises all-in, a pretty big bet, the other guy folds and there I sit, wondering what to do. If only I hadn't bet out, I would only be facing about one-fourth the bet I was now facing. Well, to make matters worse, I go over the action, scrutinize the bettor for telling behavior, and decide he is come-bluffing[38] on a KQ, or perhaps AQ or AK, any of which would give him two overcards plus the straight draw. I call. Boy, was that a mistake too. He showed down 8♥ 9♥, and I was history.

Except I wasn't. I hesitate to tell you how things ended because you might get the wrong idea. Believe me, if I were engineering this story to follow through on my point, I wouldn't tell you how it ended. But since I promised you the whole truth and nothing but the truth, here it goes: I was saved by an absolute miracle. The turn comes up J♦ giving me trip jacks, and the river comes A♠, giving me a full house. My ex-opponent (ex because he was now broke) leaped up from his chair and started stamping around in circles shouting "Jesus Christ! Jesus Christ!" over and over again. And I couldn't blame him. He'll probably add that story to his bad beat repertoire for years to come.

Now, I started this off by saying I had suffered two reversals, of which this was the first. Believe me, even though I completely lucked out, this was a reversal. I had made a *serious* mistake and I knew it.

The second reversal ended up as it should, me with egg on my face and with less money than I should have had. I have pocket kings and the flop had come up junk, 8♣ 4♦ 9♠. There are two other guys in the pot, both of whom I look over and both of whom I decide don't have anything interesting; therefore, if I don't bet they won't either. I don't want to give them the opportunity to hit an ace for free, so I bet out. One guy

---

[38.] The pros and the books written by pros call this "semibluffing." Although come-bluffing sounds a bit awkward, I feel it is more to the point. If anything should be called "semibluffing" I feel it is what I call "defensive bluffing."

folds, the other guy calls. The turn comes 9♦. I've put my opponent on two overcards, probably AK or AQ, and bet out again. He raises the max. Again, had I not bet, I'd have had only about one-fourth my current problem. I study and think and figure and can't put him on anything except maybe pocket aces, which doesn't jibe with his action before the flop, or maybe a set— which had now become a full house—and that doesn't jibe with his actions *on* the flop. Then it comes to me, that's it: he had slow-played a set on the flop and now has a full house. I fold, and he shows pocket queens. I had folded the best hand.

Well, that was enough for me. I had completely misread my opponents and led myself into four big mistakes in rapid succession. In the first instance, I bet when I should have checked, then called when I should have folded. In the second instance, it wasn't necessarily wrong for me to bet in the first place, but I had bet for the wrong reason, i.e., so my opponent wouldn't have a chance to hit a free ace. Because I was so completely befuddled about what he had, I then folded when I should have called. When you start zigging when you should be zagging, it's time to get up and go, so I got up and went. By the way, therein lies the difference between pride and pride: The "bad" kind of pride would have kept me at the table, but the "good" kind of pride (sort of like "good" cholesterol) kicked in, in that *I recognized when it was time to go and then did so*. Knowing when it's time to go is part of good poker too, a very big part.

You don't always, necessarily, have to take a particular read on a particular opponent to decide what to do; the general nature of the aggregate of your opponents may be enough. When I used to play draw in Gardena, if the game was loose, with folks opening on all kinds of trash in any position, I often adopted a policy of not even looking at my hand before the draw up to third position (out of eight). If I was under the gun or if the pot was checked to me, I would just check along blind because I knew that if anyone had anything at all the pot would be opened. This, as I mentioned back in Chapter 6, avoided the possibility that I would give anything away about my hand before the action came back around to me. On the other hand, if the game was tight I would always look at my hand, even when under the gun, and make a decision to bet or check based upon what I found and my read of the other players.

There are those who say that giving specific examples of hands is a waste of time because there are so many possible hands that those specific ones would come up only once or twice in a lifetime. Well, this isn't really true—in business and law school they give case studies to the students—but it is a point worth discussing. First, I have, I hope, chosen situations—specific hands—which are representative of a type of situation often encountered. For example, the skeptics would point out that having a full house under the gun is going to be a pretty rare occurrence. Well, read full house as "strong hand." It could be fours, a flush, a straight, or even three of a kind, and you will have one of these strong hands under the gun often enough to justify it as a case study.

I should now, therefore, include lengthy case studies about having medium and weak hands under the gun. But I'm not gonna, and this is the second reason the skeptics are wrong, at least in my case: When I give you an example of a hand, I always follow it up by saying that the cards are only part of the story anyway. One of the constants in poker is that you are always playing against *people* and the relative value of your cards will rise and fall depending on the *people* you are playing with. So here are your case studies for betting out on weak and medium hands under the gun: look around the table at your opponents and decide if your hand is a winner or a loser and act accordingly. If you're under the gun in five draw with a pair of jacks, have seven opponents lurking behind you, and think you can railroad your way to the pot, then bet those babies and see if you're right. If you're wrong, you'll find out toot-sweet because someone else will be stacking your money in front of him. Adjust your play next time.

So, when to bet under the gun? In one sentence? Okay: Bet when you think you are going to win, unless you think you can get someone else to bet for you. Sounds simple, doesn't it? But, as the preceding admonitions and tales show, it is quite a complex decision to make.[39]

If it's up to you to bet because players have checked to you, then you have to decide: Did they check because they're weak, or did they check because they're sandbagging? Let's say you're in last position with three opponents after the flop in Hold'em. The flop was A♣ J♦ 2♥, you have J♣10♣ in the pocket, and the other players have all checked to you. Now, there could be all kinds of reasons that those three guys checked to you. Among them: Someone is sandbagging trip aces or other strong hand; someone has a pair of aces but a weak kicker; someone has an underpair, like you; no one has anything; the muzak has put everyone to sleep.

Clearly, the first thing you have to do is try to figure out which of the above applies. If your read is that your pair of jacks is the best hand, then you should probably bet out. If your read is that you are being sandbagged, you may want to bet out anyway just to find out. The problem with this, however, is that the sandbagger might just *call* your bet to continue his slow play, instead of giving you the raise you were looking for. In fact—this is a generalization, of course—I might be more inclined to read a call as proof of sandbagging a very strong hand than I would

---

[39]. There are many, many books—especially the more current ones written by the new techno pros, who have discovered computers along with the rest of us—that tell you that cards are everything and, oh yes, by the way, every once in a while you should vary your play to fool your opponents and, um, while you're at it, it's a good idea to pay attention to how they play. One of the favorite things for these authors to point out is that they have set up programs *proving* that loose play—loose play defined as not bowing to the statistical card god—is less likely to win than tight play. How do they do this? Well they program some "players" to play tight and some to play loose, run a few million hands, and voilá, the tight players have come out on top. Well, of course. Their "loose" players play loose *all the time*. What you're supposed to do is play "loose" (as defined above) at the *right* times! You do that by looking your opponent in the eye and deciding: my rags are going to win, or, my four kings are going to lose. Computerized players, at the current state of the art, don't have eyes either for looking or for being looked into. *My* proof of this is that these same techy authors are often the "consulting experts" in computer poker games which, as I have said before, are all easily beatable.

a raise. The reason is that someone with a good but riverable hand like AK in the pocket would seemingly want to raise out the competition. A player who has flopped a set, however, or perhaps even two pair aces and jacks, might feel confident enough to let his competition go ahead and draw. Then again, maybe not.[40]

If all players ahead of you have checked and there are still players behind you, the situation is a little different. You not only have to decide what the players ahead of you are up to, but it now behooves you to consider what those behind you might do. The criteria for this are the same as if you had been first to bet. If Harry's behind you bouncing around on his chair—and you know his hemorrhoids have been cured—you'll do yourself a favor to wait and see what he's going to do.

When to check

Aside from the admonitions about when to bet or not (i.e., if you shouldn't bet then, obviously, you should check) there are some specific times when specific advice about checking is in order. One of these arises when: if you bet and are called you will lose. This is not as convoluted as it sounds. Let's say you're playing seven card stud and by fifth street have trip 10s *showing*. You bet and everyone folds down to one, last player who calls. He calls? And you have trip 10s showing? What the hell's he got? Well, he's either on the come or he's already got your 10s beat and is slow-playing his hand.[41] Whatever, he calls. Sixth street brings no improvement for you and no apparent improvement for him. You bet; he calls. What the hell's he got? Seventh street leaves you still with just the 10s. What should you do?

[40.] I recently read a book—and there are others like it—that said: "If you have hand X [the hands were detailed] and your opponent has hand Y and you bet, then he will surely fold." Jeez. I don't know who that author plays with but he sure has led a sheltered life. I know lots —lots!—of players who would call or even raise with the hand he described. I know I'm harping but it's true: know your opponent.

[41.] Or he's playing the now-famous Daniel move of calling on nothing. See Chapter 6 for details.

Check, of course, unless you want to run a bluff representing more than the 10s, which would probably be a mistake. Why you should check is obvious. If your opponent can't beat the trip 10s he's either going to fold or try to bluff by raising back. You will have either risked a bet needlessly, or will be facing having to call a raise. If he *can* beat the 10s he'll certainly call and probably will raise, and, since you'll probably call his raise, you will have completely wasted your money. Just check and see what he does. If he bets, you're only looking at one-half or one-quarter the money to call than if you had bet.[42] Of course, if you do improve the 10s to, say, a full house, then we're back in the "when to bet" section above, which means whether or not you bet depends on your read of your opponent. If you

1. think he will call if you bet, then bet;
2. think he will raise if you bet, then bet;
3. think he will fold if you bet, then check;
4. think he will bet if you check, then check;
5. can't decide what he might do (tut tut) then go ahead and bet.

Implied in the above example, but not specifically addressed, is the check-raise. If you have a hammer and think your opponent(s) will bet if you check, then check so you can raise back and perhaps make more money.[43] Furthermore, as we have discussed before, if you want to run a bluff and think your opponent will be more susceptible to the bluff when check-raised —and if you think he will bet, of course—then check.

[42.] Depending upon whether the game is limit or pot limit.

[43.] At one point, the manuscript for this book contained an impassioned argument as to why the check-raise is a perfectly acceptable tactic in poker, but I decided to scrap it. The reason was that if you are "against" check-raising, then you're much too obtuse or naive to be a good poker player. (Harry, who is both obtuse and naive and is a terrible poker player, thinks check-raising is just awful.) So forget the arguments. If you're against check-raising, then forget poker and take up basket weaving as a hobby. Sorry to be so blunt, but, believe me, you'll be doing yourself a favor.

This leads to the next obvious checking opportunity: when you think you're being set up for a check-raise. If you smell one of those in the air and don't have the nuts, then you don't need me to tell you that you should check.

Chocolate

When to call

There are those—the bump it or dump it crowd—who maintain you should never call. The argument goes like this: If you're going to call, then you obviously think you have a chance of winning, and if you think you have a chance of winning, then you should raise. Not only is this sophistry in a particularly heinous form, but I have never, ever run across anyone who actually practices it consistently, even or especially among those who tout it. In any case, there are a number of situations in which the right move is to call and a raise would be inappropriate.

One of these is when you have a come hand and are getting the right pot odds to call but would throw them out of whack by raising. You're in against one opponent and have a one-card draw to a flush. There's $50 in the pot, and your opponent bets $10. If you call, you'll be getting $60–$10, or 6 to 1 odds for your draw. That's good, since your draw is about a 4 to 1 dog. If you raise to $20, however, and the other guy calls, you'll only be getting $70–$20, or 3.5 to 1. Now you're on short odds and you've done it to yourself.

Another scenario in which you might not want to raise, so as not to mess up the pot odds, occurs if you think perhaps you're being bluffed. In the limit game, Tim bluffs about 20 percent of the time when he doesn't make his hand, which means—people and other factors aside for the moment—that if I can get better than 4 to 1 for my money when I call him I'll have a winning proposition. So, if there is $50 in the pot and Tim bets $10, I'll be getting 6 to 1 when I call. If I raise to $20 and he calls—which would apparently mean I was wrong this time about his bluffing—I've cut myself down to 3.5 to 1, a loser. If I raise and he folds, I'm only getting 2.5 to 1. I've risked $20 to win $50 when I only needed to risk $10. This is very bad business indeed, and even though I was "right" this time that he had been bluffing, if I keep playing like that I'll come out a loser in the end.

Another calling, rather than raising, situation is when you have a winning hand, have players behind you, and think that one or more of them might call if you call, but they may all fold if you raise. This decision has to be made quite often in high-low poker.

The other night we were playing seven stud high-low. From fifth street it was obvious that I was alone for low, and Nick and Bill were duking it out for high. Bill bets and it's up to me, with Nick behind me. Well, I think Nick is beginning to lose faith in his hand and might fold if I raise. So I just call. Nick had expected me to raise and, relieved that I hadn't, calls as I had hoped. Now, this pissed Bill right off as he had been counting on my raise to help drive Nick out. (How do I know? Because, of course, he talked all about it after the hand.) But that's his problem. I'm looking out for my own interests and, as we will see a bit later in the section about return on investment, it is important to have as many opponents as possible in high-low to avoid just getting your own money back when you win. Sixth street, same story: Bill bets, I call, Nick calls. Seventh street—now I can raise when Bill bets. (I know that Nick, though liable to fold during the course of a hand, is a bit of a calling station on the end, i.e., once he has put substantial money in the pot.) Meanwhile, I'd gotten two extra bets out of Nick that I may not have if I had raised.

A call is an excellent play to use when sandbagging. Although I wasn't sandbagging as such in the Nick and Bill story, the effects are the same. You're playing Hold'em, have pocket rockets, and the flop comes A♣8♥2♦. The guy in first position bets. You're second with two other players behind you. First consideration: What's the bettor got? Well, you hope he's got something really great like a set of 8s that will take him all the way to the river. Don't scare him off or put him on his guard by raising.

Second consideration: What do the players behind you have? Again, you hope they have something that will keep them in, and, if they do, you don't want to scare them off either. So, here, usually, a call is in order rather than a raise.

Were the flop different, your decision might be different. The flop I gave you as an example is a "safe" flop for you to sandbag. There are no flush draws yet; there are no straight draws yet, except a gutshot at the wheel, so you can probably feel pretty confident that letting the opposition draw is not going to hurt you, at least not on the turn.

You may be waiting by now for me to talk about the primary calling situation: someone bets on the last round—no more cards to come—and you figure you may be facing a legitimate hand. Well, I already did, in the Tim story above. Although I described it as a calling-a-possible-bluff story, just switch the statistics around to "when Tim bets he has a legitimate hand about 80 percent of the time." Now you have a calling-a-legitimate-hand story.

Although I made it sound simple in the Tim story, deciding whether or not to call a bet on the end may be the hardest decision to make in poker. There's no where else to go: you can't call and hope to improve on subsequent cards; you can't call and hope your opponent has a heart attack before the river. This is it. Is his hand better than mine or not? Here, the only thing you can do is round up everything you know and put it to use. Does he bluff? How often? Would he bluff me? Would he bluff me now? What could he have? Has he been playing consistently since the beginning, (consistency meaning that his bet is logical)? How much is in the pot compared to the amount of the bet? On and on.

When to call on the end? Study everything in this book and in every other poker book ever written, then play thousands and thousands of hands to acquire experience . . . and you'll still make mistakes. But the more you study, the more experience you acquire, and the more you think, the fewer and fewer mistakes you will make. And that's the best you can hope for.

When to Raise

Here's a quiz. (Don't be afraid, it's multiple choice.) You should:

1. Always raise early with a strong hand
2. Never raise early with a strong hand
3. Sometimes raise early with a strong hand
4. All of the above
5. None of the above
6. It depends.

Anyone who didn't pick number 6 should go back and reread the rest of this book. *Everything* "depends" in poker.

First of all, why raise? What do you hope to accomplish? Classically, there are several reasons to raise:

1. You have an unbeatable hand and you want to win as much money as possible.
    Problem: You may actually get more money in the pot by not raising as we discussed in the When to Call section.
2. You have a good hand, but one which could be out drawn, so you raise to run out the competition.
    Problem: Depending on the other players, their style of play, the hands they may hold that worry you, you may not run anyone out at all; thus you are just setting yourself up to lose more money if in fact your hand is out drawn.
3. You raise to test an opponent's strength, get information.
    Problem: If your opponent reads your raise for what it is he may "tell you what you want to hear," i.e., by calling or reraising regardless of what he has. Your raise has not only failed to glean any information (except that he didn't fold), it may have resulted in your getting *false* information.
4. You raise on a come hand to get more money in the pot

when the odds are in your favor.

Problem: You are still more likely than not to miss your hand and will therefore have simply cost yourself more money when you miss.

5.   You raise to bluff.

Problem: If your bluff gets called, well, there goes extra money.

6.   You raise in late position to get a free card next round.

Problem: If your opposition read what you're up to they may reraise or come out betting next round to foil your plans.

7.   You raise to shorten the pot odds to unacceptable levels for the come hands.

Problem: Many poker players don't even know what pot odds are, much less take the trouble to calculate if the odds are correct for their draw or not.

Raising, in short, can be a complex decision.

Let's say you start playing seven stud high-low, and your first three cards are A♥ 2♥ 7♥. Your probability of hitting either an ace-high flush (or better) *or* a seven-low (or better) is about 53 percent, odds-on. Should you raise? Well, it depends.

In the limit game, I would sometimes be inclined to raise the roof. This is because I know that the table will usually take one, two, or three raises in the first rounds and still have everyone call! In this case, then, I would raise to get as much money in the pot as possible, knowing that the players are much more likely to start dropping out in later rounds. Since it is much more probable that I will win only one way, I want to make sure there is a lot of early money to increase my return. I would also raise, sometimes, if I saw that someone else might have a potentially even better starting hand and I wanted to gauge his reaction to my raise.

In the limit game, I would sometimes be inclined to sit quietly and just call all bets, essentially sandbagging or slow-playing the hand. I would do this, for example, if I saw that someone else was getting excited and would do my raising for me; if I saw that a couple of usually loose players had tightened up for some reason and might drop; if I saw that some hands were especially weak and might fold even given the general looseness of the players; if I saw that someone else had a potentially even better starting hand.

Other variables (Remember, I have A♥ 2♥ 7♥): If the ace is in the door, I would usually be more inclined to use the raising options, since an ace is an undefined card in high-low, that is, they won't know if I'm betting high, betting low, just betting the strength of the ace, whatever. If the 2 is in the door, I would usually be more inclined to use the raising options as it would be read for strictly low, my three-heart high option not being evident. If the 7 is in the door, I usually would be more inclined to slow-play as a 7 is not *that* great a card for low, and, therefore, my raising might cause suspicion that I had a potential high hand, or a potential high-low swinger. On the other hand, in any of these three cases I might do the opposite if I felt it would be beneficial in getting more money in the pot, confusing the other players, etc. For example, I might *want* the others to be suspicious of my raise with the 7 showing. It is, after all, considerably more likely that I will hit for low (about 33.3 percent) than high (about 19.5 percent), so I might want the others to think I was raising on something like a big pair in the hole or even trip sevens.

In the pot-limit game, I would sometimes be inclined to slow-play because, usually, those players are much tighter, and a first-round raise will often drive out half the hands. It's hard enough to get a decent return in high-low pot-limit without scaring out the early callers.

In the pot-limit game, I would sometimes be inclined to raise the roof if I saw some other good starting hands and wanted to test their strength; if I was betting late or last and a lot of other players had called a bet, thus making them more inclined to call a raise; if for some reason I knew (from a sloppy shuffle or a flash) that I was about to get a bad card and, therefore, wanted to run out some of the weaker competition before I got it (or to try to make it fall somewhere else!); if I wanted to build the pot so that the second and third round bets could be substantial.

Notice that in the limit game, running out the competition with an early raise is not an option. Six or seven or, often, eight out of eight players will call an early raise or two and hang around to get more cards. This is fairly typical of many home games and is even typical of some low-limit casino games. In these cases, if you've read or believe that you should raise early to run out the competition and protect your, say, big pair or trips from the flush and straight draws, you're just, well, pardon the expression, pissing in the wind. It isn't going to work that way. The only thing you can hope to do is make it more expensive for your competition to keep drawing, but remember: you're making it more expensive for yourself as well. Here's an example.

You're playing $2–$4 Hold'em in a casino and get pocket rockets. You're good, you're great, you've read every poker book ever published, and you're surrounded by tourists and little-old-people wearing polyester flowered Bermudas, T-shirts that say "I lost my picture of a donkey in Las Vegas," and talking with New York accents. You raise the blind—and nine people call. Well, think you, I'm gonna win a fortune!

Probably not. The flop comes up 4♥ 5♥ 9♣. You may be beat already, but let's say you're not. Someone bets. You raise. Five people call. Another raise. You raise, and nine people call. The turn brings K♣. So here's the picture.

Mabel has a 3-6 and needs a 2 or a 7.
Fred has a 3-7 and needs a 6.
Ralph has a J-10 and needs a Q.
Blanche has a 6-7 and needs a 3 or an 8.
Irving has a Q-J and needs a 10.
Byron has a J♣4♣ and needs a club or a J or a 4.
Ziggy has a K♥3♥ and needs a heart or a K or a 3.
Elmo has a 9-8 and needs a 9 or an 8.
Mel has a 5-8 and needs a 5 or an 8.

If you add all these up, you'll find that either twenty-seven or twenty-eight of the remaining twenty-eight cards in the deck will beat your aces (depending whether or not one of your aces is a heart or a club). You're cooked.

So, should you *always* raise aces before the flop? It depends what kind of game you're in and, whether or not your opponents know what they're doing. The fact that at least four of the people in the example above are being very, very silly is not going to help you. In one million-hand computer run against nine loose opponents, pocket rockets won only 24 percent of the hands, followed by J-10 suited which won 22 percent. So, although the aces were still the best starting hand, they were only marginally better than J-10 suited and they still lost 76 percent of the time. Given this scenario, then, yes, I would still (usually—it depends) raise the aces before the flop, but I would start to get very wary if I don't trip up on the flop or get four to the nut flush. If the flop is trash and Mabel and Ziggy start looking excited, I might even fold.

How to defend against this sort of thing? Well, the only semi-sure way I have found is not to play in public games under $10–$20. Starting at that level and going up the games become somewhat less of a lottery, with skill and judgment carrying more weight. If I do find myself in a very loose game, either public or private, I then play more come hands, like the J-10. It depends. Like a chameleon that changes its color to match whatever wallpaper it's on, you have to change and adapt your poker playing to whatever game you are in.

Now, hang on. Doesn't a good player *want* to be in a game with loose players, players throwing their money about willy nilly? It depends. My extremely loose opponents in the limit game are a poker player's dream come true. But this is a private game in which, week after week, I can monitor and predict the players' behavior, control the situation, and use their looseness to my advantage. A casino game with one to four "tourists" out of ten players is also a godsend, as their collective probabilities are usually not great enough to change the odds against you. A low-limit casino game with nine Mabels and Elmos, however, comes very close to being a lottery.

In the later rounds of a hand, the decision whether or not to raise becomes somewhat more straightforward. If you've made your hand, you can raise to get more money in the pot, to run out the competition, or to make it expensive for the competition to keep drawing.

Here again, however, you're going to run into the same sort of situations described above depending on the relative tightness or looseness of the game. A good example of this is English Stud in the limit game. Let's say you've hit a flush in five cards. Harry and Nick have two pair, and, believe me, there isn't a raise big enough you can put in that pot to keep them from trying to get the full house. Depending on the situation, maybe this is good, maybe not.

We'll give Harry QQ886 and Nick KK994. They each have three cards to come, one free and two paid-for twists. Depending, again, on a lot of factors, you're looking at something between 40 percent and 85 percent possibility of being out drawn. Neither extreme offers much comfort as far as you're concerned.[44]

The first thing you should do is remind yourself that a flush in this game is not such a great hand if you have a couple of opponents trying for full houses. Next, based on your evaluation of the likelihood that they are going to hit, you can either keep raising while maintaining a wary eye as to where their cards fall; you can just trail along calling all bets while ditto; you can see if there's some way you can protect yourself, perhaps by dumping the flush and trying to hit for low; you can save some money and get out early. (Yes, I do mean fold your flush even though it's winning at that point! If you're looking at odds approaching four to one in favor of their hitting and a return on your remaining bets and raises of two to one if they miss, get out now.) There are many games, even those without wild cards, in which

---

[44.] This calculation began with the assumption that one Q and one 9 were exposed. Otherwise the low end would go to zero if all their cards were out and could approach 96 percent if none of their cards were out. Then a number of scenarios were tested with variations in the number of players still in, the number of players taking twists, etc.

a flush is a very marginal high hand, which shouldn't be tried for in the first place, since it's only going to cost you money if you get one and play it.

So, here's a summary of the basic principle: If you have a good come hand or a virtually unbeatable hammer you want **a lot** of people in the pot, calling as many raises as the traffic will bear. If you have a strong hand but one which could be drawn out on, you want *few* people in the pot calling as many raises as the traffic will bear. In the first instance, a very loose game is ideal. In the second instance, a very loose game can be deadly. First you have to decide:

If I raise . . .

a. will players get out, or

b. will the players stay in regardless of the raise?

This, as we have seen, varies from game to game and the answer to this question will color all subsequent decisions. If the answer is (a) players will get out, then you do not usually want to raise with a promising come hand. This is especially true if you're playing high-low poker as you will only get half the pot if you win, and you, therefore, need as many early contributors to the pot as possible to avoid the prospect of just getting your own money back.

If the answer is (b) the players will stay in, then you should usually raise the roof with a promising come hand. You will not be diminishing your odds; you will not be diminishing the number of contributors to your potential pot; you will simply be making everyone bet more when you are likely to win. Good, yes?

Now, let's say you already have a hand. You're playing seven stud, and by fourth street you have trip kings. Of your four remaining opponents you figure that:

Tom has a pair of aces.

Dick has two pair.

Ralph has four to a straight.

Jane has four to a flush.

If you're right about what they have, a big *if,* then:

Tom alone is about[45] an 8-1 dog to beat you.

Dick alone is about a 5-1 dog.

Ralph alone is about a 2.6-1 dog.

Jane alone is about a 2.3-1 dog.

You can see that Ralph and Jane are getting pretty close. In fact, overall, if it's you against Ralph and Jane together you're down to about even money. If *everyone* stays in against you to the end, including all scenarios, you're about a 1.4-1 dog. If everyone stays in against you and you *don't improve*—which will be about 61 percent of the time—you are going to lose more than eleven out of twelve times. Bummer. Do you still want to slow-play those trip kings? Or do you want to start raising like crazy and get as many people out as possible?

Well, that depends. (Here we go again!)

We'll do some very simple math here. Over 100 identical hands, everyone stays in, having invested $100 each to do so; therefore, $500 in the pot. 61 percent of the time you won't improve, and of those hands you will lose 92 percent. $.61 \times .92 = .5612$. So, we'll say that you lose fifty-six hands when you don't improve for a loss of $56 \times \$100 = \$5,600$. You'll lose two hands when you do improve for a loss of $2 \times \$100 = \$200$. You'll win the other forty-two hands for winnings of $42 \times \$400 = \$16,800$. Your overall outcome is $\$16,800 - \$5,800 = \$11,000$ profit. Maybe you *do* want to slow play and have everyone hang around. Then again, maybe not. It depends on whether your blood pressure and your bankroll can stand it.

Blood pressure? Bankroll? What's a bankroll? It's the money you have available to play poker with, that's what. And unless it's virtually limitless, either in absolute terms or relative to the stakes of the game—you do not want to keep putting it to the test by letting folks draw out on you, even when the math shows that, theoretically, you're going to win in the long run.

---

[45]. "About" because these numbers can vary considerably depending on whose cards are showing, whose aren't, what the kickers are, etc.

And that, once again, is the problem with mixing math and human activity: math is, one, theoretical and, two, without a soul. Ever wonder why insurance companies seem so incredibly cold and heartless? Because everything they do, *everything*, is based on cold and heartless calculations of cold and heartless numbers. They don't *care* if your baby girl needs a bone marrow transplant to live. Not only do they not care from a personal point of view, they don't care that, should she live, she may turn out to be the discoverer of the cure for cancer. It doesn't matter. If the numbers work out in favor, she lives. If not, she dies. Your baby is dead, but the stockholders are happy. It's just numbers.

So we're back to people again. If you have the bankroll and the cool to sit there and get drawn out on time after time after time after time, then, yes, in the long run the numbers will work out in reality as they should theoretically. That's exactly what casinos do. They set the odds in their favor, often not by very much—just a few percent on average, call it X percent—have virtually limitless capital, and then just sit there, minute after minute, day after day, year after year, paying out and taking in, paying out and taking in, ad infinitum. And when the auditors come, sure enough, they've taken in X percent over what they've paid out, and the directors get new limousines. Casinos operate just like insurance companies: numbers.

Well, you can do that with machines. You can even do that pitting people against machines. Casinos know *exactly* how much a roulette table or slot machine will pay off relative to the amount bet by players, which, of course, is one way they know if they're being skimmed. But you ultimately can't do that pitting people against people. Take Jane and her four-flush draw. If she's a better player than you are, she'll make you think she's hit it when she hasn't (you don't win the $400 when you "should"); she'll make you think she hasn't hit it when she has (you lose your $100 when you "shouldn't"); and she'll know when *you've* hit and she won't call (again, you don't win the $400 when you "should"). Your 58-42 calculations are out the window.

Now we come to the point of all this: Do you want to raise, or do you want to slow play your trip kings? Well, that all depends on you, and, Jane, and Tom, and Dick, and Ralph. To wit:

1. If you can read Tom et al. sufficiently well to know, say, 90 percent of the time when they've hit and when they've missed, i.e., if you're a much better player than they, go ahead and let them draw. Your results will eventually be close to the theoretical numbers. That is,

2. If you have a sufficient bankroll to withstand several or many losses in a row, because you could lose for days or weeks (or, theoretically, centuries) before the "long run" odds begin to kick in. And also,

3. If you have the gumption and cool to withstand beating after beating, knowing that "eventually," "someday" this is going to pay off.

4. If you would rather get out there and play, make things happen your way, win the pot right now, rather than risk losing it later, then raise the roof and try to get Jane and company out. Make them pay! Call down the thunder! Make them sweat and tremble and pee in their pants if they want to try to outdraw you! But, of course,

5. If you're in a loose limit game where the opposition never fold, and certainly don't tremble or pee, but happily throw their money in the pot in the exhilaration of a good old gamble, then you're back to points 1, 2 and 3: Can you read them? Do you have the bankroll and cool to withstand this? If you do, you'll win in the long run. If you don't, you'll be broke, drooling, babbling, and drinking Sterno under some bridge.

Strawberry

If you've forgotten, strawberry is the flavor you get if for some reason you can call or fold but can't raise. The least critical of these is in a limit game in which, by the time the action has come around to you, the maximum number of raises allowed has already been reached. Often, this is good: if you have an otherwise raising hand, it means that others have done your raising for you. I would *love* to be last, or near last, with pocket rockets and have the raises capped ahead of me. (I may have forgotten, but I can't think of a single time in twenty-some years that this has happened.) I could moan and groan, think and sweat, grit my teeth, and finally, reluctantly, decide to put my money in. It does mean, however, that if you have a hand like Big Slick, which you really would rather play against just one or two opponents, well, that option is gone. (Even *calling* three or four raises with Big Slick might not be advisable, depending on your opponents and what they usually raise and reraise with.) Anyway, in terms of not being able to reraise, this is a situation which really shouldn't worry you much.

When you or an opponent (or opponents) are all in, however, the situation can be very critical indeed. First we'll consider an all-in opponent.

If an opponent has had no choice but to go all in to cover the ante or the blind, his hand will be random and of no particular concern in itself. He may or may not have anything and, anyway, is no longer a threat to you or the rest of the table even if he does. However, if he is all in by choice, has been sitting there hoarding his last reserves of hope and has decided to invest them here and now, he probably has a better than average hand. Now, once you decide to call—you'll love this—all admonitions of people poker are out the window; you'll just have to hope your cards are better than his, or that your cards hit and his don't. No more bluff, no more maneuver, that's it. So, what do you think he has? Can your cards win on their own merit?

If you are all in, the same situation applies. To call all in you have to decide right now if you're likely to win the pot, either because you think you currently have the best hand or will improve to the best hand. Once you've called, your cards will have to go out there and fight it out while you root from the peanut gallery.

Now, all of this seems obvious but, as usual, is an oft-made mistake. Some guy bets all in and you think: "Hell, I've been pounding this wimp all night. Might as well call and finish him off." Well, if for some reason a warp in the cosmos has been giving you consistently better cards all night, then it's no tribute to your talent but you might be right to call on that basis. More likely, though, is that you have been *outplaying* him all night and forget this when, now, you've got him almost broke. From the moment you call, there will be no more opportunities for slick play, and you may be in for a surprise when he takes down the pot based purely on better cards, cards which, had he had more money, you may have been able to make him lay down.

So what? He doesn't have enough money to hurt me. Let him win a little one. Well, all in with one caller will double his stack. All in with two callers will triple his stack, and so on. I have, on many occasions, gone from all in to having a winning session because that one hand turned it around.

I'll never forget the five of hearts, for as long as I live. Some years ago, I had been taking a beating at $10–$20 Hold'em at the Bicycle and was down to my last $40.[46] I'm in eighth position, and by the time the action gets to me the raises have been capped. I take a pessimistic look at my cards and find 6♥7♥. Well, now or never. I announce all-in and put my last $40 in the pot. We end up with six players, including me, which means my share of the pot would be $245. (The little blind had folded, the big blind had called.) The flop comes 4♥ 8♥ 5♦. I can't believe it: I've flopped a straight, but there's nothing I can do about it. I'm in the cheap seats, watching the action from afar. And, considering there's a straight on the board (which I have, but they don't know that), there's a lot of action. Bets, raises, reraises, rereraises. Wow. When the dust settles, there are three players, besides me, to see the turn.

The turn comes 8♦. So now the board is showing 4♥ 8♥ 5♦ 8♦. Salvos from the left, broadsides from the right. The smoke

---

[46.] Now don't read *too* much drama into this. I don't mean my last $40 in net worth, I mean my last $40 in poker money for that trip. In any case, I was going to have to leave and fly back home a loser if I lost it and was loathe to do so.

clears to reveal one guy left, and me. The dealer gathers in all the chips and gives the side pot to the other guy. From the way he had been betting, I'm pretty sure I'm cooked. Clearly, he had convinced the others as well because they had all folded out of a big pot (to his detriment, he should have slow-played). Proving me right, in his smarmiest of voices he says, "Sorry this had to happen when you were all in, but . . ." and he turns over a pocket pair of 8s. (I *wish* I had said something like, "I'm not beat yet, sir. Let's see the next card." But of course I didn't; I thought it was all over too.) If you haven't guessed the end by now, sure enough, the dealer turns up the river and it's the 5♥, a straight goddamn flush. That 5♥ gave me a $245 stake, and it was up, up from there. I got up from the $10–$20 game a $900 winner, went over to the $20–$40 game and won another $1,500 before it was time to leave. Hot damn![47]

My point in sharing this with you is: you may think the guy's all-in bet is a wee, puny thing that can't hurt you, but if you call and lose, you'll be doubling his stack and maybe letting him back in the game. Do you want to do that? If not, let him take the blinds or antes and try to get him next time. There, however, is another, darker, side to this.

What if you *do* want to keep him in the game? What if you say to yourself: "I think he has some pretty big cards, so if I call that all-in bet I might lose. If I do, he'll have a stake again and that might not be so bad. There are some bad players at this table, and this guy has been playing wild, hitting lots of pots, winning money, and then giving it back, mostly to me. In fact, about 25 percent of my winnings are other people's money that has been funneled through him first. I think I'll help him get a stake back and see if he can manage to hang around for a while." If you think this is an unrealistic way to look at things, you're thinking about twenty-five levels of play below where a good player thinks. A good player—one who considers this kind

[47]. Yes, yes, there have been other times when no 5♥, nor any other card, materialized to save me and I was busted. If I choose to remember some of the happy endings, well, hell, it's *my* book.

of thing and many other options—is *so much better* than a bad player (or even an average player) that the bad player, literally, hasn't even an inkling of what's being done to him.

The other night in the limit game, the game was seven stud high-low and by fifth street I'm in the pot with just Bill and Harry. This is kind of complicated, so pay attention. Now, Bill is the "card" player, and tight. Losing money to him means there's a good chance you won't see that money again for the rest of the night. Harry, of course, is Harry: losing money to him means it will be back in circulation in the next hand or two.

I have 2♥3♥6♦ showing. Unfortunately, my hole cards are 6♣10♠. So, although I have a great-looking front porch, I've got zilch so far. Bill is showing K♣Q♠8♥. Now, although Bill is generally tight, one of his favorite ploys is to try to get alone high with garbage when it looks like the others in the pot are going low, hoping, of course, that the low players won't challenge him for high once he's run out any legitimate high competition. Harry is showing 2♦8♦8♣. Who the hell knows what he's got, except that I'm pretty sure he's got four to an 8-low.

Okay. So, I'm starting to think I'm going to lose to Harry for low. I could get out now and let Harry and Bill split the pot, but the pot is very big, as those pots go, and I don't want Bill to be squirreling away half of it. Time to start engineering a Harry win, if possible. How to do that? Well, here I could use some help from cards and, luckily, I get it.

Sixth street brings:
>   Me: 2♥3♥6♦5♣
>   Bill: K♣Q♠8♥Q♦
>   Harry: 2♦8♦8♣9♦

Bill bets, which tells me he has nothing, probably just the queens. (Why? Because if he really had anything, he would have checked to the possible straight, knowing I would bet.) Harry calls, of course, and I raise. I'm now convinced that Harry has a 9-low with a draw to an 8-low. I, if you recall, have a 10-low, a great draw, and Plan B—set it up for Harry to win it all—if I miss. Bill calls, Harry calls.

Seventh street brings me zip, a J♥, so I've ended up with a 10-low. Of course, I don't know what Bill and Harry have received. Since I missed my great draw and can't win either way, time for Plan B.

Bill bets, confirming to me that he's got nothing. Harry calls. I raise. Bill raises trying, no doubt, to keep me from going both ways. Harry calls and raises $1, killing the third raise. I call, then Bill calls.

Hands and chips go under the table for the declare. Bill comes up high. Harry comes up low. I come up high-low. Since the rule is that the high-low player bets first, I bet. Obviously, I'm representing a low straight to the 6 or 7. Bill knows he's beat for high, looks again at Harry's cards and knows two things: (1) Harry's best possible low is an 8, which means that he can't save Bill by beating me for low, and (2) I would never bluff into Harry, the five-star calling station. He folds. Had Harry folded as well, Plan B would have brought me an unexpected bonus, but of course he didn't. Harry calls and, when I turn over my 10-low, triumphantly turns over his 9-low, his last card having been a king. Harry wins the whole pot.

Bill goes nuts. Stark raving. "How could you be so stupid?" "How could you try to bluff Harry?" On and on in this vein. Well, Bill, I wasn't bluffing Harry. I successfully bluffed *you*, the plan being all along to throw the pot to Harry so that, shortly, I'd have a chance to win that money back. Neither Bill, an average-to-sometimes-pretty-good player, nor Harry, a hopeless player, had any idea that I would have or even could have engineered the whole thing for Harry to win the pot. It's kind of unfair, really.[48]

So, back to strawberry. Do you want to keep that all-in

[48.] By the way, had I not received that good scare card on sixth street, I may or may not have continued the ploy. With a 2 3 6 showing, Bill might have been harder to convince than with 2 3 6 5 showing. I don't know. That's not how it came out and, therefore, I had/have no way to gauge Bill's reaction to the "what if" hand. When the 5 came in, however, I could see he was very worried. Who knows how it would have turned out otherwise?

player in the game by helping him to increase his stack? Maybe so, maybe not. You decide.

The fourth category—there is an all-in bet to you and there are players behind you, but none of them has more money than the bet so you still can't raise—leaves you even more restricted than the heads-up situation. If you call (remember: you're already assuming that the all-in bettor has a better than average hand) and one, or two, or three, or more players call behind you, you're going to end up playing "cards" with a multitude of people. You can't raise them out now, and you can't raise them out at any point through the end of the hand. You'll be watching again, but this time you'll have even worse chances to win.

Up to now, we have only been considering the all-in bet, yours or your opponent's, from the point of view of desperation. That is, we haven't considered the all-in bet made from a position of strength. Let's say there are six of you playing pot-limit or no limit (this whole concept doesn't really apply to limit). You all have mountains of chips in front of you, and one guy shoves in his whole stack.

First, the comments made previously still apply: you can't raise him, now nor ever; from the moment you call you will be playing "cards" with him. The decision whether or not to call, however, has been taken to another plane. Many people think that betting all-in, especially in a freeze-out situation as in a tournament, will add an "I really mean it, otherwise I wouldn't be risking my whole stack" to a bluff. Well, the first thing to consider is—guess what?—who bet. If the guy who bet is a jerk, liable to do this sort of thing on a whim, you'll pretty much have to base your decision on your cards and their relative strength in that hand. If the bettor is a sound player, however, you'll have to consider more complex issues which we'll get to in a minute.

Second, how does his ex-stack ("ex" because it now belongs to the pot) compare to yours. Maybe his mountain of chips was only a mole hill compared to yours, in which case you know that if you call and lose you'll still have a commanding position. Perhaps his ex-stack was about half of yours, which means that if you call and lose you will switch positions: your stack will then be half of his. Or, his ex-stack was the Himalayas and yours is the Adirondacks, in which case if you call and lose you'll be busted, but if you call and win he'll still be in good shape. Finally, if your stacks are (were) about equal, one or the other of you will be going home.

Now, considering the sound player, which of the above scenarios might attract your opponent to bluff? Conversely, which might attract him to bet and hope for a call? The *least likely* to have been a bluff is the your-mountain-to-his-mole-hill scenario. Only a truly naive player would try that. On the other hand, maybe that's what you're supposed to think. The *most likely* to be a bluff is his Himalayas to your Adirondacks. Unless he knows you'll go all-in relatively easily, he probably would have made it easier for you to call. Any of the scenarios, however, can only lead to one conclusion: either he has the nuts, or he's bluffing that he has the nuts, or he doesn't have the nuts but thinks he probably has you beat.

This last example is dear to my heart. I was playing pot-limit Omaha at the Barracuda[49] in London. The flop comes 9♦ 10♦ 5♣ and I have J♦Q♦7♦A♣ in the pocket. (I don't actually know if an Omaha hand is called the "pocket," just to give you an idea of my limited Omaha experience. It may be called the "banana" for all I know. So what the hell was I doing in a pot-limit Omaha game? Lord knows.) I don't know if the Omaha experts—in whose number I do *not* count myself—would agree, but my hand had looked good to me and the flop made me even more optimistic. I've got a draw to the nut straight and a draw to a decent flush, although I wasn't really happy about having three diamonds in my hand. Someone bets a moderate amount, and there are two callers including myself and the guy on my immediate left. I was having a hard time putting that guy on a hand, but I eventually decided on the straight draw. The turn brings a 2♠, a dud. The player who had bet on the flop checks.

[49.] What a name for a casino.

I check, and my southern opponent bets. Weird. He bet, all right, but only enough to give me odds to keep drawing. I decided my straight-draw analysis had been right. The first bettor folded, and I'm left in the pot alone with my neighbor.

The river comes the 6♦. Now, I'm *very* happy about having three diamonds in my hand. I'm first and I push in my stack, which is about the same size as his. (This is getting too suggestive of locker room comparisons.) I figure that my having three diamonds makes it very unlikely that my opponent has two, one of which would have to be the king or ace to beat me. Furthermore, I hadn't checked because I thought he might call me had he made a lesser hand, like the straight, but would check if I checked. Hell, thought I, he might even call if he just has trips. Well, he thinks and thinks (if he was looking for tells all I could have broadcast was confidence because I actually thought my queen-high flush was good) and studies and studies and finally calls. I turn over my queen-high flush, fully expecting him to trash his hand, and he turns over a K♦2♦! I had been right he *would* call my all-in bet, and *would* go all in himself with less than the nuts! Unfortunately, his less-than-the-nuts was better than my less-than-the-nuts. Go figure. Anyway, he took down the money, and I was digging in my pocket for more investment capital.

So, your all-in opponent may have the nuts, may be bluffing, or may have simply made a mistake as I did at the Barracuda. It's up to you to decide.

Neapolitan: High-Low Poker

Most casinos and card clubs offer high-low games in such variations as Omaha, stud, and so on. As you know, I think these are a waste of time for a number of reasons. The really fast and furious action in high-low is in home or private games. High-low keeps the action going as it gives more players more opportunities to get involved in pots. This is good. This is *very* good.

You *want* lots of action, lots of players throwing their money in the pot for you to win. But high-low can also be a financial mine field, which is the reason this discussion is included here.

Unless this is the first poker book you've ever read, you probably know that the general advice in playing high-low is to go low. This is especially true if your group plays the wheel whereby low hands have far more opportunity to hit straights and flushes and to swing both ways for the whole pot. This is *especially* true if you're playing pot-limit or no limit. As you know, I rarely give dicta when it comes to what cards to play when, but here comes one: If you are playing pot-limit or no limit YOU ARE CRAZY IF YOU TRY TO GO HIGH. In a limit game, it's not so serious a consideration.

You also may have read, as I did just recently, that you should only stay in for high, in five or seven card stud for example, if your first two or three cards give you at least a big pair, like aces or kings, preferably trips. This is wrong, almost without exception. High-low stud turns up with many more straights and flushes than high-only. The reason is obvious: Opportunities are relatively rare to hit straights and flushes in high stud (virtually nonexistent in five stud—except for Edward G. Robinson), but if you're going for low and happen to hit a straight or a flush it's just a bonus—and it happens often. Therefore, if you're going high and starting off with a big pair, or even trips, you could well be setting yourself up for a trap. This is especially true if you're playing stud with a twist allowing players to change one card at the end. I have seen this happen so many times it's difficult to decide which story to tell you to illustrate the point.

A good one occurred several years ago when I nailed a friend of mine (a poker-playing friend) for over $4,000 in a pot-limit high-low five-stud-with-a-twist hand. (That may be a record for hyphens.) Out of eight players, we were the only two left in the hand at twist time. He was showing high with KKQ5, and I was low with [3] A467. There had been some big betting and loose calling early on in the hand, and there was $940 in the pot. He said, "Look, I'm high and you're low, why don't we just split?"

I said, "Dan, why should I split? Half the pot's already mine for sure and I'm gonna twist for a straight." With a disgusted, we're-wasting-time (more hyphens!) look on his face, he checked. I, of course, bet the pot. He called. So now there's $2,820 in the pot. He threw away his 5, and I dumped the Ace. He got back a 9, and—what else?—I got a five. So he's showing KKQ9, and I've got [3] 4675, a straight! So now what? He says, "I'm not gonna believe you hit that gutshot, but I'll check if you're not going to split." I said, "Fine. I bet the pot: $2,820."

Now, when Dan originally found himself alone with me with $940 in the pot, he had a pretty good gamble in calling my bet. Two 5s, two 3s and three 8s had been exposed during the hand (from my up cards he wouldn't know that I needed a five; had I a 5 in the hole, a 3 or an 8 could have made my straight). That meant that there was only a total of five cards that could (possibly) make my straight. If any other card comes up on the twist he's home free. Furthermore, there were three cards, one king and two queens, which could make him a full house or four kings. Therefore, for $940 against a return of $470, or 1 to 2, he was looking at odds of about 1 to 8 that he was going to win high regardless of the draw. But the point is: *All* the risk was his. No matter what happened, I was guaranteed half the pot, and he was the one who had to sweat. (It's worth noting here that he had no chance of winning the whole pot by hitting fours or a full house then by my going both ways and losing. Had he hit a "danger card" I would never have gambled half the pot against it. I would have been happy with my sure-thing half.)

So now, Dan is trapped. I've just hit one of the "danger" cards, which increases his risk to 2 to 5, or 1 to 2.5, that I've hit my straight, and he's got a $2,820 bet to contend with. Again, remember, he doesn't know what I have in the hole; I could have a 10 or an ace or something with no chance at all of hitting a straight, but he has to figure on a legitimate straight draw. What to do? What to do? What he should have done is folded. It just wasn't worth $2,820 to get back $1,410 by making that call. But how could he fold? Psychologically, he couldn't at that

Round One: Eight Players:	Total Bet	The Pot	Half the Pot Equals	Dan has in the pot	I have in the pot
Ante		$1			
Player 1 bets $1	$1	$2			
Player 2 calls and raises $3	$4	$6			
Player 3 calls and raises $10 (Dan)	$14	$20		$14	
Player 4 folds	$0	$20			
Player 5 folds	$0	$20			
Player 6 calls	$14	$34			
Player 7 calls	$14	$48			
Player 8 calls (David)	$14	$62			$14
Player 1 calls	$13	$75			
Player 2 calls	$10	$85			
Round Two: Six Players					
Dan bets $85	$85	$170		$99	
Player 6 folds	$0	$170			
Player 7 folds	$0	$170			
David calls	$85	$255			$99
Player 1 calls	$85	$340			
Palyer 2 folds	$0	$340	$170		
Round Three: Three Players					
David bets $300	$300	$640		$399	
Dan calls	$300	$940			$399
Player 1 folds	$0	$940	$470		
Round Four: Two Players					
David bets $940	$940	$1,880			$1,339
Dan calls	$940	$2,820	$1,410	$1,339	
Round Five (After Twist): Two Players					
David bets	$2,820	$5,640			$4,159
Dan calls	$2,820	$8,460	$4,230	$4,159	

point. The answer is something else: he shouldn't have been in there with that hand in the first place, certainly not in a pot-limit game. If you study the chart from the previous page, you'll see that Dan's absolute best case was to win $71 against a total final investment of $4,159. In other words, Dan ended up risking $4,159 to get back $4,230, or a $71 profit. Now, I know, as the hand progresses the money in the pot is nobody's. But the point is that from the very beginning of the hand, from the very first bet, you have to project a likely outcome for that hand, a likely return on your total investment. Look at the chart of the hand, and then we'll talk about it.

Now, first of all, you want a lot of players in a high-low split pot. Remember, you're probably only going to get half the pot. If there are two of you in the pot, you'll be battling to get your own money back. In the first round, I had [3] A. That, of course, is a good start, but it's early in the hand, and a plethora of bad things can happen. Besides, I want a lot of people in there to give me decent odds (potential return) on my money, so I'm just trailing along calling. Dan, with his back to back kings, is doing all the betting, which will only insure short odds on his investment.

By the second round, I have [3] A4. Looking good. But still, I could get a clinker on my fourth card, so I'm taking it easy, and I still want people in the pot to give me odds. By now, though, Dan has trip kings and only wishes the pot were bigger so he could bet more. His betting the pot drives out three of the remaining six players and shortens his odds further.

On the third round, I have [3] A46. My low competition is showing [?] 489, so when Dan bets $300, I just call hoping to keep them *both* in the pot. Unfortunately, my low competition is either weak of hole or faint of heart and folds. If you do the subtraction—the numbers are available to you in the chart—you will see that although there's now $940 in the pot, we are each now only going to win $71 on our total investment, given half the pot. But therein lies the rub. Once my low competition has folded, *my* $71 is a dead guarantee. If it costs me a million dollars, there is nothing that can happen to deny me my $71 profit.

Dan, however, is in a completely different situation: there are *lots* of things that can happen to deny him his profit and even take away his total investment.

On the fourth round, it's just Dan and me. My low is a dead cert and Dan is—or should be—sweating blood. Now, when I bet $940, I have absolutely nothing to lose. It's a totally empty gesture as far as possible loss is concerned. My only reasons for doing it are (1) to see if he will fold as he should and give me the whole pot, and (2) to see if he will call and give me a shot at a really huge pot. As it happened, he called, which was great for me, but it was the last semi-sensible thing he did, as we have seen above. In other words, he shouldn't have been in there in the first place, but since he was, this was a reasonable call for him to make. The odds were in his favor that he would get his $940 back, plus the $470, which would be his from the pot.

On round five, after I had hit my 5 for a straight and bet $2,820, Dan should have folded. He still had the absolute odds in his favor since he had no idea if my hole card made a straight or not, but that isn't the point. The point is: he had trapped himself.

So what do you do? If the game is high-low five-stud and you start with kings wired, do you just chuck it in? Well, yes, probably, especially in a pot-limit or no limit game. So what happens when everyone has read poker books and only plays low? Won't that be the end of high-low? Well, no, it won't. For one, many poker players don't read poker books, and many who do don't learn anything anyway. They keep making the same old mistakes. For another, there is a high strategy for high-low games: go for straights and flushes, not pairs, trips, etc. This strategy is completely anathema to high stud, but it is the correct one for high-low.

In the end, the potential return on your total investment is *not* usually going to be worth your hanging around to try to win high. It is a very rare case indeed where this is worthwhile.

Considering a limit game, the situation is different, especially if the game is pretty loose, as many home games are. We have discussed high-low hands previously, and they provide great action. With a lot of players in the early rounds, it is often worthwhile to stay in for high. Take the situation I described earlier in which I nailed my friend for some $4,000. With, say, $150 in the pot and an end bet of $5, or 15 to 1 (figured on half the pot), he has a good bet all the way. When I dump my ace to try for the straight, he just checks, waits for me to bet $5, shrugs and throws in his call, and waits to see if I hit or not. At 15 to 1, his pot odds are far and away enough to let me draw, call, and shrug if he loses. In terms of his total investment, he may double his money if he wins (this postulates a lot of callers in early rounds, remember), so that $5 represents a 1 to 15 shot at getting back his money and making a good profit.

You're *still* better off going for low, however, even in a limit game, but the advantage is not so great, and going high can give you opportunities to set traps. This is especially true if you're playing seven stud, going high, and have a shot at making a high straight or flush. Not only will you probably win high, but you may even win the whole pot if some low player hits a low straight or flush and swings. Most low-hand flushes will have an ace in them, though, so make sure yours does too—and some good high cards to go with it.

You've heard that the money in the pot belongs to no one. You've also heard that your pot odds at any given point are calculated on the total pot verses what you have to put in, irrespective of how much of that money is yours. In the later rounds of a hand this is true. But when the hand begins, you have to look at the overall picture. How much am I going to put into this hand in relation to how much I can expect to get out? If you're putting a lot of money in pots with little return potential, you're going to walk away a loser even though you've won a lot of pots. This seems obvious, but you'd be surprised how easy it is to forget—and how many players never think about it. This is one thing that happens to overly tight players. Everybody sees them coming, folds and, sure the tight player wins, but he wins peanuts. Look at the example on the next page for five-stud high-low.

Five stud, high-low, limits: 2,3,4,5

Round 1	To Pot	Pot	Player One's Investment
Ante	$5	$5	
(Tight) Player 1 bets	$2	$7	$2
Player 2 folds			
Player 3 folds			
Player 4 folds			
Player 5 folds			
Player 6 calls	$2	$9	
Player 7 calls	$2	$11	
Player 8 folds			
Round 2			
Player 1 bets (showing low)	$3	$14	$3
Player 6 raises (showing high)	$6	$20	
Player 7 calls (showing low)	$6	$26	
Player 1 calls	$3	$29	$3
Round 3			
Player 1 checks	$0	$29	
Player 2 bets	$4	$33	
Player 7 calls	$4	$37	
Player 1 calls	$4	$41	$4
Round 4			
Player 1 checks	$0	$41	
Player 2 bets	$5	$46	
Player 7 folds	$0	$46	
Player 1 calls	$5	$51	$5
Player 1 wins	$25	On	
		investment of	$17
Profit of	$8	= return of	47%

By the time the hand is over, Player 1 has won $8 on a $17 investment, which is about 47 percent. Now a 47 percent return on your investment in XYZ Widgets, Inc., is a good deal. For a poker hand it is the pits. If Player 7 hadn't hit a bad end card, he could have won and Player 1 would have been out his $17. With a 47 percent return, he would then have to win two hands just to make up for that one loss. Depending on the looseness of your poker group, in high-low it's usually very difficult to make more than a 100 percent return unless you're able to swing and win both ways. That means that one loss and one win will come out even. Often, winnings at high-low are in the 70 percent to 90 percent range of rate of return. This is what makes high-low so deceptively dangerous: it's easier (more action) to win pots,

English Stud (high-low split)							
Round	# of Players	Bet	Raises	Total Bet per Player	# Taking Twists @ $5	Total to Pot	Total Pot
Ante	8						$5
1	6	$2	1	$4		$24	$29
2	5	$2	1	$4		$20	$49
3	4	$3	1	$6		$24	$73
4	4	$4	1	$8		$32	$105
Twist	4				3	$15	$120
5	4	$5	1	$10		$40	$160
Twist	4				3	$15	$175
6	3	$5	2	$15		$45	$220
Declare							
7	3	$5	2	$15		$45	$265
Total Invested per Winner if paid for twist:				$72			
Total Return:				$132			
Profit:				$60			
Return:				83%			

SPIT BUY (high-low split)

Round	# of Players	Bet	Raises	Total Bet per Player	# Taking Twists @ $5	Total to Pot	Total Pot
Ante	8						$5
1	7	$2	1	$4		$28	$33
Widow	7						
2	6	$3	1	$6		$36	$69
Draw	6						
3	5	$5	1	$10		$50	$119
Twist	5				3	$15	$134
4	3	$5	1	$10		$30	$149
Declare	3						
5	3	$10	2	$30		$90	$239
Total Invested per Winner if paid for twist:				$65			
Total Return:				$119			
Profit:				$54			
Return:				83%			

BUY THE DECK (high-low split)

Round	# of Players	Bet	Raises	Total Bet per Player	# Taking Twists @ bet	Total to Pot	Total Pot
Ante	8						$5
1	6	$2	1	$4	4	$32	$37
2	5	$2	1	$4	3	$26	$63
3	5	$3	1	$6	3	$39	$102
4	5	$4	1	$8	3	$52	$154
5	3	$5	1	$10	2	$40	$194
Declare	3						
6	3	$5	2	$15		$45	$239
Total Invested per Winner if paid for twist:				$63			
Total Return:				$119			
Profit:				$56			
Return:				89%			

ENGLISH STUD, BUY THE DECK (high-low split)

Round	# of Players	Bet	Raises	Total Bet per Player	# Taking Twists @ Bet	Total to Pot	Total Pot
Ante	8						$5
1	6	$2		$2	4	$20	$25
2	5	$2	1	$4	4	$40	$65
3	4	$3		$3	3	$27	$92
4	4	$4	1	$8	3	$47	$139
Twist	4				4	$20	$159
5	4	$5	1	$10		$40	$199
Twist	4				4	$20	$219
6	3	$5	2	$15		$45	$264
Declare							
7	3	$5	2	$15		$45	$309

Total Invested per Winner if paid for twist:	$78
Total Return:	$154
Profit:	$76
Return:	97%

SEVEN STUD, HIGH-LOW

Round	# of Players	Bet	Raises	Total Bet per Player	Total to Pot	Total Pot
Ante	8					$5
1	6	$2	1	$4	$24	$29
2	5	$2		$2	$10	$39
3	4	$3	1	$6	$24	$63
4	4	$4		$4	$16	$79
5	3	$5	1	$10	$30	$109
Declare						
6	3	5	2	$15	$45	$154

Total Invested per Winner:	$41
Total Return:	$77
Profit:	$36
Return:	88%

FIVE STUD, REVERSIBLE TWIST (high-low split)							
Round	# of Players	Bet	Raises	Total Bet Per Player	# Taking Twists @ Bet	Total to Pot	Total Pot
Ante	8						$5
1	6	$2	1	$4		$24	$29
2	5	$2	1	$4		$20	$49
3	4	$3	1	$6		$24	$73
4	4	$4	2	$12		$48	$121
Twist	4				4	$20	$141
5	4	$5	1	$10		$40	$181
Declare	4						
6	4	$5	2	$15		$60	$201
Total Invested per Winner if paid for twist:				$56			
Total Return:				$100			
Profit:				$44			
Return:				79%			

but it's harder to make any money. The charts below illustrate the average rates of return in high-low and high-only variations played in the limit game. A few things to remember: (1) In this group, the dealer antes $5 for all players (rather than each player anteing each hand). (2) This is an exceptionally loose game, as illustrated by the number of players calling the first-round bets and raises, so if your group is tighter your returns will be even more measly. (3) This game has a betting round after the declare, which makes the returns even better.

What you have in all the above charts is an average return ranging from 79 percent to 97 percent of your total investment; this in a very loose group with some impressively large pots considering the betting limits. When Harry the Asset wants to try to recoup some of his losses, he invariably deals English Stud, Buy the Deck, and says, "Let's get a $300 pot!" It isn't evident to Poor Harry that his love for games with lots of buys and twists, high-low, is one of the big reasons he can't win. If the niggardly return in the above charts is not immediately evident to you, have a

HOLD 'EM (high only)

Round	# of Players	Bet	Raises	Total Bet per Player	Total to Pot	Total Pot
Ante	8					$5
1	6	$2	1	$4	$24	$29
2	4	$3		$3	$12	$41
3	3	$4	1	$8	$24	$65
4	2	$5	1	$10	$20	$85
Total Invested:				$25		
Total Return:				$85		
Profit:				$60		
Return:				240%		

OMAHA (high only)

Round	# of Players	Bet	Raises	Total Bet per Player	Total to Pot	Total Pot
Ante	8					$5
1	6	$5		$5	$30	$35
2	4	$3	1	$6	$24	$59
3	4	$4		$4	$16	$75
4	2	$5	1	$10	$20	$95
Total Invested:				$25		
Total Return:				$95		
Profit:				$70		
Return:				280%		

look at the few high-only games played in the limit game, below.

Look at that! Returns over 200 percent, sometimes approaching 300 percent! If Harry were really looking to recoup—and not so impressed by inflated pots—that's what he should be dealing. Lest you think these returns are only available in a very loose group, below is a typical hand from a casino Hold'em game.

I hope this clarifies what I've been trying to say: it's hard to make money at high-low. So, what to do? Play very tight so you

SEVEN STUD (high only)

Round	# of Players	Bet	Raises	Total Bet per Player	Total to Pot	Total Pot
Ante	8					$5
1	5	$2	1	$4	$20	$25
2	4	$2		$2	$8	$33
3	3	$3	1	$6	$18	$51
4	3	$4		$4	$12	$63
5	2	$5	1	$10	$20	$83
Total Invested:				$26		
Total Return:				$83		
Profit:				$57		
Return:				219%		

CASINO HOLD 'EM 10-20 (high only)

Round	# of Players	Bet	Raises	Total Bet per Player	Total to Pot	Total Pot
Blinds	10					$15
1	5	$10	1	$20	$100	$115
2	3	$10	1	$20	$60	$175
3	3	$20	1	$40	$120	$295
4	2	$20		$20	$40	$335
Total Invested:				$100		
Total Return:				$335		
Profit:				$235		
Return:				235%		

can at least "guarantee" your itsy-bitsy return? Yes and no. You need to play only hands that are almost sure winners, while not letting the other players know that that's what you're doing. If the others think you are really tight, your return will be so poor that you won't be able to make any money at all. This is true in any form of poker but especially so in high-low.

How does this rate of return relate to whether or not you should invest in a hand? Well, if for example you are playing limit draw with eight people, you already know that you shouldn't draw to a flush unless you are going to get about 5 to 1 for your money; therefore, if you win you can usually expect a return of around 3 to 1, or about 200 percent. This makes a 50 percent return in high-low seem pretty paltry. If you go back to the Dave-beats-Dan example of pot-limit high-low, Dan's rate of return would have been 2 percent *had he won*. Having lost, he would have to win fifty times at the same return just to break even. (Pot limit and no limit games also tend to have a return closer to 100 percent, even in high only. This, of course, means that you can afford to be wrong more frequently in a limit game, where one win might cover two or three losses.)

This all should have shown you that thinking of your total investment in advance is extremely important. And calculating, in advance, your expected rate of return on that total investment is absolutely crucial in high-low. You should be thinking something like this:

(POTENTIAL TOTAL POT × PROBABILITY OF WINNING)/TOTAL
INVESTMENT REQUIRED = PLAY/NO PLAY

Let's first take the ubiquitous and easy-to-figure flush draw in high as an example.

1. Potential Total Pot: $400
   Total Investment Required: $100
   Probability of Winning: .191
   Ergo: ($400 × .191) / $100 = .764 (no play)
2. Potential Total Pot: $523
   Total Investment Required: $100
   Probability of Winning: .191
   Ergo: ($523 × .191) / $100 = 1 (break even:

play / no play is a toss up)

3. Potential Total Pot: $600

   Total Investment Required: $100

   Probability of Winning: .191

   Ergo: ($600 × .191) / $100 = 1.146 (play)

Considering long-term, multiple-event investment: At 1, you break even. Under 1 you lose. Over 1 you win.

Now let's consider a high-low game, but we'll stipulate the winning chances and an average rate of return of 50 percent. (That is, if you put in $100, you get $150 back, representing a $50 profit.) Remember that the $150 represents half of a $300 pot.

1. Potential Total Pot: $150

   Total Investment Required: $100

   Probability of Winning: .400

   Ergo: ($150 × $400) / $100 − .600 (no play)

2. Potential Total Pot: $150

   Total Investment Required: $100

   Probability of Winning: .667

   Ergo: ($150 × .667) / $100 − 1 (break even: play/no play is a toss up)

What this means is that, with an average rate of return of 50 percent, you need a 67 percent chance of winning before the hand even starts *just to break even*. 67 percent chance of winning means you are odds-on. When you get your first two or three cards, you have to be the favorite, you have to be the horse to beat, *just to break even*. (If your group is particularly loose and you think your rate of return is closer to 100 percent, you still have to have a 50 percent chance of winning—out of eight guys or however many are in your game—with your first two or three cards.)

But wait a minute, didn't I say that poker was a people game, to forget the math? Yes, I did. And just as the people factor changes—even nullifies—the card odds in the "Matt" chart on page 102, your personal ability as a poker player, your edge, will change the above equations in that it will enter into the "chances of winning" number, making it higher or lower. For example, the chance of winning in high only with a one-card flush draw is not really 0.191. It is 0.191 plus the likelihood that you can win without hitting! (It is also 0.191 minus the possibility that you will hit your flush and lose.) I have won so much money after *not* hitting flushes that sometimes I think it's better to miss! Well, not really; it's almost always better to hit, but your chances of winning after not hitting definitely have to enter into the equation. After all, missing your flush happens more than four times as often as hitting it, so what are you going to do with all those useless cards?

The same applies to your chances of winning the high-low hands, but don't get excited: be careful. If your cards aren't so hot, but you figure you can maneuver, manipulate, bully, and bluff your way to the pot, you still have to remember you're going after a small return, probably 100 percent or less. Are you really that good? There are eight guys in the game, which means that in a pure lottery you have 12.5 percent chance of winning. Can you mess around and out play your opponents to the point of giving yourself the odds-on advantage that you need? Remember the hand that I played from the food table? For one, I played it high, which as I said at the time wasn't the greatest, and two, I only made just short of a 100 percent return, actually about 95 percent. Further, I could have lost (gasp!) and my having won depended on a whole range of factors involving people, cards, position, etc.

So the point is that you have to be very, very sure of yourself if you're going to try to buck the low returns in high-low, and it's not only you, it's who you're playing against as well, and what cards they have, and . . . well, you get the idea. No one, except the "Matts" of this world, sits at the poker table with a computer in his lap, or in his head, solving equations for every situation. Once you have the basics down, experience will give you the answer without your having to excuse yourself from the game while you consult your mathematical tables.

For example, let's say you're playing seven stud high-low with your regular group. Since you've been playing with that group, this is about the eight thousandth time someone has dealt seven stud high-low and you should know by now about how big the pots usually are and how much it costs you to see the hand all the way through. In the limit game, the pots average $210 and cost an average of $50. So, when Bill says, "Seven stud high-low," I know automatically within a few dollars of what my investment and potential return will be. I also know, for example, that if Harry is showing the same way I am I wouldn't be able to bluff my way to the pot even if I bet my house at him; if Nick is showing mishmash he will fold; if Edgar has a bad hole card he will fold; three others guys are showing the other way; etc., etc.

A quick look around the table tells me everything I need to know to figure my chances of winning. If the cards are good and the situation is good, start shoveling that investment into the pot! If the cards are so-so but the situation is good, ditto, but be careful: you'll have to work much harder. If the cards are so-so and the situation is bad, get out. Therefore, a marginal answer in terms of strict numbers can be changed by the "people" input. If you get an answer of "1" or "break even", the people input could push it one way or the other: play or no play. If you get a low "play" answer, like a 1.05, the people factor may make you decide to fold anyway. If you get a high "no play" answer, like a 0.95, the people factor could make you decide to go ahead and play.

The idea of looking at your whole potential investment, then, has to be broken down step by step. Go back to the example above of the player who puts $17 in the pot to win $8. If this is an average return for him in high-low stud, then he's got to be very careful before getting involved, even to "see another card or two." He could easily blow $9 just to see the next couple cards—and that represents his average winnings from an entire hand!

All of this is a matter of money management, and it is absolutely crucial in high-low where the returns are low. If you start throwing money into the pot in the early rounds of a hand, deciding from card to card what to do, you can easily waste away the potential winnings from several hands. It's easy enough to start out with good cards and get blasted along the way, so it behooves one not to throw away money uselessly. Following are two more examples, one high only, one high-low.

High only: The game is five stud. You have [K]Q. There are eight of you, and your nearest apparent competition has [?] J. From the way his eyeballs are rolling, you're pretty sure he has jacks wired. Should you stay in there and try to out draw him? Well, you know that five-stud pots run to about $120. You figure that to stay in to the end you'll have to put in about $30. If you win, that's a return of 300 percent or 3 to 1. Right now you're about a 2.7 to 1 dog. Since your potential profit is 3 to 1, you should (without considering other factors) probably go ahead, especially if any "people" factors are present to give you an extra edge.

High-low: Everything is the same as above, except the pot will be split high-low. You know that five-stud high-low pots run to about $200, which means the winners get $100 each, and you will have to invest about $50 to go all the way. If you win, that's a return of 100 percent, or 1 to 1. Now your 2.7 to 1 shot at out drawing the Jacks doesn't look so good. Without considering other factors, it's a loser.

Summarizing high-low, it is popular, fun, interesting, gets the action going, gives you lots of room to maneuver, makes people play more loosely, builds bigger pots—and is usually a very shaky investment with lousy returns. I don't know how many times (thousands) I've seen everyone fold down to two guys, one high and one low, and they're slugging it out, throwing tens or hundreds or thousands of dollars in the pot for the privilege of splitting the ante between them. If you get involved in something like that, just make sure you're the low hand because, as we've seen, the high hand has nothing to win and everything to lose, which in my book is a pretty bad proposition.

Chapter 8

our image at the poker table is either going to help you or hurt you. Better if it helps you. And the easiest way to do that is to project an image that will make the other players misread who and what you are. Maybe your own sterling personality is sufficient to all situations and you don't need to worry about this aspect of poker. I doubt it, though. If you sit down to a game with your everyday self hanging out, it's going to take good players a very short time to figure out what that "self" is, and use it against you. "But I am what I am!" you say. Fine, be what you are, but if your poker-playing style is simply an unconscious, invariable extension of what and who you are, you'll be a sitting duck. As we have seen repeatedly throughout this book, predictability is poker death.

Not considering specific moves for the moment, the two most common, general manifestations of this predictability are "tight" and "loose" play. If you always play one or the other, the other players will draw a bead on you, and you won't have a chance. If you can *look* like one and *be* the other, however, you're on the road to poker success. Now, as I alluded to above: *most people equate types of behavior, personality, with style of play*. If you sit there quiet, stoic, stony, sullen, or even meek, timid, and unsure, people are going to read you as rock-tight, at least until they get further evidence. If you're flamboyant, extroverted, maybe having a drink or two, chattering away, telling jokes, enjoying yourself, you'll be read as loose, at least until ditto. And loose, most of the time—certainly in private games— is what you want to be read as. Why? Let's see how many reasons I can come up with.

241

1. Tight players look like they're trying to win money and don't add to the overall "enjoyment" of the other players. If you're new to a private game, the other players won't like that, and you may get disinvited.

2. Tight players don't get any action. They bet, everyone folds, they win the antes.

3. When tight players do get action, they are often beat. Their opponents know they're tight and aren't in pots with them without hammers.

4. The presence of a tight player often tightens up the whole game: less action all around.

5. "Loose" players are welcomed and valued in virtually any game, public or private.

6. "Loose" players get lots of action. They bet and opponents call.

7. Opponents will often get into pots with marginal hands because they think the "loose" player probably has a weak hand as well.

8. The presence of a "loose" player often loosens up the whole game: more action all around.

It should be evident from the above that appearing "loose" is going to be an advantage most of the time, unless you have a particular strategic reason for appearing tight.

Let's say you're in a game with a bunch of real tough cookies. Well, you're no wimp yourself, but it might be in your best interest to appear to be one. I did this the other day when I found myself in a $50–$100 Hold'em game in Las Vegas. These guys looked as though they could all have gotten roles as the chief bad guys in the next Mad Max movie. Tough, real tough. Through a series of little squeaks, moans, worried looks and questions like, "Gee, are *all* you guys pros?" I let them know I was just about wetting my pants. Why? Because I wanted to start off winning to give myself the luxury of playing with their money. Therefore, I needed them to respect my bets. If I was in a pot, they had to know that wimpy old me wouldn't be doing anything risky; I must have the nuts. Also, since I'm never in a pot unless I think the odds are in my favor, I wanted them to think they could scare me out with lots of aggressive raising. Hell, if the odds are in my favor, I *want* more money in the pot—but I didn't want them to know I was thinking in those terms.

Sure enough, if I was in a pot, there would either (1) be a few early calls but then they would all get out if I persisted; or (2) be two or three players who would start raising like crazy, hoping collectively to drive me out through scare tactics. Further along, my nut-player persona insured that when they did bet into me, I knew they had a good hand.

In one hand I have A♥K♦ and had raised before the flop. When the flop comes K♣J♥6♠, I bet out and get two calls. The turn comes 8♥. I bet out again. The guy on my left folds, and the third guy raises me back. I'm thinking, now, wait a minute. He's got to figure me for the ace-king, so he's either bluffing or he's got a pair of kings beat. I couldn't figure him for the bluff since (1) I had by this time shown the table that I would call down a bluff if I thought I had the best hand, and (2) if he was reading me for top pair with top kicker, he surely wouldn't expect me to fold. That meant he must have me beat. I folded. Sure enough, this guy showed his hand to his buddy across the table, as many players are wont to do, and he had the J♦8♦, two pair. Here's the point: I made the right move, because I knew he had me beat, because I knew what he thought of me, because I had made him think it.

I ended up doing well in that game and grunts and murmurs of "lucky" were rumbling around the table. Well, about 25 percent of my win had been on bluffs, which they never once suspected a "guy-like-me" would be pulling. Right in the middle of one of the bluffs, a guy I had become friendly with came up behind me, on a break from his own game, wanting to chat.

He saw my cards and saw what I was doing. When the bluff was successfully concluded, he leaned over and said in one of the various languages we both spoke: "Dave! You've got to show them what you did! After a move like that they'll call you forever." I told him, "Not now. I'm not catching that many cards and, meanwhile, I've got them right where I want them." It wasn't broke, so I didn't want to fix it. And I never did "expose" myself. When I got up from the table, they were all thinking there goes the scared nut-player who got lucky.

I often like to use the meek and mild image as it induces players to try to bully me on the one hand, and respect my bets on the other. I might point out that this is not easy for me to do since, physically, I am somewhat imposing and have been told that I am rather stern and forbidding of countenance. There are times, however, many times, when another image is more appropriate. It all depends on the folks you're playing with. In casinos or public card rooms, you can get away with a lot more image shenanigans than you can in a private game. To illustrate, following are some of my favorite casino poker personas.

• *Relaxed, friendly, chatting with all the players, telling jokes, just another joe in a friendly game of poker.* Purpose: I want the other players to think I'm just out for entertainment, treating this game like I would my private game "back home." In other words, I want them off their guard, not thinking that I'm there for "business."

• *Sullen and sneering, shut up, don't bug me, just play cards.* Purpose: This can be a defensive posture when I'm feeling unsure of my ability relative to the other players. It can be an offensive ploy if I think there are some inexperienced players in the game who will be easy to bully.

• *Aggressive and mean: you mess with me and I'll bust you.* Purpose: Again, this is primarily a defensive posture. Typically, early in the game I'll wait till I have some pretty impressive cards and try to catch someone on a marginal hand. (If these criteria don't present themselves, I'll switch tactics.) Then, I'll lure him into a real hammering and sort of look around the table with a "this could happen to *you* too" air. Clearly, what I want is for the other players to be wary if I'm in a pot, thus giving added protection to my future bluffs. If someone persists, i.e., doesn't back down at my "presence in the pot," I'll know he's got a pretty strong hand.

- *Flamboyant and devil-may-care: the stakes in this game really mean nothing to me.* Purpose: One, to put opponents off their guard. I don't want them to know that this is "business" for me. Two, opponents will tend to read me as loose, as not really paying attention, and will call my bets.

- *Pensive and philosophical, thinking for several seconds about each play, looking at the ceiling, studying the board.* Purpose: If I've spotted one or more players behind me who have tells that give away their intentions, I want to delay my play long enough to give them an opportunity to "tell" me. Sometimes, too, a player behind me will have a habit of acting out of turn if I don't act right away. Either way, I need an excuse to delay and "pensive" gives it to me. Different from "absent minded" below, it makes opponents think that here's someone who's thinking about the game and opponents' moves.

- *Preoccupied and absent minded, "Oh! Is it my turn? Did somebody raise?"* Purpose: This affords me the same opportunity to delay my play and look around for tells as with "pensive" above, but it has the added attraction of making opponents think I'm not paying attention and not really of any concern to them. Note: Very often your opponent to your immediate left will wait to look at his cards until it's your turn to play and, sometimes, you will be next to someone who inadvertently shows his cards when he looks at them. That means you need to give yourself time to see his cards and both "pensive" and "absent minded" will do the trick. Beware, though, of the traps we discussed in Chapter 5 about seeing other players' cards.

- *Rock tight and quiet, hiding behind my dark glasses[50] and*

[50.] You'll see a lot of folks wearing dark glasses in public poker. Yes, as much you *never saying a word.* Purpose: Much like "mean and aggressive", I want to be "feared" if I'm in the pot. Usually a defensive move—or protection for future bluffs—it actually means I'm unsure of myself and feeling my way in that game.

Sleepy, disheveled and unshaven, just barely able to keep my eyes open. Purpose: To put opponents off their guard. There is further discussion of this "act" below.

Inexperienced, curious, always asking about the rules and "How much can I bet?" Purpose: To put opponents off their guard, again, trying not to be spotted as an experienced, businesslike player.

Wild and loose, frantic for action, calling every hand, raising on nothing. Purpose: Primarily this is to insure my bets get called when I have a hand. Since wild and loose is perhaps *the* best of all image ploys in both public and private games—and since it is the most difficult as it involves *appearing* loose without actually *being* so—there is extensive discussion of it below.

One, no, two personas I don't use, but which many people in public poker do, are the drunk and the idiot.

The drunk: if you're at a game in Vegas or California or wherever and a new player comes lurching over to the table, tripping over people and chairs, reeking of alcohol, slurring his speech, knocking over his chips, sloshing his drink, fumbling hopelessly with his cards—nine times out of ten this is an act. Don't fall for it. Figure the guy knows exactly what he's doing until you get substantial evidence to the contrary.

The idiot: To illustrate this I'll use the genuinely sad case of a player I've run into several times in California who clearly has some neuromuscular disease. The result is that he acts and talks like a complete idiot, sways around in his chair to the point of

may want to ignore it as an image ploy, it makes the player look more "dangerous" and "businesslike." I wear the glasses but mostly for another reason: they really do hide your eyes, which are any human being's weak spot in terms of giving away what's going on inside.

having to be rescued from falling off, can't stack his chips or handle his cards, and his speech is all but unintelligible. When he bets, all the players who don't know him call and raise like lemmings. The players who do know him all get out because, his affliction notwithstanding, this guy is as sharp as a tack. Not only is he a good poker player, he is also aware of the image his affliction causes him to project, and he uses it to the maximum. In his case, I say good for him; more power to him. I hope he can keep winning until, well, as long as he can keep playing. But, there are other people who fake this sort of thing for effect. And to them I say: Fuck you. I'll redouble my efforts to get your money, and I'll get it, too.

As to the fake drunks, I am hard pressed to explain exactly why I find this distasteful when I'll happily use a dozen different personas myself. I guess it's because most of the various personas I put on are still really me, in the end. I just bring out different aspects of myself that I think are more strategically appropriate at the moment. Just like with my kids: there's a time to be outwardly stern, even though my heart may be melting. All I can say is that I don't use the drunk act, and I have a hard time mustering respect for people who do. (Although, in the limit game, I will have a few drinks from time to time. See below.) My main complaint is that it tends to slow down and disrupt the game, a discourtesy to all.[51]

The one act I do use that is purely an act is the sleepy, disheveled, unshaven one listed above. Sometimes, I really *am* sleepy, disheveled, and unshaven, but not usually. What I'll do is, after a day's playing I'll disappear around ten o'clock at night and go to sleep, leaving a wake-up call for, say, 4:00 a.m. Upon wakening I'll have some coffee and a shower, but I will be careful to put on yesterday's clothes and not shave. Yesterday's clothes on a clean bod are truly yucky, but business is business. I'll then show up in the card room trying not to appear as bright-eyed and

---

[51.] There is, usually, an overall code of (outward) behavior in public poker. It is that if you are trying to bust someone, starve his family, and make them homeless, you can at least do it in a gentlemanly fashion.

bushy-tailed as I am, and proceed to make feast of the players who have been up all night. To all who then see me the next (actually, later the same) day and who ask, "My God, have you been playing all night?" I, of course, say yes. This is an excellent ploy. Works like a charm. You profit from the all-nighters and then again from those who think *you* are an all-nighter. Time was when I could play for days and nights on end and not lose a single degree of sharpness. Can't do that anymore. After about forty hours at the table, I start to lose it. So, as always, adapting to new conditions and situations, I try to make the most of my newly acquired need for shuteye. Strategic sleeping!

There are many more acts you'll see around public card rooms that I don't use, just because, well, they are so lame, so stupid, that I would be embarrassed to look at myself in the mirror. Also, they are blatantly, obviously acts. The most prominent of these is the nut or the weirdo. You'll find people mumbling and talking to themselves; spouting inanities to other players; making signs as if calling down spirits; drooling; using mechanical, robot-like movements; tearing up napkins and sprinkling the resulting confetti on their heads; chanting mantras. It goes on and on. I've even seen people tear up (or light cigarettes with) money. Whenever I see this kind of crap, I just have to chuckle to myself and think these folks are truly interpersonally challenged. If you find yourself in a casino or public card room just ignore the players' window dressing but, as with everyone else at the table, *watch how they actually play!* The guy with napkin confetti in his hair is just as likely to hit and bet the nuts, or check-raise, or bluff as a "normal" player.

In contrast to what you can get away with in public poker, in a private game such behavior is likely to get you disinvited. Furthermore, since you're seeing the same folks week after week, your behavior has to be more consistent, at least it must appear so. In the limit game, I do use some of the personas listed above, but they all come under the heading of temporary aberrations in my usual behavior, which is, as you know by now, the wild and loose player. For example, sometimes I show up grumpy and sullen. This inevitably evokes questions of "What's the matter with you tonight?" to which I reply something like "I'm in a bad mood" or "I'm grumpy" or "I'm not feeling well." In other words, in contrast to public poker, the result is not: "This is a mean, aggressive player." The result is: "Wild and loose Dave is grumpy tonight (or not feeling well, or whatever)." See the difference? It's a big one.

You may have noticed that I didn't say that I show up *acting* grumpy and sullen. In fact, when I show up that way, it's often because I really *am* in a foul or irritable mood for some reason, and I figure I might as well make the most of it. I go out of my way to let people know. This is another part of my cover: If I know that for some reason it's likely that I'll be off my game, and, therefore, playing much tighter than usual, I want the other players to write this off as an aberration due to a temporary mood swing. I don't want any of them thinking, "Hey, Dave can play like a rock if he wants to."

On the other hand, sometimes I *am* acting. I'll act grumpy and sullen but still go ahead and play my "loose" game. Why? Again, I don't want any particular card-playing behavior associated with a particular mood. It's protection, really, for future sessions when I may actually be grumpy: I want the other players to think "It doesn't matter that Dave isn't himself tonight, he still plays loose when he's like that." Imagine a football player who has a chronic bad knee that acts up, say, two or three times a season. Then imagine his opponents saying, "Hell, his knee was acting up last week and he still played like a demon." Was his knee really acting up last week, or—perhaps—did the team just *announce* that it was acting up? Get the idea?

Now, wait a minute. You're playing with your regular crowd. One thing is playing poker better than they do. But to go as far as adjusting your behavior, your persona, your character to win? Is this an honorable thing to be doing? Good question. We talked about this in Chapter 4 where I warned you that if you started playing poker to win, poker would never again be a "night out with the boys."

For the serious player, the good player, a quandary develops. Perhaps you have been playing poker as a boys'-night-out, enjoying the repartee and a bit of gamble, confident in the knowledge that this is all harmless fun. Sure, sometimes you lose more than you would like to, but then the next week, or the week after that, you win it back. Or do you? Perhaps not. Perhaps you've begun to notice that one or two players in the game definitely seem to win more than they lose, and perhaps you've had a few weeks of particularly hurtful losses, and this or these have led you into keeping track of your own wins and losses and those of the other players. Your findings: you're not winning it back. Good old Joe and good old Ted are adding money to their household incomes from poker, whereas you're always having to figure out—and explain and make excuses about—where the money is going.

You're not a patsy by nature—even though the losses are affordable you don't like the idea that others are lining their pockets at your expense—so something has to be done. Perhaps you quit playing poker. Nothing wrong with that. I know some fine, healthy, intelligent, manly, macho, winners-in-life who have told me, "I've played poker some, but I'm a lousy player and always lose, so I don't play any more."[52] When I have given the occasional admonition in this book that some folks should just give up poker, I have meant it sincerely as sound advice. In fact, if there are Harrys and Clarences out there who read this book, recognize themselves, and give up poker as a result, I'll have done a good job, and a good thing.

Perhaps that's you, but logically, if you've read through to Chapter 8 in a poker book, you have at least decided to try to improve your game first. So, you read this and other poker books. You study and you apply what you learn. Perhaps, given time, your game gets better and better. As it does, and if it does, something else may happen: you *become aware* as a poker player.

[52] Notice that these people are able to admit to being bad players, not victims of bad luck.

Like a child who can't grasp a concept then one day leaps in the air and shouts "I understand!" you *see* poker for all that it is. You *see* that poker is pitting you against other people, that someone is going to win and someone is going to lose, and that people who win don't win by chance. Now you know that *you* can win. Now you *know* that you can win.

At this point you have crossed a threshold. Before, poker was innocent because you were innocent. It was a gamble: lose this week, win next week, same story for all the players. Now you know different and you have lost your innocence. Now you know that there are and always have been people out there who can and do sit down with average or bad players and win at will. **At will!** And you know you are now one of them! You also know there is no separating money from serious-stakes poker.

A recent poker book[53] which otherwise has a lot of very good things to say, blows it here. The author essentially says (paraphrasing): what the hell? "Entertainment" poker rarely involves losing more than the value of dinner and a show. Well, say I, dinner and a show at, say, $150 a pop can lead a weekly bad player to lose $5–$6,000 a year. In the moderate-stakes limit game discussed in this book, Harry loses $15–$20,000 a year. The author, furthermore, says that even a high-stakes private game isn't likely to represent swings of more than 1 percent of the players' yearly salary. I say: 1 percent of your annual salary lost every week for a year is 52 percent of your total. Given that even a horrendous player will win occasionally, let's say it only represents 30 percent of his total annual income. That's a hell of a lot! And you, the winning player, are taking this money from him, not by chance but purposefully.

Even at "dinner and a show" level, you now know that you'll be taking your wife out once a week, whereas the loser is staying home because he's paying for *your* night out. And therein lies the quandary. Is this fair? Is it right to sit down with people and play poker *knowing that you can take their money at will?*

53. *Thursday-Night Poker,* by Peter O. Steiner (Random House, 1996).

If you are so inclined, go back and read the discussions in Chapter 4 about who I'll play poker with and who I won't, but you really—now that you've lost your innocence—must make your own rules and decide for yourself.

Suffice it to say, however, that if you're playing in a group for serious stakes and you think everyone's playing the same game, you're wrong. One or two of you are winning regularly, one or two of you are losing regularly, and the rest of you are floating around in between. Might as well be one of the winners, yes?

I really have fewer problems in practice with the moral implications of poker than my occasional agonizing over ethics would make it seem. As I have said before, poker is no more ruthless than basic capitalism. As you may have guessed by now my occasional agonizing is, in fact, over the general ruthlessness of human interaction and—basic capitalism.

You're a real estate agent and have just sold a house to that nice young family for $200,000 *knowing* that the owners would have accepted $185,000. That $15,000, and the interest on it over the span of the mortgage, may mean their children won't be going to college. Do you care? Do you worry about that? If you sell short on the stock market and make a fortune, all it means it that someone else has lost a fortune. While you're counting your dough, the loser is perhaps selling his house and pulling his kids out of school. Free-market capitalism is incredibly nasty, but, as we have been privileged to witness this century, the alternatives seem even nastier. What to do? Shut up and deal.

And to that end, the answer to our original question is: yes, fiddling with your image, your persona, is nothing more than another arrow in a good player's quiver and is perfectly acceptable. Besides, it is more of a defensive measure than an offensive one—perhaps I should have referred to it as a *shield* rather than as an arrow.

For starters, let me say that developing an image of being wild and loose does *not* mean you want to look like a calling station. If you do, people won't bluff into you—and, usually, you *want* them to bluff into you.

Here's what you want to be at the poker table: Tight, disciplined, alert, observant, manipulative, calculating.

Here's what you should *appear* to be at the poker table: Loose, wild, devil-may-care, unobservant, naïve, fun-loving.

Now how do you do that? You do it the same way a "guru" has convinced thousands that he is a master poker player when he is, in fact, totally inept. You do it the same way that mass-production hamburger chains have convinced millions their burgers are delicious when, in fact, they taste like paste and sawdust. Marketing and promotion. Advertising. PR.

The other night in the limit game, the game was English Stud. I had folded early in the previous hand and, although I hate to do it—leave the room, that is—I had had to go take a leak. The new hand starts and a summons is yelled from the table: "Are you in?" "Of course I'm in!" I shout back. I have actually finished my business and zipped up but decide to hang around in the john a little and see what happens. A few seconds later, another shouted summons: "It's checked to you, what do you do?" "Bet $2!" I say, "I'll be right there!"

I didn't even ask what my door card was. Pretty loose, right? Not even a little. I know that English Stud pots average right around $220 with $110 going to each winner. This usually represents an overall profit of about $60 each. My blind, loose, wild $2 bet is, therefore, made at potential odds of 30 to 1 if I win one way, 85 to 1 if I win both. If the game were a pure lottery I would have 3 to 1 odds of winning at least half (two winners out of eight players). My only disadvantage in being in the bathroom is that I miss seeing flashed cards on the deal and the expressions on the players' faces as they get and look at their cards. In any case, regardless of *what* my first cards are, calling $2 at minimum odds of 30 to 1 in this situation is a good, sound, tight bet. But it certainly *looks* wild and loose, and all the other players think so too. (The particular structure of this game, English Stud, allows for a lot of screwing around in the early betting rounds, as we'll see in a minute.)

Considering that I almost never leave the table more than

once in a ten or twelve-hour session, one little call-from-the-bathroom stunt obviously goes a long way. Now Harry, the asset, the calling station, pops up and down as if his chair were repeatedly catching fire. If he's out of a hand, or even in the small interval between hands, he'll be running around the room doing something. He runs over and watches the news, or sports or cooking programs, whatever, on TV, or pokes around the food table, or just walks around the room. About three hands out of four he is not in his chair when his cards are dealt, but he will *never* call even a one-dollar bet without dashing back to the table and looking at his cards. Then he calls nine times out of ten.

So do I call *all* first round bets? Of course not. But I do call more first and second and third round bets in this group than in others. The reason is that the structure of this game makes it easier to project the wild and loose image. As you know, first round bets are $2, progressing to $5 or $10 depending on the game. Furthermore, this group plays a lot of games with twists or "buys." This is good. This is very good. Hope springs eternal, and guys like Harry will stay all the way through a hand with garbage hoping to save the situation with the twists. Since the twists are expensive—each twist costs the equivalent of a bet at that round, usually $5—and with end bets being bigger than those of earlier rounds, there is proportionately more money going into the pot toward the end of the hand than at the beginning. The English Stud chart on page 226 illustrates this. Summarizing the chart on the following page.

This is a big pot for a $2–$5 game and many run bigger, well over $300; however, look at the amount of money in the pot on fifth street: $73 represents only about 25 percent of the final pot, although you've seen 83 percent of your final hand if you're not going to take any twists, and 63 percent of your final eight cards if you are (hand of six cards two of which are replaced with twists). In the "average" scenario shown in the chart, each player still active on fifth street has put $14 in the pot. If a player wins one way, his half will be $132, showing an overall profit of $60. This means you can break even by going to fifth street and

Ante		$5	Pot	$5
Players have 3 cards	Bet	$2	Pot	$29
Players have 4 cards	Bet	$2	Pot	$49
Players have 5 cards	Bet	$3	Pot	$73
Players have 6 cards	Bet	$4	Pot	$105
Players have 6 cards	Twist	$5	Pot	$120
Players have 6 cards	Bet	$5	Pot	$160
Players have 6 cards	Twist	$5	Pot	$175
Players have 6 cards	Bet	$5	Pot	$220
	Declare			
Players have 6 cards	Bet	$5	Pot	$265

dropping four times, then winning once. Anything better than one win in **five** attempts and you will make money. (I'm not talking about pot odds here which are astronomical but include your money. I'm talking about *profit*.) Now this allows for some pretty "loose" play—as long as you tighten up on fifth street. If you get yourself caught up in buying twists and the big end bets, you'll then start risking more than you can recoup in one hand.

Now, clearly, this contradicts some of what I said in Chapter 7 about high-low and where you have to be at the start to try to insure a decent return. Well, it only sort of contradicts it. If you go all the way to the end in most high-low scenarios, you'll be getting a lousy return on your investment. But, if your game is structured like this one with progressive limits, expensive twists, and lots of betting rounds at the maximum bet *then* you can play just about anything that has even the slimmest chance of winning in the earlier, cheaper rounds. But, even then, you must be careful, and you must discipline yourself to chuck it if it looks like it's not going to work out.

Another game that is particularly conducive to "loose" play is Spit-Buy. If you look at the chart on page 227, you will see that before the draw each active player has put $10 in the pot for a chance to draw and win half of $239 for a profit of about $60. Here, you can pay through two betting rounds to draw (calling one raise each time), fold after the draw *six times,* win and break even in the seventh. Anything better that one win in *seven* attempts is profitable. This is conducive to *really* "loose" play. It drives Bill, the card player, absolutely insane when I call two bets in each of the first two rounds, draw three cards to an ace, and end up winning low. It apparently hasn't occurred to him why I can get away with this in that game. (Remember, there's a twist after the draw, so all I have to hit on the draw is three, rather than four, to the low hand.) And believe me, the wild and loose image skyrockets. He, and others, *never* believe I have a hand and call down everything when I pull stuff like that. (Which, on the average, actually gives me odds to "break even" about one in *nine* times.)

And yet, in both the English Stud and Spit-Buy scenarios I've got the potential pot odds on my side the whole time, therefore, it is the essence of tight play. Again, though, it is very important to remember to fold before buying the twist and getting involved in the big end bets.

Other games in the limit game are not, per se, so conducive to "loose" play, so I don't play them that way. I pick and choose my script, make sure the stage lights are on and the audience is watching, then shout my lines as loudly as possible.

If you can read one or more of your opponents extremely well in certain circumstances, that is, *know* with nearly 100 percent accuracy when they have a hand and when they're bluffing, you have an excellent opportunity to make ridiculously "loose" plays. This occurs often in the limit game when playing five stud high-low with a reversible twist. Two tales follow.

The other night we were playing five stud high-low. My first two cards are [A] Q. An ace showing bets; I raise and get six calls. (Most players might say, "I raise, representing a pair of queens," but I know, and I know the other players know, that my raise *may* represent a pair of queens or it may represent that I'm just raising for the hell of it. My loose image makes it virtually impossible for my opponents to put me on a hand or even gauge my intentions—which is what this chapter is all about.) Of the six callers, four are showing 8 or lower. One is showing a king, and one, the original bettor, is showing an ace. My next card is a jack; the king gets a ten, and the ace gets a nine. Two of the four low-looking hands get paired, one on sixes and one on sevens, So here's what we're left with:

Carl	[ ] K 10
Bill	[ ] 6 6
Harry	[ ] A 9
Jack	[ ] 7 6
Mc	[A] Q J
Nick	[ ] 8 5
Tim	[ ] 7 7

Tim checks. Carl checks. Bill checks. Harry checks. Jack bets. I raise. Nick folds. Tim calls. Carl raises (!). Bill folds.[54] Harry calls. Jack raises (last raise). I call. Tim calls. Carl calls. Harry calls. Get all that? If not this will make it easier: The next card brings

Carl	[ ] K 10 8
Harry	[ ] A 9 4
Jack	[ ] 7 6 J
Me	[A] Q J 10
Tim	[ ] 7 7 3

And here we go again. Tim checks. Carl bets. Harry raises. Jack calls. I raise. Tim raises one dollar to kill the last raise. Carl calls. Harry calls. Jack calls. I call. Time for some analysis here.

Carl is clearly representing a pair of kings and probably has them.

Harry is betting and raising on the strength of being the leading low hand, but I happen to know he has a pair of 9s. How? Because when the 9 hit, he first looked optimistic, checked his

---

[54.] I was going to say "wallets" instead of "Bill folds" but decided not to.

whole card to make sure, then looked around the table and saw my higher cards and Carl's higher cards, looked pessimistic, had another look around the table, found he was showing the best low hand, and looked optimistic again. His thought processes weren't actually that bad; his problem is that everything he is thinking pops out on his face as if it were a TV screen.

Jack has a good hole card for low, probably a 2, certainly not worse than a 5. Since Jack never bets or raises into the nuts, he is just hanging in there, calling Harry's possible 9-low.

Me—well, we know what I have—so why am I raising into Carl's kings? Because if it ends up that I can't beat the kings by hitting either an ace or the gutshot, I'm planning to go low. What? Just hang on a minute and I'll explain.

Tim also has a good hole card for low and is hoping his last up card won't spoil his chances for dumping his superfluous 7 and drawing for low. The last up card (before the twist) brings

Carl	[ ] K 10 8 J
Harry	[ ] A 9 4 Q
Jack	[ ] 7 6 J 8
Me	[A] Q J 10 10
Tim	[ ] 7 7 3 2

I bet. Tim calls. Carl calls. Harry raises. Jack raises one dollar to kill a raise. I raise (last raise). Tim calls. Carl calls. Harry calls. Jack calls.

It's twist time. Remember: in this game you have the option of turning up your hole card and taking your twist down. Furthermore, the twists are not dealt until everyone has dumped a card and stated which way he wants it, up or down.

Carl dumps his 8, and asks for his twist up, which would be normal procedure.

Harry dumps his queen and asks for his twist up. Since, if he really had a draw to a 9-low he would opt to receive his twist down, this reinforces my read on his pair of 9s.

Jack dumps his jack and asks for his twist to come down, i.e., he will be turning up his hole card.

I dump my extra 10 and ask for my twist to come up. This gets everyone in an uproar. You're dumping your 10? You don't have two pair? If you don't have two pair what are you doing in the hand? Why are you taking your twist up? Only Carl, the card reader, says, "He's going for low and just trying to mess with your heads." (If Carl would just listen to his own advice more consistently he would be a practically unbeatable player.) Bill, the card *player,* says, "How can he be going for low? He's got two guys drawing better!" (I love it. I really do love it. I get such a kick out of this. Remembering hands like this will make me break out in giggles even years later.) What Bill doesn't know is: *I will know, and I do mean* **know**, *if they make their hands or not.*

Tim dumps his extra 7 and asks for his twist down.

The twists are dealt and we are left with

Carl	[ ] K 10 J 3
Harry	[ ] A 9 4 K
Jack	[ ] 7 6 8 2 (the 2 had previously been his hole card)
Me	[A] Q J 10 6
Tim	[ ] 7 3 2 5 (the 5 had previously been his hole card)

So now what? Harry checks. Just as he does, thus making it Jack's turn to bet, Tim says to Jack, "You can't bet, I've got the nuts." Whenever Tim says something to try to stop you from betting, he's got a busted hand. Every time. So now I know Tim's gone. Jack goes ahead and bets. Whenever Jack bets into the nuts *he* has a busted hand—not just a lousy hand, mind you, like a 10 or something, but a real bust. Had he truly had an 8-low he would have checked into Tim's possible 7-low, regardless of what Tim had said. So: I've done it; I've got a winner for low. I raise. Bill goes nuts: "How can you raise? You're not winning either way!" Tim folds. Carl raises. Harry raises one dollar, killing the last raise. Jack calls. I call. We declare with Carl and Harry going for high, and Jack and I going for low. Now Jack is in a quandary. Harry checks. Jack bets. I raise (more howls from Bill). Carl, saying irrelevantly to his bet, "I wish *I* knew what Jack's tell was," raises. Harry raises one dollar killing the last raise. Jack, befuddled and showing it, calls. I call. I turn over no pair and Jack turns over a pair of 2s. (Harry, of course, loses to Carl's kings.) My loose image takes a quantum leap.

A general poker note here: You, the reader, might think that the other players would react something like, "Holy shit! Dave is reading us like open books." The reality is: *most players in the bad to average categories—and sometimes even up into the "pretty good" category—refuse to believe they are being outplayed.* They refuse to believe they have tells that are being read by other players. They convince themselves they're losing either to bad luck on their part or to good luck on the winner's part. Of course, when they win it's because they're skillful players. This is what I discussed back in Chapter 4 about "denial." When I was losing at squash every week, there was only one answer: my friend is a better squash player. If Fred constantly loses the 100-meter race to Tom, there is only one answer: Tom is a faster runner. If you play golf every week and always lose to Bob, there is only one answer: Bob is a better golfer. However, to get most poker players to admit, even to themselves, that they are losing consistently because they are up against better players is almost impossible. There is enough luck (the pros call it the short-term luck factor) in poker that bad players will keep coming back for a whipping because their losses are due to—bad luck. And since the "short-term luck factor" will allow even the most horrendous of players to win occasionally, it only serves to reinforce their denial: "See? I can win at this game."

Sure, I had to get "lucky" that neither Jack nor Tim made his hand. Had one of them made it, I would have simply grumbled something about missing my gutshot (and let Bill lecture me about it) and folded. But having both high and low options—due to the fact that I can read when I'm beat in this situation—increases my "outs" enormously. Speaking of gutshots, which was one of my outs—albeit a distant one—in the above hand, in the next tale I did hit a gutshot. I won't detail the whole hand, suffice it to say that the cards and players were very similar—almost identical, really—to the above-described hand. The main difference this time was that it was Bill, rather than Carl who was showing the high strength, this time with a pair of aces showing. I was pulling the same old shit as described above, but on the twist I hit a king for a gutshot straight to the ace. Not only did Bill go nuts when I won for high, but Jack also started deriding me from the peanut gallery: "You must be getting desperate, Dave, trying for an inside straight," and so forth. Again, sure it was lucky to hit the gutshot (although not as lucky as they all thought: there hadn't been a king showing anywhere on the board). But I *want* to appear lucky. Appearing to chase "luck" is part and parcel of appearing "loose."

You can send your loose image soaring by hitting gutshots and other long-shot hands, or by making seemingly impossible plays, and sometimes there is very little luck required indeed. These situations arise when you know what cards are coming due to sloppy shuffling. Many home-game players don't give the cards a proper shuffle between hands and, thus, give the observant player an opportunity actually to know what cards are about to come off the deck. This happened the other night in a hand of five stud high-low. We'd come to the last round when it's time to decide whether or not to twist, and I was in a weird situation. I have [6] 5 3 2 A, and Tim, behind me, has [?] 5 4 3 A. The dealer was to my immediate right—I would be receiving the twist first if I took one—and here was my problem: I was pretty sure Tim was going to twist his hole card, and—*I knew there was a 2 coming next off the deck.*

The dealer was Harry, and Harry doesn't shuffle for beans. He holds the cards in such a way that anyone on his left can see every card in the deck. This is so incredibly stupid that I've told him about it on several occasions, but he keeps doing it. Well, among the cards I had seen were the 2♣ and the 2♠ stuck right together, and Harry had just dealt the 2♣ to himself. Well, obviously, I couldn't let Tim get a wheel, so I decided on making a show-play out of the whole situation. I throw my 2♦ and ask to receive my twist up. Tim throws his hole card. Sure enough, I get the 2♠. The fourth 2 hasn't shown, and Carl (thank you, Carl) says, "You threw a 2 and got a 2. Too bad. You'd'a had trips. Should'a taken it down! Now we all know you have a pair. Why'd you take it up? That was really stupid!" There was more derision from around the table, and Tim was cackling, as he is wont to do when he thinks he's got you. I didn't know where the fourth 2 was, but I did know it wasn't in the vicinity of the ones I had seen in the deck, so I wasn't worried about Tim getting it.

You know how it all ended: everyone betting and raising like crazy, especially Tim, and then a stunned silence followed by all manner of "it was still a really stupid play" "Dave's really lucky"-type comments from around the table. More loose-image fireworks.

You may be thinking that your group doesn't offer the same opportunities for "loose" play as the limit game. But I'd bet it does; just look for them. A pot-limit game with a small starting ante or blind can be ideal for apparent "loose" play because the first and, sometimes, second round bets are very small compared to the end bets when the pot—and, thus, the limit—is much bigger. No limit is another matter and depends on the overall nature of the group. Some groups will bet conservatively even though, officially, there is no limit; thus you know that if you call a $5 blind you will probably not be raised more than, say, $10 or $20. Other groups, however, will tend to get tough right off the bat, so that when you call a $5 blind you may get smacked with a *huge* raise. You have to know how your opponents behave and react. Still, end bets in no limit are, well, unlimited in size, and if you can get away with playing through the first couple rounds cheaply then "loose"[55] play may be an option. Finally, if you're against players whom you can "read" well in certain situations you can use those situations to appear "loose" whenever they arise.

Irrespective of the structure of your game you can always adopt non-card-related ploys, like the assorted personas, which

---

[55.] I keep putting quotation marks around "loose" because, as you know, I don't really believe in loose play—just the *appearance* of loose play.

tend to make your opponents think you are loose. Here are a couple more of those.

About twice a year I'll have a few drinks while playing in the limit game. *Everyone* notices that. They lick their lips and wait for me to drop fortunes. In fact, I usually won't start drinking on these occasions until I'm well up, and then I do tend to make a show of losing back some of the winnings. (No, I don't spill my drink, knock my chips about, be rude, delay the game, or fumble the cards as do the fake drunks I've criticized. I just enjoy myself— and really do drink what I appear to be drinking.) Not only do the others notice, they remember for the rest of the year—"Dave drinks at the game"—and the effect of this is to add just one more bit of evidence that Dave isn't taking this seriously, call him when he bets. Now *this* is advertising, not running weak bluffs to get caught.

Another thing you can do is lie a lot. Say you're playing five draw. The pot has been opened by a player you suspect of having a pair of aces. There's maybe one call to you and you have two pair, queens and tens. You raise, the opener and the other guy call. The opener draws three (aces for sure), the other caller draws one (probably a flush draw), and you draw one which turns out to be a 3—a dud. You take your three and put it between a ten and queen. The opener bets out, and you know he wouldn't do that unless he had hit at least trip aces. The other guy folds. You're going to fold, all right, but first . . . You squeeze out your cards as if hoping to see that draw you were after. You squeeze them out so that one queen, one ten, and the three are exposed in the fan, with the three between the ten and the queen. "Shit!" you declaim, as you show those three cards to your neighbors, "I needed a jack!" and you quickly muck your hand. Well, you've just told all your neighbors that you had raised and drawn to an inside straight and, unless you're the worst actor since Ronald Reagan, they may well believe you. Use your own imagination. There are plenty of opportunities to lie about what you've just done in order to project a wild and loose image.

Now, a word—not much more—about bluffing. Of course

you have to bluff, and be *seen* to bluff, if you want to appear loose and get your legitimate bets called. But, as you know from Chapter 6, I am not in favor of bluffing just to advertise. My opinion is that you should bluff to win the pot and that bluffing should be a profitable enterprise in itself. So, follow the precepts from Chapter 6 and *only bluff when you think your bluff has a good chance of working,* and, *only bluff if it's necessary.* You'll get called often enough in any case. If you really want to make a point of getting caught, then bluff successfully and show what you've done after the hand.

Bet from the bathroom, play hands blind, make "loose" plays (when the pot odds or potential pot odds are in your favor), be devil-may-care, have a drink occasionally (if you're into that sort of thing and can handle it—it won't help to have a drink if you're going to get blotto and lose six month's winnings), lie every chance you get, and the world will be yours, at least the poker world, because you can then play as tight as you want and no one will notice.

Chapter 9

Who *Are* These Guys? Public Poker

Casino Poker

Comparing the typical home poker game to casino poker is like comparing your dentist's tropical fish aquarium to the shark tank at Sea World.

At feeding time.

At feeding time on a day when someone has screwed up, and the sharks haven't eaten for three days.

The unsuspecting are lined up and thrown in, and when it's all over, as Brother Dave Garner used to say, there's hair, teeth, and eyeballs all over the place.

But, if you're the kind of poker player, like me, for whom the six days between your weekly game are known as "the void," for whom just waking up and realizing it is game day adds an extra tingle to the morning, for whom every hour on game day takes a year to go by until the six-o'clock starting time, then casinos and public card rooms are your dream come true. You're in L.A., at any time of day or night, seven days a week, and you get the poker itch. Well, you can just freeway yourself to any number of poker heavens in twenty minutes. (Except at rush hour when it's more like six hours. "Rush" hour is misnamed, wouldn't you say?) My favorite poker room is the Bicycle Club, just off the Long Beach freeway in Bell Gardens. If you're in Las Vegas and get a room at the Mirage, it is *always* game day, and the game is just an elevator away. Bliss! Joy! Wonder!

When in L.A., I usually stay with my friends Gary and Sharlene in Long Beach, just an L.A. hop from Bell Gardens, and the lure of the Bike has caused me to miss many a dinner engagement with them, to the point that I'm surprised they'll still have me. (Sorry, guys, for both past and, inevitably, future trespasses.)

When I pull into the Bike's valet parking area and the attendant gives me a ticket and takes off with my car, I often don't know if I'll be getting back in the car in three hours or three days. First buzz. As the doors to the Bike swish open and I walk into the cool air, the clatter of chips at scores of tables reaches me and makes my heart race and my palms sweat with anticipation. Second buzz. As I round the corner from the entrance and the floor comes into full view, I often just stand and gawk at hundreds of people playing poker. This is no Wednesday night game for which a dozen phone calls and a series of negotiations are required to get seven or eight people together. Third buzz.

At this point, I usually try to take some deep breaths, walk around, check things out from the rail, see if anyone I know is around—in other words, I try to get over this initial excitement, this adrenaline rush. This is business after all. But it often doesn't work. I check out the games and think I find a good one. Fourth buzz. I get my name on the board. Fifth buzz. I watch the list of names ahead of me dwindle. Sixth buzz. On and on and on, until I finally sit down and am dealt in. Buzzbuzzbuzz. Now, it's show time, and I do get down to business, but, hidden from my new adversaries and, hopefully, locked away where it won't inhibit my game, some inner part of me just keeps grinning from ear to ear the whole time the cards and chips flow. And I've felt this way since, a lifetime ago, I first wandered into the Normandie club in Gardena out of curiosity and couldn't believe what I was seeing: eternal poker. Do I love this game!

My usual highest limit game in casinos is $20–$40 Hold'em. In English casinos I play pot limit, but those games actually tend to be smaller—less action/overall risk—than an American casino's $20–$40 limit game. In the old days, I used to play pot-limit and no limit in American casinos as well, but I haven't done so regularly for some time. Just to let you know the lengths to which I have gone, have sacrificed myself, to research and bring verity to this book, during my last foray to Las Vegas I played quite a bit of $40–$80 and even got into a $50–$100 Hold'em game. I did this for you, my readers, and I felt like a steak at a USDA inspectors' barbecue.

Sixteen sharp, soulless eyes flashed their glint of pleasure and expectation as I sat down.

Eight merciless and mirthless countenances gave me empty welcoming smiles.

Four night-stalkers tried relentlessly to raise me out of pots.

Two extremely pissed-off local pros went for a walk when, twenty minutes later, I was ahead $2,000.

One sphincter, mine, will never be the same.

Actually, it wasn't so bad. It's just poker. And those eight mirthless countenances were just folks. And my opinion of the experience might be other had I not beaten their socks off, but I did. And you can too but you do have to know what you're doing.

You may recall from Chapter 1 that I said an advantage of Las Vegas is that it's full of gamblers. Another advantage is that the casino rake—the percentage they take from each pot—is extremely reasonable, at least in the bigger games. In California you pay by the half hour for your seat, so as soon as you sit down you begin accumulating overhead. In Vegas, although the theoretical rake is as much as ten percent, which would be untenable, in practice the maximum rake is $2–$3. In a $20–$40 game where pots often reach many hundreds of dollars, a $2 or $3 rake is not a bad deal at all. And for a tight, conservative player, a small rake is a much better deal than seat rental. If you don't play a hand for an hour (which happens) in California, it's costing you the blinds plus the seat rental. If you don't play a hand for an hour in Las Vegas, it costs you only the blinds.

More about the rake. An exorbitant rake is a game-killer, no doubt about it. A *reasonable* rake is not. Poker authors, including the late, legendary John Scarne, have preached against the rake mercilessly. The argument goes like this: You sit down with nine other guys to play poker, each with twenty dollars on the table. Total money: $200. The house rakes $2 per hand. In 100 hands the house has all the money, and all ten of you go home broke.

This seems like a sound argument, but it isn't. Let us analyze:

1. At the stakes implied by the fact that the players sat down with $20, two dollars would be such an exorbitant rake that they would all get up again and leave.

2. Assuming that, for some reason, they kept playing, the game would be over in thirty to forty hands with six or seven of the players broke, and the winners sharing the $140 or $120 that the house hadn't yet grabbed.

3. Points 1 and 2 notwithstanding, the real reason the argument doesn't work is that, when you're playing in a casino you're not playing against nine guys with $20 each; you're playing against all the money in the world, $180 at a time. The argument that the house will have all the money in 100 hands assumes that there are only ten poker players and $200 in the universe. In fact, as one guy loses his $20, he may very well pull out another $20 and put it on the table. If he doesn't, if he gets up, then another player will sit down with another $20. As the second guy goes broke, if he gets up, yet another player will sit down with yet another $20. The casino can take its rake, and the winners can go on winning, forever.

I read somewhere, paraphrasing now, "It's hard to make money at poker when you have to pay to play." What a crock! How can you play poker without somebody's having paid something? Someone has to buy the cards. You've got gasoline or taxis or buses to get to the game and home again. Wherever the game is—say it's at your house—someone is paying the light and heating/air conditioning bill and providing food. I could go on and on about this whiny attitude, but you get the point. Rakes, seat rentals, food for the guys playing at your house, the light bill, the air conditioning bill, gasoline to and from the game—it's all just overhead, and you simply have to take it into consideration when planning or counting your poker profits. If you find, like in any other business, that the overheads are too high then you can either do something to cut them back, or change businesses.

So, what Las Vegas offers over California is lots of loose money and player-friendly rakes. What California offers over Las Vegas is a lot more action. Both California and Las Vegas also offer cheaters but not in numbers that you really have to be concerned about, especially if you pick your venue carefully. If you're playing in lower-stake games, it doesn't really matter where you go. If you're playing $10–$20, $20–$40 and up in Las Vegas, go to the Mirage. The Mirage management will cut off cheaters' heads and display them on pikes around the poker room. (Okay, they won't really, but what they *will* do is take their pictures, throw them out, and ban them from Mirage properties.) I have been told, although I do not know from first-hand experience, that some other places are less rigorous. In California, stick to the bigger, well advertised card casinos. If you go to Slick Willie's Bar & Card Club, you're on your own. (That was a completely made-up name. If there really is a Slick Willie's Bar & Card Club out there, it is pure coincidence and I'm sure it is a fine, upstanding place.)

If you do run into cheating, 99 percent of it will be player-player collusion, and this is pretty easy to spot. Whenever you're in a pot, if two or three particular guys at the table seem to be in against you more often than normal, they may be in collusion. If you're winning when this happens (colluders are often their own worst enemies) then don't worry about it. Also, don't leap to conclusions. If three or four experienced players have identified you as a fish, it may well be that they've all, independently, simply decided to put their hooks in the water at the same time.

Very, very rarely will you run into dealer-player collusion, as mentioned before. In fact, in limit games it is so rare that it's probably not even worth worrying about. In pot-limit and no limit, well, just keep it in mind. This is simple logic. In a limit game, except for the very, very big ones, the amount extractable from a victim is limited. The victim would have to be hit repeatedly to make it worthwhile, or, the same move would have to be tried against a lot of people. Either way, the chances are increased that someone will blow the whistle. In pot-limit or no limit, colluding dealer-players could conceivably set up just one hand, which would make enough money that they wouldn't have to do it again for some time.

In a recent book, such a hand is described in a pot-limit game. The author describes it as bad luck, a very bad beat. He doesn't mention the possibility of having been cheated, either because he really doesn't think he was, or, perhaps, because he didn't want to appear to be a sore loser, or for some other reason. In any case, when *I* read his description of that hand the very first thing that popped into my head was: you been had, bro. Not wanting to jump to conclusions, however, I whipped out the old computer.

You may recall that back on page 192 I recounted a hand in which I had been saved by an absolute miracle. So why couldn't a miracle have happened to the author's opponent? It certainly could. Then again, there are miracles and miracles. I have analyzed both hands, based on the cards alone and the order in which they came. You be the judge.[56]

	Me	A.H.'s Opponent	
Before the Flop	1.7-1 favorite	3.8-1 dog	
On the Flop	36-1 dog	499-1 dog	(four hundred and ninety-nine to one against his winning!)
On the Turn	3.4-1 dog	43-1 dog	
On the River	Win	Win	

[56.] Without giving details of the hand, suffice it to say that the author flopped top set, hit a full house on the turn and lost to four of a kind on the river. You'll trust me as to the details of what the actual cards were and how they fell; the author mentions a couple of names of people involved in the game and, well, you get the idea.

The "mere" fact that the author would win that hand, given the flop, a minimum of 499 out of 500 times is not in itself sufficient to prove chicanery. (Though it sure makes you stop and think.) These odds, however, combined with the fact that it was the biggest pot of the night, the second one in which the author had gone all in,[57] that the other player called a raise on very weak cards, the way the cards came on the board, and *the fact that although the author had had the absolute nuts with very little else showing on the board and* **three** *people had kept calling until he was all in then did* **not** *call the ultimate winner's side bet*[58]—well, all I can say is how it looks to me. Again, *the author* made not even a hint in his book that it was other than bad luck, and maybe it wasn't. Oh, wait. One other statistic I forgot to mention: In analyzing these hands I ran them through several million-hand simulations. *The author's* longest winning streak after the flop—straight wins without a loss—was 4,135 hands. His opponent did manage one streak of two hands in a row, so—hell!—we could have asked for a replay of the same pocket cards and flop cards and Mr. Lucky might have lost again! (Let's see . . . Where did I put the deed to that bridge?)

One other factor, although this one comes strictly from the rumor mill: the author was playing in one of the "side games"—that is, "real" money games—that go on during tournaments for players who have been busted out or are waiting for their particular tournament to begin. I have been told—warned, actually—by experienced acquaintances who claimed to know, that these games are far more susceptible to cheating than the "normal," everyday, card room games. Exactly why this would be so I don't know, except that perhaps big tournaments are at the confluence of many powerful dreams and desires. One casino-poker-playing friend of mine who, because I gave up being a true denizen some years ago, has accumulated perhaps a hundred times more field

---

[57.] Typically, this would mean he had been "set up" on the first all-in pot to make him feel secure and confident—and not suspect what was happening.

[58.] This, typically, is to show the "mark" that he was not alone in losing to this "lucky" player.

experience than I have, flat out told me: "Stay away from _____ at tournament time." I won't mention which place he indicated lest he was wrong and I would, thus, be doing an injustice by naming it. He is, however, as journalists like to say, a "reliable source", so, well, just watch your ass wherever you may be.

It's time for a word about tournaments themselves, which have become so popular in public poker. I have only ever played in one, smallish[59] Hold'em tournament, and I won it. I have always considered that (1) my having won it was a fluke, and (2) tournaments are an unprofitable way to spend my poker time. The main thing, as Anthony Holden found out—repeatedly—and related in his book *Big Deal*, is that you can play good, solid, creative, imaginative, winning poker for hours or even days— and then get busted out by one mistake or, worse, a fluke. You have nothing to show at all for your investment in time and money. Had you been playing in real games—in the milieu these are now called "ring" games to differentiate them from tournaments—and playing good, solid, creative, imaginative, winning poker for hours or days, you'd be showing a nice profit. It probably wouldn't be the pot of gold that lures so many to tournaments, but, especially in large tournaments with a couple hundred players involved, that pot of gold is just an illusion for most of us anyway. The fact that Mr. Holden based virtually his entire stab at professional pokerdom on tournaments raised within me a couple of questions that I took up with an *extremely* knowledgeable acquaintance who shall remain nameless. We'll call him Deep Poker. This guy knows everything. Following is that conversation:

> ***Me: You know, I've really wanted to ask you: Why did Anthony Eden base his whole stab at being a pro on tournaments?***
> *DP: Holden.*
>
> ***Me: What?***
> *DP: Tony Holden.*

[59.] about forty players/$500 buy-in

> *Me: Yeah, Holden. I know. For some reason whenever I say his name "Eden" pops out. I guess it's because he's a Brit and it kind of rhymes! Well, how come? Aren't tournaments a long shot?*
>
> *DP: Well, I don't like to play in tournaments, and that's one of the reasons. But Tony was trying to be a professional and tournaments are the name of the game now.*
>
> *Me: But why, if they're such long shots?*
>
> *DP: Look, there's a group of top pros who travel around and play in these things. They all have a piece of each other, and one of them usually wins.*
>
> *Me: If they all have a piece of each other, don't you think there could be some collusion going on?*
>
> *DP: Of course there is. (Long pause, thoughtful look becoming a wry smile). But they're the only tournaments in town.*

This may be a total figment of imagination, but Deep Poker is not prone to that sort of thing. So, for those of you who are considering playing in tournaments, well, I have done my duty to you by reporting this conversation. (Tony—sorry for the familiarity—you may not have had a chance.)

I have spent the last few pages first telling you that cheating in public poker is nothing to worry about, then telling you possible horror-story scenarios. Well, the possibility of being cheated is the eternal nightmare of all poker players, including yours truly. All I can tell you is that in twenty years of playing with strangers in casinos, the only time I can say for sure I was cheated was in the card-flasher story related on page 134. Well, let me qualify that. In the old days in Gardena, three types of cheating used to happen with some regularity:

1. Players would slip extra cards into play. I'd say about once or twice a week someone would be dealt a hand with two identical aces, say two A♥s, which would mean, of course, that in some earlier hand, some player had slipped in an extra ace. Once, I was dealt a hand with two 10♣s. Why someone would bother to slip in a 10♣ I don't know. This, of course, was the era

when players were dealing themselves. I haven't seen this since virtually all casinos and card clubs started employing house dealers, but others have reported it happening still.

2. Players would call or bet short, that is, would "splash" their bets in the pot having thrown in only, say, $15 instead of the requisite $20. This, too, has all but disappeared with the advent of house dealers. (It is now more likely to be found in home games, so keep an eye out.)

3. Players would bet or call, putting their money right in front of them and leave some excess chips just an inch or two behind the bet, then if they lost would withdraw the whole amount. Say someone had to call $20. He would put $40 in chips in his hand, place the $20 call in approximately the right place—right in front of him but maybe a little closer to his chips than normal—announce "call" and deposit the excess $20 on the table right behind the bet. If he lost the hand, he would then reach out, grab the entire $40 and put it back in his stack. If caught, he would then claim to have made a mistake thinking he was just reclaiming the "excess" chips. Again, the presence of house dealers generally precludes this sort of thing happening today.

I, however, was instrumental in getting a player thrown out of the Mirage, and banned, for making a similar type of move. It's the final round of betting in a $20–$40 Hold'em hand. The player to my right bets out. I take a few extra seconds to deliberate whether or not to call (this wasn't a delaying tactic, I really was deliberating), and the remaining player on my left says "call" and puts his money in. I say, "Wait a minute, I'm still thinking" and subsequently decide to fold. As I fold, the player to my right turns over his cards—and the player on my left takes his money out of the pot! Neither the dealer nor the other player seemed to notice. Two things: (1) I had played a lot with the guy on my right and liked him; (2) I had played a lot with the guy on my left and didn't like him. For one thing, he was always pulling stuff like this. In this case, he had called out of turn trying to put a move on me to get me to fold, although it hadn't influenced my decision, had then pulled his bet back when he saw he was beat and, I was positive, was going to allege that his out-of-turn bet wasn't binding *if anyone objected*.

Well, in Vegas an out-of-turn check, bet, fold, call, or raise *is* binding, even if you just *say* it and don't even put any money in, precisely to thwart moves like this. I said to Mike (on my right), "That guy just took forty bucks out of the pot. I'd complain if I were you." Sure enough, Shithead starting squawking and whining that it hadn't been binding since he had made a mistake. We ended up getting a floorwoman over to the table (the dealer, also a woman, was being especially timid for some reason). The floorwoman ruled in Mike's favor, Shithead refused to put the money back, and they threw him out and banned him. Hooray!

Anyway, as I said earlier, the card-flasher was the only real case of being flat-out cheated I can remember, at least since the coming of house dealers. There have been a handful of times when I've *suspected* but haven't been certain. Sure, I've lost some pretty unlikely hands, but I've won some pretty unlikely hands, too, hands that might have led my defeated opponents to wonder if *they* had been cheated.[60] Certainly, in public poker, I have been "ganged up on" many times as in the $50–$100 game mentioned above and related in more detail on page 242, but it's difficult to say when this is true collusion or just several people having the same idea at the same time. In any case, this stops when the gangers-up realize it isn't working on me.

I was cheated big-time once in a *private* game with *people I*

[60.] There is an even uglier side to this cheating thing: when people accuse you of cheating. Some years ago in the limit game there was, first, a very bad player who lost all the time. Then, he was joined in the game by another, even worse player— an out-of-control compulsive gambler who lost thousands. The two of them got to talking one day down at the local pub and decided they must be getting cheated. This might have been laughable except that they started telling all who would listen that the limit game was rigged. Ugly, very ugly, but there is really nothing you can do about it except to weather the storm, refute the slander—and have a few score people who knew the limit game players spontaneously and vociferously back us up. However, this is a (another?) dark side of being a good player: those players I told you about who won't recognize superior skill will sometimes come up with—and spout—other reasons why they're getting beat.

knew—but had been warned by others not to play with. I was just so interpersonally challenged at the time that I ignored their warnings: I *knew* these people and, more to the point, had too inflated an opinion of my own ability (which some say continues even to this day!). I was even cheated small-time once playing with two *friends* who said "we were just kidding you"—after I caught them at it.

How do you know if you're being cheated? That's a tough one. In a big pot-limit or no limit game, where everyone has mountains of money on the table, watch out if you're dealt a huge but beatable hand, such as four of a kind or a straight flush. Also watch out if, as we've discussed before, you've got the nuts for now but there are more cards to come. Don't jump to conclusions: just be careful. Hell, the other night in the limit game, Tim drew out on other players nine times in a row—a true phenomenon!—and five of those times were against me! (Result at the end of the night: Tim, about even; Dave, winning. Luck really won't do it for you in the end.) In a limit game, it doesn't really matter a whole lot if you're being cheated, which seems like a pretty strange thing to say, but it's true—as long as you are critically analyzing what's happening. Why? Because if you're being honestly outplayed or being cheated, you'll be losing hand after hand, in which case you should just get up and leave anyway. The management at places like the Mirage and the Bicycle will look out for you to the best of their ability, but they can't be looking in all places all the time. There's only one human being who can spend *all* of his or her time looking out for your ass and you know who that is: your ass's owner. No, I don't mean your spouse; I mean *you*. And to that end, following are a few helpful hints:

1. If you show up at the casino with, say, $1,000 to play, don't plunk it all down on the table at pot limit or no limit. Aside from my having advised against this as a bad *playing* move, if you're in the wrong sort of game and get sucked into a hand for all of it, you'll just have to go home. You won't have left yourself

the option of getting up and trying another game. This won't keep you from being cheated, of course, but it will keep you from being hurt too badly if you are cheated. If you want to put it all on the table in a limit game (some folks like to buy in for lots of chips since they think it increases their power presence at the table), there's no particular harm in it as long as you are sufficiently disciplined to get up and change games if you think you're being fleeced. As I've mentioned before, however, I think you're still better off putting just a part of it on the table and, if you want to make an impression, just make sure the other players see you have plenty more.

2. Don't show your hole cards to *anyone,* certainly not while you're still in a hand. The friendly guy next to you has introduced himself as Ron and has become quite chatty with you. When you're out of a hand, he starts showing you his hole cards as a friendly gesture—"Hey, look at this, think I'm gonna win?"—and, after a while, lets you know one way or the other that he'd like to see your hole cards when *he's* not in the pot. Problem is, of course, Ron's buddy Fred is in the game, and Ron is now signaling your hand to him, just as Fred has been signaling his neighbor's hole cards to Ron. Don't even show Ron your hole cards when you fold. Not only would this help him get a fix on how you play, but he may still signal Fred what you folded. This in turn may help Fred beat someone else, and why help cheaters?

3. When you first sit down, have a good look around at everyone. I mean look each player over from head to toe and in the eye and in the ear, and examine his navel, and count the hairs in his eyebrows, and really study each and every one of them—and make sure they see and feel you doing it. This is good practice anyway as it will (1) acquaint you with your adversaries and (2) make a good number of them nervous about you. If a couple of them are cheaters it may also make them decide you're not the one to pick on.

4. This is partly a "how to spot": If it's late at night, few tables are going and the dealers are circulating and coming back

fairly quickly, pay attention if one of your opponents always seems to win more than normal with a particular dealer. And partly a "how to remedy": Just say something like, "Oh no! Not you again! Whenever you show up seat six wins all the hands!" If you say it in the proper, friendly tone it will just sound like table chatter. If, on the other hand, there is something going on, it will likely stop. If seat six keeps winning more than his share of hands, time to get up.

5. If you spot someone pulling stuff like "Shithead" above, even if you're not involved in the pot, sing out. For one thing you'll be helping to clean up poker in general, and, for another, you'll put other possible cheaters on notice that you have your eyes open.

That's about all you can do: protect your money, protect your cards, and let the other players (and the dealers) know you're no patsy. If you're suspicious, it means one of two things: you're either losing to honest play and beginning to look for excuses, or you really may be getting cheated. Either way, it's time to go.

This whole subject of cheating and rigged tournaments leads me to interrupt Chapter 9 with the following essay.

An Essay

Whither Professional Poker?

A lot of people in the biz have high hopes for tournament poker. They want to see corporate sponsors, televised events, the works, just like golf and (in England, at least) snooker, which is the Brits' version of pool. Interestingly enough, if you can believe the literature, golf and pool are professional poker players' favorite nonpoker scams.

Scams?

There's the problem. People like . . . well, suffice it to say "very well-known professional poker players" will swear up and down that they've never cheated at poker, but they will then blithely recount how they've mercilessly swindled people at golf or pool or other betting activities. From *their* point of view, all they're telling you, really, is that they've outsmarted someone, and all they're doing at poker is outsmarting their adversaries in the same way.

That may be so, but to most people the impression is that if the pros are "outsmarting" you at poker the same way they describe having "outsmarted" someone in another gamble, then you don't want any part of it. And this is the principle reason that Western society and professional poker are going to have to change an awful lot before poker tournaments are sharing time on ABC with golf: the amateur, poker-playing public equates "professional poker player" with "scammer"—if not outright cheater—and it's the pros' own damn fault. It seems most of them—not all, mind you—are just too damn ignorant of how other people think and behave to realize that, when they tell a story about taking someone to the cleaners in a betting scam, the public might think this is mildly romantic but will not, ultimately, admire the scammer; they will despise him.

Let's stop pussyfooting: Is there collusion in tournaments? Jeez! There is *documented* collusion in tournaments! That at least the final two, or three, or four, or however many, players in a tournament are simply *expected* to start making deals is shown by the published fact that the modern "gurus" of poker have written articles *presenting the proper calculations for making such deals*. Need more proof? Here's an excerpt of an interview from *Card Player* magazine.[61] Dana Smith (DS) is interviewing Matthias Rohnacher (MR) who has had some good finishes in some World Series of Poker and other tournament events:

> MR: . . . *I was happy about my [second place] finish two years ago, and I am happy about it this year. I never made a deal, although other players almost always try to make them* . . .
>
> DS: *So, you don't like to make deals on the end?*
>
> MR: *No, because it takes a lot of the challenge out of a tournament. If I win a first-place title, I want to really win it and not be involved in a deal.*

Firstly, let me say: Hooray for Mr. Rohnacher! Secondly, let me say: Great Mother of God! And you want this shit on Sunday-afternoon TV? Would I find an interview in *Sports Illustrated* in which Greg Norman is saying, "Well, Faldo wanted to make a deal to end it before the final nine holes, but I decided to play this one out." How about Steffi Graf at Wimbledon: "I know I was the favorite going in, but Martina really wanted to win one more, so our managers got together before the match and made a deal so she could win." How about the Super Bowl? It's the opening of the Super Bowl and John Madden is announcing to the world:

The two head coaches are now meeting in mid-field to discuss who is going to win and who is going to lose. The 49ers are the favorites by fourteen points, so they'll be going for a larger

---

[61.] July 26, 1996; p. 43.

chunk of the purse. Uh-oh, there seems to be a disagreement. Jimmy Johnson is getting out his calculator and appears to be upset. He's gesticulating wildly and pointing at the numbers. George Siefert has pulled out his laptop and is sticking the screen right in Jimmy's face . . . Jimmy seems subdued. He seems to be nodding. Yes! They've reached agreement and have called in their quarterbacks for a briefing. Of course, we won't know what the deal was or who is going to win until it's all over, but we'll try to get the inside information and pass it on to you on the post-game show . . .

Well now that the Dolphins have pulled off a stunning upset, we have word from reliable sources in the Dolphins organization that the sticking point in the negotiations was that the Dolphins had had to promise one-sixth of their Super Bowl take to the Broncos so the Broncos would throw the playoff game and let the Dolphins go to the championship. Jimmy Johnson felt that George Siefert wasn't taking this into consideration at first but finally arrived at an agreement that would let the Dolphins win since they had not won a Super Bowl in a quarter century. Johnson felt that a Super Bowl ring would mean enough to his players' future careers that he was willing to cut his Broncos allowance down to one-twelfth. Siefert agreed to this, and the Dolphins players subsequently agreed to hand over two-thirds of their prize money to the 49er players, with a further one-twelfth going each to Siefert and Johnson. They further agreed to pay over one-sixteenth of their future incomes to the 49er players for the next three years and one-sixteenth each to the two coaches with an advance cash payment going to the Broncos players. It was a tough, complex negotiation, but that's the Super Bowl!"

Furthermore, take Anthony Holden's description of Johnny Chan, two-time "world champion"—this in quotation marks because even 200+ people do not represent the world's poker players[62]—in *Big Deal*:

[62] It is written that many of the entrants in the "World Series of Poker," the so-called "World Championship," are just amateurs with $10,000 to burn who want

"Chan seems to be in a mean mood. Immediately he is irritated at walking straight into the big blind . . . After a bad beat Chan gets even meaner . . .Then Chan is rude to the dealer . . . As his stack grows ever smaller, so Chan's mood grows fouler; he is hideous to another dealer . . . As the dealer leaves in tears, we calm down and resume play.

Now, tell me, is this the sort of person you want your child to emulate? Can you see Coca Cola giving this guy a contract? Can you see Mom and Pop and the family sitting down on a Sunday afternoon to watch this guy drive a dealer to tears? Can you see the United States Playing Card Company (Bee and Bicycle brands) putting his picture on boxes of cards? Wheaties?— forget it.

Okay, okay, other professions have their bad boys and girls too. There was McEnroe and there was Connors; there is Rodman. There was once an entire team of "bad boys" in the NFL: the Raiders. Pepsi made a *huge* mistake with Michael Jackson. Coke got it right with Ray Charles.

Anyway, this doesn't excuse professional poker because most of the other spectacle industries (with the exception of rock music) at least *try* to project a modicum of respectability. Professional poker doesn't even know what "respectability" is. Take the ironic examples cited above. Surely no one on the planet would even *think* that Greg Norman made some kind of deal with Nick Faldo to throw the Masters Tournament in 1996. Right?

Wrong.

Las Vegas is *full* of people who would believe that *because that's exactly what they would do.* And they wouldn't think twice about it. They would publish articles about how to calculate the payoff properly given the total size of the first and second place prizes, Norman's lead and the odds against Faldo's winning. Are

---

to rub shoulders with the greats and don't have a hope in hell of winning. It's a bit like taking ten teams from the NBA, fifty or so CBA (basketball's minor league) teams and 150 high school teams and calling one of the NBA teams "World Champions" when they win the tournament.

the PGA, NFL, MLB, NBA rife with deal making? Well, I suppose it's possible, but I sincerely doubt it. The "Black Sox" threw the World Series in 1919, and, nearly eighty years later, it is still a smudge on professional baseball. To the poker players and article writers of Las Vegas the Sox "wouldn't be maximizing the full value of their position" if they *hadn't* sat down with someone to discuss a deal. There would then be follow-up articles discussing whether or not they had made a *good* deal. The problem with professional poker players is that: they think this sort of thing is normal and they want it on TV with golf, and they want the "World Champ" to receive a check from Mutual of Omaha (which, come to think of it, being an insurance company, is pretty much in their league).

Come on, all you folks out there in professional pokerdom. Get out of your casinos, take a deep breath of nonhyperoxygenated air, and have a look around at the real world. Poker is even worse than chess as a spectator sport because the audience can't see the hands and, therefore, can't get involved in the play.[63] If, to add to that handicap, you're going to keep carving up tournament purses to suit yourselves and then give proud interviews about how you "made it" in life through a series of scams, cons, and rigged bets that allowed you to fleece the suckers, you're not going to make it on ESPN. Everyone loves reading Damon Runyon, but no one in middle-America (which is where the money is) is going to let Sky Masterson marry his daughter.

Remember, these opinions have been expressed by a lover of poker—a lover of poker who wishes that right now he were at a table at the Bike or the Mirage playing instead of sitting here at the computer writing about it. If things look this bad to me,

---

[63.] If the networks could come up with a way to show the "audience at home" what the hands were without showing the players—sort of like some quiz shows do in showing the answers—it would take only until the next issue of *Card Player* magazine for someone to start running ads for special receiver head phones that "transmit this vital information to the players which will allow you to maximize the value of your position." The various gurus would then write serious-sounding mathematical articles about the proper way to apply the information gleaned through the headphones.

what is the Christian Coalition going to think? You have a long way to go, poker brethren.

End of Diatribe

Back to the matter at hand.

One of the problems facing the occasional poker visitor in casinos is that, not being a denizen of those places playing against other denizens, you don't have the opportunity to make the personal behavioral evaluations that you have in a regular private game. That's okay. Don't panic.

Human behavior is remarkably standardized and, through pervasive mass media, is becoming more and more so. This trend is insidious and, perhaps, eventually dangerous to our individual freedoms, but it is also very convenient. Any marketing person or political pollster knows this. I'm sure you have noticed that modern political polls can predict very accurately what a nation of 250,000,000 will do by polling 2,364 people. They can tell you how millions of African Americans will vote by polling a thousand or so. They can tell you how white, blue-collar Southerners will vote the same way. And, by golly, they do, every time. If a market survey of 1,500 people between the ages of eighteen and twenty-five shows that 41 percent of them are wearing Superpuffer tennis shoes, you can take it to the bank that the percentage figure in that age group for the nation as a whole will be essentially the same. There is usually a disclaimer in polls and market surveys that the margin of error is plus or minus 3 percent or so. If you stop to think that they are extrapolating sample statistics by factors of tens of thousands, that is pretty damn close.

So, yes, that's right: me, you, all God's chillun, can be labeled, categorized, predicted, filed away, folded, bent, spindled, stapled, and mutilated. If you know your demographics, you can't miss. Watch sports on TV. As a rule, if you're watching football (except for the Super Bowl) you'll see commercials for beer and pick-up trucks. If you're watching tennis, you'll see commercials for BMWs and mutual funds. You, sitting in your living room watching sports, are being labeled, categorized, and having your habits, behavior and probable future predicted all the time—with astounding accuracy. (If you watch football *and* tennis, there's a category for you, too, though the demographers know it's a small one. Furthermore, there are exceptions in sports like football, depending on which team is playing. Some teams tend to have a proportionally higher or lower socio-economic class following than others.)

This is why, nasty fellow that I am, whenever someone calls up or appears with some market, political, or social survey, I lie and give false information. I don't like them doing what they're doing. But, you know what? There's a category for people who will do *that*, too, (the interpersonally-challenged file), and it's all calculated into the results. So in the end, my sabotage does no good, except that it makes me feel a little better. At least I can try to be part of the 3 percent margin of error instead of one of the lemmings.

And therein lie the points hereto: 97 percent of players who show up occasionally in casinos are not experienced enough to vary their play, vary their image, or vary their moves. They are predictable, and that's what the pros count on. The well-read pros are armed with all manner of treatises on how to prey on the unsuspecting. But I said "points"—plural—and that's the other side of the coin. As I said back in Chapter 6, since the pros are all reading the same books and taking lessons from each other, 97 percent of *them* tend to play alike as well.

Now, the 3% "margin of error" among the pros are truly, truly folks you don't want to mess with. They have gone well beyond the poker treatises and manuals. They will look right into your brain, predict your every move and intention, and bush-whack and hog-tie you before you've even realized you're lying on the ground. (Has this ever happened to me? Is the pope Catholic? What did I do about it? Got up, brushed myself off and changed tables.) If, however, you can be among the 3 percent "margin of error" among the *visitors,* you can take 97 percent of the pros to the cleaners. And that's a fact.

First, how do you spot the three-percenters (we'll call them "stars")? Fortunately, there aren't that many of them around, and, mostly, you won't find them messing around in the games you're likely to be playing in. In stakes like $3–$6, $4–$8, $1–$4–$4–$8, $2–$10, $5–$10, and $6–$12, you'll virtually never find one. *All* the pros in those games will be 97 percenters (we'll call them "regulars") except for the very occasional fluke appearance—maybe he's just waiting for a "real" game to start— of one of the stars. Even then, you don't have to worry much: typically, he may be so bored with the stakes—and antsy for his real game to start—that he won't be paying attention and may even lose a hand or two! I've seen this happen on a number of occasions.

The games that represent the fulcrum of public poker—low stakes teetering on one side and high stakes tottering on the other—are the $10–$20 limit games. At this level, you will start playing with the upper echelons of the regulars—they're definitely still "regulars", however—and there may occasionally be a smattering of stars but, still, not usually.

It's in the $20–$40 games where you run into the best regulars, and the stars begin to appear in the firmament. We'll get back to this, but the odd thing here is that the quality of play seems to deteriorate from there (!) through $30–$60, $40–$80 and even $50–$100. After that it picks up again through the higher limits, through pot-limit and, finally, to the biggest no limit games, in which the number and concentration of stars is like a moonless desert night. Unless you have a *lot* of money to burn and are willing to pay dearly for the thrill of being bushwhacked and hog-tied by the big boys—okay—or think you are perhaps a potential star yourself[64]—stay away from those games.

Aside from just playing the odds, about 32 to 1, and hoping you won't run into one of the stars, there is another way to spot them: ask. If my true aim for the day, or evening, is $20–$40 Hold'em, I'll usually start off in $10–$20. One reason for this is

[64] If you're kidding yourself, you'll find out real quick.

that I can (usually) count on making some money there and then moving to the bigger games with other people's money. Another reason is that I can get information about the bigger games. I play enough in casinos to recognize some faces and know some players, but I no longer play often enough really to know, and be able to spot, all the "dangerous" ones. So, getting friendly and chatty with the $10–$20 regular (both regular and "regular") players often saves me from making a big mistake. After a while, I ask my new "friends" what they think about the players at the neighboring $20–$40 games. I've never had occasion to be rebuffed. If they can, they'll be informative. "Well, lessee . . . table 19 is mostly tourists except for Patrick and Martin and they're not so tough; looks like a pretty good game. Hmm . . . That guy in seat 3 at table 20, that's Michael; wouldn't wanna play with *him* in the game. See those two women at table 13? That's Monica and Nicole; they're real tough cookies. If I were thinking of moving it'd be to table 19." In and out of poker I've always found: if you want to know something, ask. Try it; it works.

Now that you know how to avoid the stars, we'll have a look at beating the regulars, both the regular pros and the regular visitors. The first thing you have to know is how they play and, as I've said before, that means you'll have to do some supplementary reading. If you're going to be playing low limits, there's a book called, straight-forwardly enough, *Winning Low Limit Hold'em*, by Lee Jones (ConJelCo; 1994), which is reputed (and endorsed by some big names) to be full of good advice. I have read it a couple times, and it *seems* to me, too, that it contains good advice, but I am not a good judge. It's been a number of years since I played low limit Hold'em much. Now, I am bored to absolute verge of insanity by any public games under $10–$20, so I have not had the opportunity to apply Mr. Jones's advice in the $3–$6 games to which he principally addresses himself. Generally speaking, he reinforces the following several points that I have made previously in this book (which, of course, makes me feel good).

1.   In low limit games, you're not going to raise anyone out.
Mr. Jones (and Pokerdom in general) refers to these games as
"No fold'em Hold'em" and that's pretty accurate. If you're going
to start raising in the early rounds, all you're going to accomplish in a $3–$6 game is to turn it into a $6–$6 game.

2.   Medium pairs—anything below a pair of kings, really—
and high-card hands like Big Slick have significantly less potential. Drawing hands like J-10 suited or even 7-6 suited are often
a better prospect. Ace-rag suited also becomes a good drawing
hand as long as you remember that you're after the flush and not
the aces, which, if an ace flops, can be easy to forget. There are
two reasons for this: First, as I outlined back on page 204, if you
have a tableful of people calling with rags before the flop, *collectively* they're going to hit their rags quite often. If you've hung
in there with a pretty big pair or Big Slick, you may be tempted
to keep calling when someone's 9-4 off-suit has already hit two
pair. You'll be in danger of losing more money because you're
sucked in. Second, if you hang in there before the flop with, say,
9-8 suited, you'll either have proper pot-odds to keep drawing if
the flop gives you something to draw to, or you'll be able to
dump it with no qualms if the flop misses you completely.

3.   You're going to have to pretend you're a casino or an
insurance company and just play the numbers, the "percentages,"
which means that if you're careful and pay attention and know
your odds you'll win in the "long run"—but you may go through
some pretty big swings in your financial fortunes before you get
there. Take pocket rockets—please. On page 204 I outlined the
dangers of aces in a no fold'em game, and back on page 83 I
said that in a million-hand run against nine random hands
pocket rockets had had one losing streak of thirty-four hands.
Mr. Jones concurs that your aces might get outdrawn in no fold'em
sometimes (actually, they'll get outdrawn about 70 percent of
the time), but he says that you shouldn't worry about it because
if you only got aces all the time, you'd make a "ton of money."
Well, I just ran aces on the computer *again* against nine random
hands, and *again* (!) they had one losing streak of thirty-four

hands. (Hmm . . . Must be something statistical about that. I'll have to check it out.) So yes: if you have the patience *and the bankroll* to sit through getting your pocket rockets cracked as often as thirty-four times in a row, you'll win "a ton of money"—eventually.

4. Bluffing—forget it. You'll simply have to have the best hand to win.

5. Position is of little importance in these games, certainly in the first round before the flop. (Mr. Jones would take exception to this.) Whereas in bigger games late position lets you know what other players have done first, and, thus, lets you decide what you can/should do, in these games you are pretty safe to assume that essentially the whole table will be in and that there may be a couple of raises. Knowing that, it doesn't really matter if you're first or last when deciding which hands to play. The exception to this would be if there is a whole flock of pros in the game (say, more than three) who are more circumspect about calling before the flop.

Our lessons here are:

1. Only the very regular regulars will be in these games.

2. They will be playing mostly with big pairs and suited connectors (connectors being two cards to a straight).

3. They may or may not raise before the flop with big pairs.

4. If they do raise before the flop they will probably have pocket big putzes (remember?) or rockets, or more likely, big suited connectors, 10-9 and up.

5. If they are in late position and call a bunch of raises but don't reraise, they probably have either small suited connectors or big unsuited connectors.

6. The "tourists" will have a hodgepodge of everything, so play like the pros to win on the "percentages."

7. If the flop brings you four to a flush or four to the NUT straight and there are more than two people in the pot against you (which will be just about all the time in these games), raise

and reraise like crazy; the pot odds are in your favor. If you miss your hand, however, don't try bluffing it; you'll just be costing yourself another bet.

8.   The *one* exception to not bothering to bluff is if, first, you have spotted the pros in the game, second, are in on the last round with one or two of them—no more than that and no tourists at all, third, are pretty sure they have both missed, fourth, have been playing with them long enough to have shown them that you are "playing like they do," and, fifth, have seen them fold to last-round bets before. In other words, this *one* exception will practically never occur—maybe once a day at the most.

9.   If the flop brings you a complete hand from NUT straight up, bet, raise and reraise like crazy. Slow playing a really big hand on the flop is just going to cost you money in these games. If the opposition has anything at all to draw to—even though *you* know they're drawing dead—they'll hang in there. The reason I have emphasized the nut straight twice is that in a game like this, if you have the low end (to give you an idea of how bad this is, it's known as the *suck* end) of the possible straight on the board, or even the middle of it, you're probably beat if any other players are showing any enthusiasm.

10.   Until you get information to the contrary, against fellow "tourists" call end bets if you have even as far down as fourth or fifth best (category of) hand if the pot-to-call ratio is big; against the pros, call end bets only if you have second, or sometimes third, best category of hand. Let's say the board is 10♣10♦6♠8♥4♣. The potential hands here are: one set of four tens, six full houses, one straight to the 10, one straight to the 8, then an assortment of trips, two pair and one pair hands. Notice no flushes made it. In this case I would almost certainly call a "tourist" if I had the low straight or trips if the pot were big enough. I would probably only call the pros with one of the full houses, maybe sometimes with the high straight. Many people don't grasp this concept. They want to know why the pros are likely to hold better cards than the tourists if it's all random. They're *not* likely to. But a "tourist" is more likely to *bet* with a weaker hand,

whereas a pro would probably just check or wouldn't even be in the pot. That's the difference.

11. To find out who are the pros and who are the tourists, start gabbing with the players. The ones who (in the case of Las Vegas) say they live there are probably either pros or semipros. If you're in a "normal" town like L.A. (L.A. normal?) the ones who say they come and play "a lot" or "all the time" are probably retirees or other frequent-playing amateurs who are trying to impress you. The ones who say "off and on"—and are generally kind of grumpy about conversing with you—are probably the pros or semi-pros. If you're not sure, keep chatting. You'll find out.

12. It won't help you so much in these games, but you still have to size up your opponents. Generally, the range of skill among the "tourists" will be from average to none. Among the pros the skill level will tend to range from low to pretty good—in the terms of these games. (Remember: *never risk underestimating your opponent out of hand*—these are just general guidelines.) This will help you, mostly, on the end when you think maybe someone is being silly enough to try a bluff.

Now you may have an inkling as to why I'm bored silly with low stake games like this. The first consideration, of course, is that if I've shown up to play, I've often got at least an airline ticket and hotels as immediate overhead, and a $3–$6 game isn't going to cover it, much less show a profit for the trip. But that's not why I'm bored. I'm bored in low limit casino poker because—ready for this?—it's a *card* game! Sure, you have to play better than your opponents, outsmart them in terms of playing better cards than they do, read them properly when you think your cards are beat, but it doesn't have the people-manipulation factor, which is what makes poker really interesting. It's mechanical. You just have to sit there and wait to get cards. The "tourists" think they're playing poker. The pros know they're just playing the odds, the numbers. So, on to more interesting stuff.

If you're going to be playing higher stakes, from $10–$20 and up into the stratosphere, you'll need to read a whole boatload of books.[65] Rather than detail them here, I've put a selection in the bibliography with remarks about, in my opinion, their strengths and weaknesses.

By making three big mistakes, the pros create their own Achilles' heel. The second biggest mistake made by the pros in casinos is to assume that higher-stakes limit poker is just as mechanical as low stakes poker is. The third biggest mistake they make is to assume that visitors don't know the mechanics of the game. Now, neither of these is actually a mistake 97 percent of the time because 97 percent of the visitors *don't* know what they're doing and, against them, playing mechanically will work. The pros' *biggest* mistake, as I've mentioned over and over in this book about players in general, is to assume that this applies to 100 percent of the visitors. If there's a book out there, of those written by and for pros, that says "Watch out: a small percentage of those tourists can play rings around you," I have yet to see it. And the reason I have yet to see it is that the pros refuse to believe it. Although the pros' books are constantly advising how to play against "strong" and "weak" players, the overall assumption is that all the "strong" players come only from within their own ranks. Underestimating your adversary is the biggest mistake anyone can ever make in *any* of life's encounters.

So, if you're part of the 3 percent "margin of error" among the visitors, that's where you can bushwhack the pros. They may, after a while, recognize that "for some reason"—probably a lucky streak—you're winning, even to the point of asking for changes from your table. But only the best of the regulars will

---

[65.] Don't be disappointed or surprised that I'm not telling you that this, my book, is sufficient for you to read and then go out and win, win, win. It would be very irresponsible of me—or any other author—to attempt to give that impression. There is a plethora of books out there and, although I feel mine covers areas and explains some things better or in a more enlightened way than others (which is why I wrote it in the first place), there are many other authors with many other points of view that a complete poker player should know and study. In fact, part of my "advice to you" in this book in terms of "learn how to play winning poker" is: *read as many poker books as you can get your hands on.* Furthermore, and more to the point here, you (we) need to read these books to know what the opposition is reading and, thus, may be thinking!

actually stop and consider that they've come up against a worthy opponent among the "visitors." You know that has happened when they start asking you about your poker history—You play a lot? Where do you play? What do you do?[66]—and it won't happen until you've beat them out of quite a few hands, beyond the point of being written off as lucky flukes.

Before we go any further, a word of warning which should be obvious: Don't *you* go underestimating the pros. If you are, say, completely ignorant about coins and show up at the National Numismatists' Convention to sell the 1882 silver dollar that used to belong to your great-great grandmother, you're probably not going to make a very good deal. If you study the subject a little bit before hand, you might make a little better deal. If you study some more you might make an even better deal. The more you study and prepare yourself . . . Well, you get the idea. Still, because you don't have the same level of experience, you will probably not make as good a deal as a "pro" would; you'll find that you got your best price and the "pro" you sold it to will still go and make a profit on it. This means, of course, that you didn't get the maximum possible out of your coin.

But that's probably okay. I have no idea what an 1882 silver dollar is worth, but let's say you get $100 for it, and the "pro" turns around and sells it for $130. How much more time would you have had to spend studying and acquiring experience in his milieu in order to extract that extra $30? Probably too much to be worth it. You have other things to do; he doesn't. He's making dozens of deals a day, every day, and those $30 each time add up. If, on the other hand, the "pro" turns around and sells it for $10,000, or even $500, you were woefully unprepared and got fleeced.

Now, suppose your people skills are turned on and tuned in; this will help you make up the difference in knowledge and experience. You'll be able to look the "pro" in the eye and make

---

[66.] The first thing they're likely to think is that you're a visiting pro whom they haven't seen before!

a judgment, *feel* perhaps, that "this guy is offering me as much as he thinks he can and still be a reasonable deal for him," *or,* "I'm not sure what this coin is worth, but I can tell for sure this guy thinks he's about to pull a big one on me."

One of the reasons I have hammered away at the people aspects of poker throughout this book is that human nature is the great common denominator in all human activities, specific skills, knowledge, or experience notwithstanding. Showing up at the casino to play poker is just one example. Those big, bad poker players out there are just folks with the same range of talents and foibles common to us all. The advantage they have over the occasional player is that they play all the time and have acquired a lot of experience and, among the better ones, knowledge.[67] You would have to play (and study) as much as they do—which is basically all the time—to be on an equal, let's call it "technical," footing with them. Furthermore, they have the experience of that particular *kind* of poker—casino poker with its fast and furious pace and decisions that have to be made in nanoseconds—which most visitors don't have. Do not ever underestimate these advantages of theirs. They're very big ones. But now the fun part: most of the pros are real easy to sneak up on and bushwhack.

As a group, professional poker players tend to have some basic character flaws and occupational hazards that make them vulnerable. One of the biggest character flaws we have already seen: because they tend to be arrogant about what they do and how they do it, they tend to underestimate opponents, especially "visiting" opponents. Of the occupational hazards that hurt them and make them vulnerable, by far the biggest is: *they* have

---

[67.] Actually they have one other advantage: the fear caused by the mystique of the "professional poker player," which I have done my best to demystify—demystiquefy?—in this chapter and throughout the book. They're just folks, readers; really, they are just folks. A lot of them are so insecure, and so needful of projecting self-assurance and success, that they decorate themselves with lots of jewelry and assorted finery. They think this impresses and intimidates. Don't let it bother you. You could wear lots of expensive junk too if you were equally insecure—and if you really wanted to be so crass.

to win; that's how they live. If you show up in Vegas and have allocated, say, $1,000 to play poker and you lose it—so what? You'll go back to whatever it is that you do and start saving up for your next poker adventure. If a pro loses his bankroll, he's out of business and, even if his bankroll is substantial, whenever he loses a bit of it he starts to fear for the rest of it. Every little bit he loses puts him closer to having to start borrowing, hustling, or scamming his way to a new stake, because, unlike you, many of them don't really know how to do anything else.

Now, some will say that this "life or death" view of the game is an advantage; that the "tourists," flippant about their money and willing to gamble, are the pros' biggest asset. And of course they're right most of the time. But if you, the visitor, can be both comfortable—not "flippant" but "comfortable"—about your money and wily about your play, you'll have an almost insuperable psychological advantage over the pros.

Now to some specifics. We'll talk a bit about play of the cards first, just to sort of get it out of the way. (For in depth discussions on how the pros play their cards you'll have to read the books indicated in the bibliography.) The pros are very much into "knowing" what cards should be played from what position.[68] *Position* means where you are in a given hand relative to the first and last players to act. Its influence on your decisions varies depending on which betting round is taking place.

Before the Flop

Most pros will base their initial judgments on the relative strength or weakness of an opponent's play by the cards he calls and bets with before the flop. If you're first or near the first— "early" position—you're told to play cards that are likely to stand up with little help from the board. This means big pairs, from QQ up, and big-card hands like Big Slick. Minimum, you

---

[68.] By the way, if you haven't noticed by now, in terms of casino poker games this chapter is virtually completely dedicated to Hold'em. Altough some would take exception, my opinion is that Hold'em is really the only game in public poker worth playing.

should have an ace with a big kicker, preferably suited. If you have hands like this in early position and bet out, it's supposed to mean two things: one, no one behind you is likely to have a better hand with which to raise you, and, two, since the rest of the table will assume you have a big hand, more players will tend to fold, thus leaving you with fewer opponents and a better chance of your big cards standing up. (Get a pencil and make a mental note that this latter attribute of betting big cards early implies an assumption of behavior with a cause/effect relationship to others' behavior.)

If you're about in the middle between the first and last players to act—"middle" position—you are told you can lower your standards somewhat in deciding what cards to play. If there has been action ahead of you, you can "gauge" the strength of that action and decide to play or not. If the players ahead of you have folded, you know they are already *hors de combat,* and you have fewer players behind you to worry about. Here, depending on what has happened ahead of you, you are told you can lower your standards of playable cards to pairs of 10s, sometime 9s, can allow yourself somewhat weaker (down to Js) and unsuited kickers to your aces, and can occasionally start limping in with drawing hands like J-10 suited or, if you're feeling especially bold and daring, maybe even something like 10-9 suited.

In the "late" positions, with the advantage ever increasing in proportion to your proximity to last place, i.e. the dealer or "button," you can really go to town. Depending on what has happened ahead of you in terms of players in, players out, raises and calls, you can lower your card standards to such hands as—gasp!—J-10 unsuited, 7-6 suited, any pair, maybe, occasionally, just to show how risqué you are, you might play hands like 5-4 suited. You might even be able to play one- or two-card gapped connectors like J-9 or J-8 suited.

In any position the "unplayable" hands are unsuited non-connectors like K-7, 10-5, 8-2 and the like. Three-card gapped connectors, those with the bottom and top cards of their implied straights like J-7 or 9-5, are generally considered equally unplayable, although some "authorities" allow them in late position if suited. Of course, as everyone knows, the worst starting hand in Hold'em is said to be 7-2 off suit,[69] the two lowest cards you can put together that can not make a straight. Ace-rag has a special place in poker lore, but generally, the dictum is to dump it if it's not suited and to play it in late-middle through late positions if it is suited and you can limp in with it cheaply in a pot with many callers.

On and After the Flop

Here, the variables are too numerous to summarize without risking oversimplifying. You'll just have to hit the other, specialized books. Suffice it to say, however, that just as in every other form of poker, at this point you either have a hand or you have a draw, or both. You can gauge the absolute value of your hand using your overall poker experience. You can gauge the relative value of your hand based on an analysis of your opponents. A weakish hand might be a winner against a weak player; you may need the nuts to beat a strong player. If you have a draw, you should know what your outs and odds are because the pros know these well and, again, will be passing judgment on your play based on what kinds of draws you try to make. Appendix 1 has a summary of various draw odds.

Now, armed with the above and, of course, having read all the recommended books, you are ready to sneak up on the pros. There are two ways to do this: (1) Start out playing like they do, then switch gears on them and begin using "amateur" tactics; (2) Start out playing like an "amateur" then switch gears and begin using "pro" tactics. Either way will befuddle your opponents, but I usually find the first strategy to be the most effective.

Extract your pencil from wherever you had inserted it to make your mental notes and look back to the second paragraph

---

[69.] Actually, this depends. Heads up against random hands, 7-2 off suit is about 7 percent better than 3-2 off suit. Against nine random hands, however, which would represent a full table, 3-2 off suit is indeed better than 7-2 by about 17 percent.

under "Before the Flop." That tells most of the story: If you play like the pros play and they "see" this, your actions will generate a certain set of predictable reactions on their part. When you first sit down to a game, the pros will start testing you. For example, if you've recently sat down, are in early position and open with a bet, you will almost always be raised. Somebody back there wants to know: what does this guy play with in early position and how does he respond to a raise? If you fold, call or raise him back, he'll have the latter part of his question answered. If the hand is seen through to a showdown, he'll have the former. Those first hands can tell the pros at the table "all they need to know" about you. So just make sure that what they know is whatever you want them to know.

This is why I say sneak-up option 1 is usually best. If the first few hands you're involved in are "by the book" and the pros see that, by and by you can start getting away with weird moves that they wouldn't let you get away with if they thought you were just a wild and sloppy player. Moves like

1.   Raising on rags in early position. I love this one. Because you've raised, a large portion of the opposition will fold. Those who stay will have big ol' pairs and high cards. If your rags come on the flop, the other players haven't hit and they won't think you've hit either. They'll call your bets forever. If big cards hit, you can still keep betting because, remember, your raise before the flop has made them think that's what you've got. Since, however, these are the players who called your raise they've probably got some pretty impressive cards themselves. If your first bet gets called, you're probably going to have to check and fold on the turn.

2.   Raising on small connectors like 5-4 in early position. This is great too. The flop comes A-2-3 and, again, they'll call you till doomsday—especially the ones with aces—not believing you have that little stuff.

3.   Calling either a bet or a raise with rags in middle or late position. The principle is always the same: have cards that your

opponents won't expect you to have. Say you're in middle position, have 9-4 off suit, there has been an early bet and raise before you and you call. The flop comes 9-7-2 off suit. Your two pro opponents *will not have any of that junk,* and they won't think you do either. If one of them bets he may have an overpair in the pocket, but it's much more likely that he has something like A-K—and thinks this is good! When you raise, as you certainly should, he'll either figure you for an overpair in the pocket, trips, or a counter bluff. If you're careful on two fronts this sort of move will make you a lot of money. First, you must read your opponent correctly in deciding that he hasn't got an overpair; second, if an ace, king or queen hits on the turn or the river, you're probably beat. A jack would be a toss up.

So, sneak-up option 1 allows you to lull the pros into a false sense of knowing how you play and then slamming them with outrageous moves. The best *theoretical* proof that this stuff works comes from one of the pros' favorite books by one of their favorite authors. Therein, the author says categorically that if the flop comes, say, Q-J-J you may well be facing a full house, but if the flop is 8-3-3, you don't have to worry about a full house *because nobody will be playing an 8 and a 3.*[70] Well, folks, guess what: I hope they've ALL read that and believe it because *I'm* the one who will be sitting there with the 8-3. And when it hits, they'll all call my raises and bets right down to the end of time—or at least to the end of bankrolls. The best *practical* proof for me that this works is that I attack through the Ardennes all the time, and I regularly leave with what used to be other people's money. (I'm now on a three-trip winning streak for Las

---

[70.] Lest some readers miss the significance of this: Before World War II, *all* the French war experts and theorists declared—and wrote—that a German attack would *never* come through the Ardennes forests. Needless to say, perhaps (but here it is anyway), the Germans spent a lot of time reading what those French experts had to say—and then attacked through the Ardennes. Before D-Day and Operation Overlord, the German war experts and theorists declared that an Allied invasion would *never* start in Normandy. Ike read those opinions and, needless to say . . .

Vegas, and it's been years since the last time I left L.A. in deficit. That includes air fares and other expenses and I come from a *long* way away.) Don't take my word for it, though. Try it yourself. If it doesn't work, you've misread your opponents and will have to go back to the drawing board.

That reminds me: I've made some pretty categorical statements here myself about what people will have and what they won't have in given situations. Don't make the same mistake the pros make by categorizing people out of hand. Use generalities as a rule of thumb but always size up the individual, um, individually.

Furthermore, don't get the idea that I'm telling you to sit down with the big boys and to start playing 8-3s willy nilly. If you do that, you're going to lose your backside. First, remember that I said you have to have shown them you're playing good, "solid" poker. Second, you have to pick your occasion carefully and make sure you're not walking into big pocket pairs or other traps. Third, when you've gotten away with these moves a couple of times, you may then have to tighten up again and wait to spring another trap later on. One of the things you're trying to do with "trash" moves is to confuse your opponents. *Another* thing you're trying to do is to *get them to start modifying their play* to counter yours. Then, by the time they've switched to your gear, you've switched back to theirs. Presidential candidates, boxers, generals, businessmen, football coaches—anyone facing an adversary—are constantly trying to get their opponents to *re*act rather than letting them take the initiative and act first. Poker is no different. You want your opponents trying to react to you: "What's he doing?" "What's he up to?" Keep them guessing. An opponent on the defensive is already half-beaten. Sorry, I mean half-beat.

Here come some more generalities, this time regarding tells. You may recall the story back on page 31 and the relevant footnote on the same page wherein I mentioned that my theory of how I would be perceived depending on how I put my money on the table had turned out to be professional doctrine and had appeared in a magazine article. Well, these professional doctrines concerning behavior abound in Pokerdom. The generally arrogant attitude of the pros is also exposed in that same article, which refers to these particular opponents as "nerds" and "dorks."

Anyway, all you have to do is know what these doctrines are and adjust your behavior accordingly to confuse the hell out of your professional opposition. The pros *do* have a category in which people who are pretending to display these traits or their opposites are listed as well, but we'll handle that in a minute. Here are a few of the dicta and their countermeasures.

1.   People who look away from the table, or are otherwise feigning boredom or a lack of interest in their hands, actually have very strong hands and are trying to hide it.

> Countermeasure: Look away when you really aren't interested and are going to fold. Also look away when you have a hammer and are going to raise.

2.   People who put their bets in the pot very aggressively are bluffing or at least are very weak.

> Countermeasure: Put your bet in aggressively when you have a hammer.

3.   People who, when asked a question, stammer and spout incoherencies are probably bluffing.

> Countermeasure: Stammer and spout incoherencies when you have a hammer.

4.   People who answer questions forthrightly and coherently after they have bet have very strong hands.

> Countermeasure: Since you don't know what the question will be (they usually like to ask a nonpoker question like "What did you think of the fight last night?") you have to prepare nonanswers like, "I'm terribly sorry, but I don't like to engage in conversation in the middle of a hand," and practice it to come out coherently and forthrightly—when you're bluffing of course.

5.   People who try to "stare you down" after they bet are probably bluffing and are trying to get you to fold.

Countermeasure: Stare people down when you have a hammer.

6.   People who grab for their chips when you're about to bet have weak hands and are trying to get you to check into a showdown.

Countermeasure: Grab for your chips when you have a hammer. (We've discussed this one before.)

7.   People who show their cards to nonplaying onlookers probably have a strong hand.

Countermeasure: You may recall that I recounted on page 244 that I let my friend see my hole cards during a bluff in the $50–$100 game. This is why I let him see my cards in mid-bluff: the others would read it as strength. My friend was an unwitting partner to my bluff.

8.   People who glance at their chips when a card comes on the board have just hit something.

Countermeasure: Remember to completely ignore your chips when a board card has made your hand.

9.   People who hem and haw and delay and ponder and then bet out or raise have strong hands.

Countermeasure: Hem and haw, delay and ponder, when you have a weak hand.

10.   People who read at the table are "nut players" who might go through *War and Peace* rather than play a weak hand.

Countermeasure: If you want to appear tight to disguise some "loose" play, read at the table. (Some places don't allow reading at the table, so ask.)

11.   People who stack their chips carefully are likely to be tight players. Conversely, sloppy chips on the table mean loose player.

Countermeasure: Stack your chips neatly if you're planning some "loose" play; scatter them about in an amorphous pile if you're planning to be "tight."

12.   People who look at their hole cards when a card turns have probably just hit something, or have something similar in the hole that they're checking out.

Countermeasure: Here's a general principle: Try, try, try to train yourself to look once at your hole cards and then never look again throughout the hand. If you can't do that—and there's no need to feel bad about it—just train yourself to look at your hole cards after *every* new board card. That way you can't give anything away. Now, in particular to this "tell": look at your hole cards when the new card is meaningless.

13. People who have just won a hand and are busy stacking their chips from that hand (which with a big pot can be quite a happy chore and take up the time of the entire next hand to do) are not likely to play the next hand with weak cards, nor to run a bluff.

Countermeasure: Might be a good time to run a bluff.

14. People who stare at potential bettors to their right are weak, whereas people who studiously do not look at potential bettors to their right have hammers.

Countermeasure: Studiously avoid looking at the bettors to your right when you are weak and would like them to check. Stare at them when you have a hammer.

15. People who bet and then look back at their hands when an opponent seems about to call are bluffing.

Countermeasure: Look back at your hand when you have a hammer.

16. People who bet and then seem about to show their hands prematurely are bluffing.

Countermeasure: Bet and seem to be about to show your hand prematurely when you have a hammer.

17. People who shrug when they bet as if to say, "Oh well, I don't know, but here goes," have hammers.

Countermeasure: Shrug and look that way when you are bluffing.

Okay, that's enough. You surely get the idea. Find out what the pros think various behavior means and use it to mean the opposite. But won't they catch on? Won't they see what you're doing? Of course they will. They're not stupid, after all. And—they're even on the lookout for people who will use these tells "backwards." So why did I bother telling you all this? Well, for one thing, you can just avoid these tells altogether and make the pros look for something else to read you by. But, if you're really, really clever about how you go back and forth between using them "forwards" and using them "backwards" you can confuse the hell out of your opponents. And the way to be really, really clever is to be random. And the way to be random is not to be clever at all but to let a random factor govern what you do. Here's how I do it, sometimes.

The first time I decide to make use of a "tell", I'll usually do it backward. Being "visitors," you and I have the added advantage that the pros will be underestimating us and, therefore, assuming that our tells are genuine. At least, the first time. Once won't blow our cover; they're more likely to think that that particular tell didn't work just because, for some reason, it happened not to apply. However, when you've used tells backwards two or three times they will think "Oh ho!" and start looking for other signs of not-so-stupidness in you. Now's the time to start randomizing your tells, and I do it thusly; I'll look at my first hole card, and, if it's red, I'll use a tell forward; if it's black, I'll use a tell backward. If, for some strategic reason I don't want to go along with the random mandate, I just won't use it at all—one makes one's own decisions, after all—but this is rare.

Let's take an example: the thing about grabbing your chips. This is a good example because even inveterate "forward" chip-grabbers don't necessarily grab them all the time. The first time I do it, it will be backward: I'll grab my chips when I want to encourage someone to bet. *If I'm sufficiently satisfied that my opponents have noticed this,* I begin randomizing my chip-grabbing, to the point that it will be absolutely meaningless. I'm grabbing my chips when I'm both weak and strong, and I'm *not* grabbing my chips when I'm both weak and strong. It gets to the point that after a while I'm not grabbing my chips just because I've grown bored with the enterprise. Strong, weak, weak, strong, bored: who the hell knows? That, of course, is the point, and believe me, it drives the pros stark raving. Even if I've abandoned the charade, it sets their minds in high gear: "He's not grabbing his chips, what does that mean? Let's see. The last time he had it, the time before he had it, the time before that he didn't have it, the time before that he didn't have it . . ." You can see the gears turning.

The reason I put *"sufficiently satisfied,* etc.*"* in italics is, as we have discussed before, you have to be playing with observant people for your maneuvers to be observed. The pros are, usually, sufficiently observant. If you try all this convoluted stuff at your home game, however, most of it will just be wasted and you'll end up outsmarting yourself. Just remember: if you randomize your behavior using a truly random factor—if you have a digital watch, for example, you can go "forward" on even minutes and "backward" on odd minutes—no one has any hope of reading you. When they guess right, well, they're doing just that: guessing.

One last caveat: there are those among the pros astute enough to realize that you are using some random factor to randomize your "tells." When they realize that they will simply start ignoring that particular "tell" and start looking for others. Well, if you think there are pros in your game who are that good, it's a good time to start appearing with other "tells."

That's about all I can tell you without writing another 500 pages on casino poker. Clearly, my message is that casino poker is beatable, but it takes study, experience, concentration and people skills. But, hey, what doesn't require effort to be done well?

A final word along some lines I have mentioned before. As you can probably tell from the content of this chapter and the tenor of the entire book, I don't play casino poker to have a good time, win or lose. I have a wonderful, exquisite, mystical, transcendental, primordial, devastatingly FUN time playing casino poker—but I play to win. When I dive into the shark tank, I fully intend to emerge with shark hair, teeth, and eyeballs in my pocket. Losing ain't my idea of a good time, not in home games and not in casinos. I have told you why I feel this way, and I have tried to tell you why I think *you* should feel this way. If, however, you persist, if you would prefer to adopt or maintain the attitude that, "What the hell! I played some poker, lost some money, but had a good time," well then—what the hell!—let me shake your hand and more power to you. Just get out there and have some fun!

Oh, by the way, will you drop me a line and let me know when and where you'll be playing? After the game, be sure to give me your address. I'll send you a postcard from the Caribbean.

Appendix 1

Where Are You And Where Are You Going?

Unless otherwise noted, all figures given in this Appendix of probabilities, percentages and odds are based on results from runs of several million hands on the The PokerWiz simulation program, rather than on mathematical calculations. For this reason, if you compare some of these figures with theoretical tables you will note some small differences. In case you're wondering, these million-hand statistics are actually more useful than calculations.

DRAW

Five Card Draw

Ace   Draw 4 cards

Drawing four cards to an ace isn't always such a wild and crazy move as it seems to be. If you are against an opponent whom you suspect of opening weak, say on the minimum pair of jacks, it can be a winner. You'll hit a pair of aces or better about 25 percent of the time, which is only 3 to 1 against. However, the fellow drawing to jacks will improve occasionally too (see below) so your actual odds of beating the jacks are about 3.4 to 1.

Pair   Draw 3 cards

This is your basic, common or garden draw. You'll get two pair about 16 percent of the time (a little over 5 to 1 against), and you'll get trips about 11 percent of the time (8 to 1 against.) Full houses (99 to 1) and fours (359 to 1), well, they aren't going to happen very often. The sum of all these (i.e., any improvement at all) is a little worse than 2.5 to 1 against. A low pair will out-draw and beat a higher pair about 23 percent of the time, or about 3.3 to 1 against.

Pair + Kicker   Draw 2 cards

If you draw three cards to a pair, you're giving yourself the best opportunity to improve your hand. You're also pretty much telling your opponents what you've got. A good remedy for this is to keep a kicker with your pair. Your odds to improve drop a bit, but not off the chart. It's still about 5 to 1 against hitting two pair. Trips get more difficult: 12 to 1. A full house goes up to about 130 to 1. Fours are the only ones really to skyrocket at about 1,250 to 1. The deceptive value of keeping a kicker is often worth the sacrifice in probability: Is it a pair or is it trips?

Two Pair   Draw 1 card

Not much mystery here. Odds against hitting a full house are about 11 to 1 against.

Trips   Draw 2 cards

You can either pull in a pair for a full house, about 15 to 1 against, or you can get four of a kind, 23 to 1 against. Usually (usually!) you won't have to worry about it too much as trips will win more often than they lose, without improvement.

Trips + Kicker   Draw 1 card

This is a good idea as it disguises your hand even better than keeping a kicker with a pair. They might think you have, besides trips with a kicker, two pair, a flush draw, a straight draw. Your odds against hitting a full house are actually the same at about 15 to 1 against. Odds against hitting fours double to 46 to 1.

Four to a Straight (open ended)   Draw 1 card

If you have 9-8-7-6 you can hit either a 5 or a 10 to make your straight; that makes 8 cards. (47–8) / 8 = 4.875. So call it 5 to 1.

Four to a Straight (gutshot/one end)   Draw 1 card

If you have 9-8-7-5, you have to hit a 6 to make a

straight, which is only 4 cards. You might expect this to be twice as hard to get as the open ended straight, but actually it's worse than that. $(47-4) / 4 = 10.75$. Call it 11 to 1.

Four to a Flush   Draw 1 card

This one you know. It's about 4.2 to 1 against.

Three to a Flush   Draw 2 cards

If you're really desperate, on tilt, masochistic, or just feel that the cosmos may be leaning in your direction, here's a draw to try; it's only about 25 to 1 against. However (there always seems to be a however), let's say your three-flush is A♠K♠Q♠, and you think you're against an opener who only has jacks (or even lower if there is no opening qualifier). Well, you'll hit a pair of Qs or better about 39 percent of the time, about 1.6 to 1 against. You'll hit two pair or better about 8 percent of the time, or about 12 to 1 against. Since the jacks will improve sometimes too, you'll actually outdraw them and win about 30 percent of the time, or a bit worse than 2 to 1 against. Be careful and keep an eye on your opponents and the pot odds, both actual and potential, but making draws like this occasionally can send your wild and loose image skyrocketing.

Four to a Straight Flush (open ended)   Draw 1 card

If you look down at your hand and find 10♥J♥Q♥K♥ looking back at you, it may be difficult to keep from getting a bit excited. Don't get *too* excited, however. You're still about a 2 to 1 dog to hit anything, i.e., a straight or better.

Three to a Straight Flush (open ended, two cards on each end)
    Draw 2 cards

Hands like 9♥10♥J♥ look a lot better than they really

are. You'll only hit a straight or better about 7.6 percent of the time, or a bit worse than 12 to 1.

Five Card Draw Lowball (Wheel Low)

A word about lowball. If you're playing with a wild and loose group, then it's going to be difficult to draw any conclusions from their behavior. If you're playing with a pretty tight, competent group, however, you may be able to make some judgments concerning drawing possibilities. Let's say that, hand after hand, the players are folding, leaving maybe three players out of eight to contend for the pot. All of a sudden, this hand, the guy under the gun bets, the next guy raises, the next guy calls, someone else calls, another guy raises, another guy calls—and then the action comes to you, and you have a one card draw to a six low. Whatever the probabilities below tell you is likely to happen, bump it up by a factor of a lot. Why? Because, obviously, a lot of low cards are out, i.e., no longer in the deck. It's almost like stud, where you can see cards out that might have helped you had they still been in the deck.

Four to an 8-low   Draw 1 card

> You have sixteen cards to hit your 8-low, which makes it about 2 to 1 against.

Four to a 7-low   Draw 1 card

> Now you only have twelve cards to hit a 7-low, so you're a 3 to 1 dog to hit.

Four to a 6-low   Draw 1 card

> Getting harder and harder, now there are only eight cards. It's about 5 to 1 against hitting your 6-low.

Four to a wheel   Draw 1 card

> You look at your hand and see A♥2♣3♠4♥. I'm gonna hit a wheel! you think. Probably not. You've only got four cards that will do it for you, which is the same as

trying to hit an inside straight, 11 to 1 against, which in fact is what you're doing. The difference here, is that you don't have to hit your inside straight to have a hand. If a 6-low or 7-low or 8-low will win it for you, then you're back to sixteen cards to hit, or about 2 to 1 against.

Three to a Wheel   Draw 2 cards

You sometimes can get away with draws like this if you're playing with an extremely loose crowd, the bets after the draw are substantial, and there's a lot of betting, calling, and raising after the draw to boot. Sure, you're only going to hit that elusive wheel about 1 percent of the time (about 70 to 1 against), but you'll hit an 8-low or better about 14 percent of the time, which is a little worse than 6 to 1 against.

STUD

A word about stud. Below are a lot of probabilities and odds. They're as right as I can get them, but they have to be seen in terms of *ideal*. This "word about" came after I found myself writing all the information below and including, "if none of your cards are out" and, "depending on how many cards you have seen" over and over again.

As soon as a stud hand is dealt, you start seeing a bunch of cards. If you're heads-up, you see your cards plus the first up card of your opponent. If there are three of you, you see your cards and two more. If there are six of you, you see your cards and five opponents' cards. Let's say there are seven of you. On the first round you see your cards and six opponents' cards. On the second round, how many cards do you see? I don't know: I don't know how many of your opponents folded on the first round. Third round? Who knows? There were seven of you to start off. Are there now six of you in the hand? Five? Four? Three? Two? Dunno.

Because it's impossible for me to know how many players are left in the hand, it is equally impossible for me to know how many cards you have seen. Therefore, it is equally impossible to know how many of your helping cards are out—that you can see.

What you have to do is this: THINK. Think about what your odds are. Think about what cards you need to help your hand and how many of those are no longer available—because you can see them on the board. You have a pair of kings. The theoretical odds on your getting a third and fourth king depend on those kings being available. If Harvey has a king showing, and Pete has a king showing, your pair of kings are going to stay a pair of kings for all eternity.

You're playing seven stud. There are seven people in your group. The sixth card has been dealt. If everyone has hung in there, you can see as many as thirty cards: your six and twenty-four of your opponents' cards. Now, you have four to a spade flush, and there isn't a single, solitary spade on the board. Is the rest of the deck loaded with spades? Um . . . yep, it is.

So. If I try to tell you your odds are X if one of your cards is out, Y if two of your cards are out, Z if three—well, it isn't going to work. Your drawing odds still depend on how many cards you have seen in the course of the hand to that point, which depends on the number of people who have hung in or folded since the first round. Can't be done.

So, THINK. Figure out how many cards will help you. Five stud, third card has been dealt, you have K-K-J. There are two kings and three jacks that can improve your hand—a total of five cards. Think of these as "points." Five points. If a king then shows somewhere on the table, you have four points, and so forth.

Playing low, you have 7-4-3-2. To hit a 7-low, there are four 6s, four 5s, and four As—twelve cards, twelve points. If one ace is out, you have only eleven points. If one ace, one 6 and one 5 are out, you have only nine points. Your odds against hitting have gone up by 25 percent, but are lessened by the number of cards you can see. Just THINK. That's all. And you'll be okay.

Five Card Stud High

Hole + First Up Card

A♠K♣ (Two unpaired cards)

Any time you have two unpaired cards to start with, you'll end up making a pair of one or the other of them, or better, about 33 percent of the time, or about 2 to 1 against. If you're up against a pair, however, as we've seen before, you need to consider that the pair will sometimes improve right along with you. Therefore, you're actually looking at about 2.7 to 1 against out-drawing the pair. (This depends somewhat on *which* pair you're up against. Certainly, in this scenario, if you're up against a pair of aces or kings, you're pretty thoroughly cooked and might as well muck it.)

9♣9♥ (Pair)

Any time you start out in five stud with a pair you're a favorite over anyone who doesn't have a pair, even if they have overcards. Surely I don't need to point this out, but here it is anyway: the higher the pair, the better off you are. Whatever your pair, however, you'll improve to two pair or better about 28 percent of the time, a little worse than 2.5 to 1 against.

Three cards

A♠K♣Q♥ (Three unpaired cards, higher than suspected pairs)

I'm not showing A-K-Q as an example to make you start thinking about going after straights in stud! I'm showing them as an example because at this point because if your unpaired cards are lower than an opponent's suspected pair, it's time to pack up and get out. If all of your cards are overcards to an opponent's pair, you might want to keep trying. At this point, with two cards to come, you'll beat a lower pair about 28 percent of the time, or about 2.5 to 1 against. By the way, if at this point you think you need trips to win, forget it. It's about 46 to 1 against outdrawing trips.

A♠K♣3♥ (Three unpaired cards, two of which are higher than suspected pairs)

Getting harder. You'll only outdraw the lower pairs about 20% of the time, or about 4 to 1 against.

9♣9♥J♦ (Pair and X)

You're still the favorite if you're the only one with a pair. You'll improve to two pair or better about 26 percent of the time, a little better than 3 to 1 against.

9♣9♥9♦ (Trips)

Forget about trying to improve. If you've got trips at this point and someone has better trips, just lament your fate and muck it. Lower trips will draw out on higher trips a little less than 10 percent of the time, or a little worse than 9 to 1 against.

Four Cards

A♠K♣Q♥10♦ (Four unpaired cards, higher than suspected pairs)

If all you're up against is lower pairs, you'll draw out on them about 31 percent of the time, or about 2.2 to 1 against. Yes, in this case that includes hitting the gut-shot straight among your outs. If you don't have the gutshot possibility, something like A♠K♣Q♥9♦, you'll out draw lower pairs about 20 percent of the time, or about 4 to 1 against.

9♣9♥J♦7♥ (Pair and two Xs)

You're getting down to the end and, theoretically at least, your competition is getting tougher. But, still, if you're the only one with a pair then you're odds-on to win it. At this point you'll improve to two pair or better about 17 percent of the time, or about 5 to 1 against.

9♣9♥9♦J♦ (Trips and X)

Same as before: if you're not winning at this point with your trips, pack it in. If you are in the lead, then all you can do is sit there and hope the probabilities behave themselves and don't let someone draw out on you. It's about 11 to 1 against smaller trips drawing out on bigger trips.

Five Card Stud Low (Wheel Low)

Hole + First UP Card

9♣4♥ (Two cards to a 9-low)

You'll hit a 9-low about 11 percent of the time, about 8 to 1 against.

8♦2♠ (Two cards to an 8-low)

You'll hit an 8-low about 6.5 percent of the time, over 14 to 1 against.

7♦2♥ (Two cards to a 7-low)

You'll get a 7-low a little over 3 percent of the time, about 30 to 1 against.

6♥3♣ (Two cards to a 6-low)

A 6-low will appear about 1.3 percent of the time.

5♥2♦ (Two cards to a Wheel)

A Wheel is pretty hard to get at five stud. It will occur about 0.3 percent of the time or over 300 to 1. But look at it this way: a wheel low is just as unbeatable as a royal flush is for high. If you start out in five stud with two to a royal flush, your odds of actually ending up with one are around 20,000 to 1. In comparison, a wheel looks pretty easy to get.

Three Cards

9♣4♥3♣ (Three cards to a 9-low)

> With two cards to come, you'll hit a 9-low about 20 percent of the time, or 4 to 1 against.

8♦2♠4♥ (Three cards to an 8-low)

> You'll get an 8-low about 13.5 percent of the time, about 6.5 to 1 against.

7♦2♥5♦ (Three cards to a 7-low)

> You're not there yet. A 7-low will show up about 8 percent of the time, or about 11.5 to 1 against.

6♥3♣2♠ (Three cards to a 6-low)

> You'll get a 6-low about 4 percent of the time, about 24 to 1 against.

5♠2♦A♠ (Three cards to a wheel)

> Looking pretty good to hit a wheel, only about 72 to 1 against at this point. (Continuing our royal flush comparison, if you had A♠K♠Q♠ at this point, you'd be down to only about 1,200 to 1 against hitting.)

Four Cards

9♣4♥3♣2♠ (Four cards to a 9-low)

> You're getting close to even money to hit a 9-low: about 41 percent or about 1.4 to 1 against.

8♦2♠4♥3♥ (Four cards to an 8-low)

> You'll hit your 8-low about 33 percent of the time, about 2 to 1 against.

7♦2♥5♦A♣ (Four cards to a 7-low)

You'll hit a 7-low about 25 percent of the time, about 3 to 1 against.

6♥3♣2♠A♥ (Four cards to a 6-low)

The 6-low will come in about 17 percent of the time, about 5 to 1 against.

5♠2♦A♠3♣ (Four cards to a wheel)

What, we're still trying to hit a wheel? I guess so, and we're getting closer: it'll happen about 8 percent of the time, about 11 to 1 against.

Seven Card Stud High

Third Street

A♠K♣10♦ (Three connected [one-way], unsuited cards)

Starting out with these cards, you'll hit two pair or better about 33 percent of the time, or about 2 to 1 against.

A♠K♠10♠ (Three connected [one-way], suited cards)

Lest you think having suited cards doesn't make that much difference, with these starters you'll hit two pair or better around 47 percent of the time. That's nearly even money at about 1.13 to 1 against.

J♦10♣9♥ (Three connected [both-ways], unsuited cards)

Because of your increased capacity to make straights, the statistics show you'll hit two pair or better over 43 percent of the time, about 1.3 to 1 against. Take note, however, that since your cards are lower (of necessity to allow hitting a straight both up and down) you're on much shakier ground unless you do in fact hit your straight.

J♦10♦9♦ (Three connected [both-ways], suited cards)

Now here's a heck of a hand to start off with. You'll hit two pair or better about 55 percent of the time—that's odds-on—which means you're more likely to hit than not. You'll hit a straight or better about 34 percent of the time, and a flush or better about 20 percent of the time. Sounds like a raise a-comin'.

Q♠Q♦7♥ (Pair with X)

So, you think a pair is a good start? You're right. You'll hit two pair or better about 61 percent of the time. Raise it up, unless you think there is a higher pair, or perhaps some trips out there . . .

J♠J♦J♥ (Trips)

Unfortunately, this doesn't happen very often—about 0.24 percent of the time or about 424 to 1 against. Oh, well. But if you do get trips wired you might want to start looking for the deed to the ranch, because you're going to win about 75 percent of the time. Even if you don't improve, you'll win about 60 percent of the time. If you do need to improve, you'll hit a full house or better about 40 percent of the time. It's a pretty good hand to start with.

Fourth Street

A♠K♣10♦J♥ (Four connected [one-way], unsuited cards)

Three cards to come. You'll hit two pair or better about 40 percent of the time, or around 1.5 to 1 against. Wondering about the straight? You'll hit it about 23 percent of the time, about 3.3 to 1 against.

A♠K♣10♦7♥ (Three connected [one-way], unsuited cards + X)

This doesn't look so good. You'll hit two pair or better about 24 percent of the time, or a little worse than 3 to 1 against.

A♠K♠10♠J♠ (Four connected [one-way], suited cards)

Well! Four to a royal flush! How good is that? Well, it's pretty good. You'll hit two pair or better over 70 percent of the time. Straight or better: 59 percent. Flush or better: 47 percent. The royal flush is still fairly elusive at about 6 percent, about 15 to 1 against (*if* the Q♠ is still alive and stays that way).

A♠K♠10♠7♦ (Three connected [one-way], suited cards + X)

What a letdown was that 7♦. Three good cards, lots of excitement then—a dud. One little card and you're only going to get two pair or better about 33 percent of the time, about 2 to 1 against.

J♦10♣9♥8♦ (Four connected [both-ways], unsuited cards)

You're in pretty good shape. Two pair or better will come in about 58 percent of the time, the straight about 43 percent.

J♦10♣9♥5♦ (Three connected [both-ways], unsuited cards + X)

Look at that. Change an 8 to a 5, and all of a sudden you've got a dog. You'll hit two pair or better about 30 percent of the time, worse than 2 to 1 against.

J♦10♦9♦8♦ (Four connected [both-ways], suited cards)

Four to a both-way straight flush. Looks good to me. You'll hit two pair or better about 79 percent of the time. Straight or better: 69 percent. Flush or better: 48 percent. Where *did* I put that deed to the ranch?

J♦10♦9♦5♣ (Three connected [both-ways], suited cards + X)

Once again we see the difference a card makes. Here, you'll hit two pair or better about 38 percent of the time, about 1.6 to 1 against.

Q♠Q♦7♥5♦ (Pair with XX)

You'll hit two pair about 57 percent of the time, odds-

on. Please note, however, that in seven stud, with three
cards to come, there could now be some pretty dangerous hands out there.

Q♠Q♦7♥7♦ (Two Pair)

You'll hit a full house or better about 23 percent of the
time, about 3.3 to 1 against. Whether or not two pair
queens up is a decent hand on its own depends on how
many players are in the pot against you. It's a big favorite
heads up. Against four opponents, when there is no
improvement, it will win about 30 percent of the time
which is about 10 percent over average. Two pair aces-
up is a better deal: it will win against four opponents
without improvement about 50 percent of the time.

J♠J♦J♥5♣ (Trips + X)

You probably don't need me to tell you this is still a
pretty good hand, especially with three cards to come.
You'll improve to a full house or better about 39 percent of the time, or about 1.6 to 1 against. With no
improvement, you'll still win against four opponents
about 61 percent of the time.

Fifth Street

A♠K♣10♦J♥5♣ (Four connected [one-way], unsuited cards + X)

You'll hit two pair or better about 26 percent of the time,
about 2.8 to 1 against. The straight will come in about
16 percent of the time, a bit worse than 5 to 1 against.

A♠K♣10♦7♥5♣ (Three connected [one-way], unsuited cards + XX)

Not so hot. You'll get two pair or better about 11 percent of the time, about 8 to 1 against.

A♠K♠10♠J♠5♣ (Four connected [one-way], suited cards + X)

That 5♣ was a bit of a disappointment, but don't give

up hope. You'll hit two pair or better about 53 percent of the time. A straight or better will come in about 45 percent of the time, or about 1.2 to 1 against.

A♠K♠10♠7♦5♣ (Three connected [one-way], suited cards + XX)

Two disappointing cards in a row and things don't look so good anymore. You'll get two pair or better only about 15 percent of the time, a bit better than 6 to 1 against.

J♦10♣9♥8♦5♣ (Four connected [both-ways], unsuited cards + X)

You'll get two pair or better about 41 percent of the time. The straight will come in about 31% of the time, about 2.2 to 1 against.

J♦10♣9♥5♦2♣ (Three connected [both-ways], unsuited cards + XX)

Well, this hand is now a dog, trash, toxic waste. You'll hit two pair or better about 14 percent of the time, or about 6 to 1 against. Even heads up, this hand at this point will lose about twice as often as it wins.

J♦10♦9♦8♦5♣ (Four connected [both-ways], suited cards + X)

This hand is definitely not trash yet—unless all your helping cards are out, but I said I wouldn't keep repeating that. You'll hit two pair or better over 62 percent of the time, a straight or better about 54 percent, and a flush or better about 35 percent.

J♦10♦9♦5♣2♥ (Three connected [both-ways], suited cards + XX)

One of the hardest things to do in poker is to start off with a promising hand, watch it go down the drain, and abandon it. The tendency is keep trying. But it looked so good to start! Yes, well it doesn't any more. You'll hit two pair or better about 18 percent of the time, worse than 4 to 1 against. With all those lowish cards your two pair is going to be pretty trashy too. To win anything you'll probably have to hit the straight or the flush, and the odds against that happening are about 11 to 1 against.

Q♠Q♦7♥5♦2♣ (Pair with XXX)

You'll hit two pair or better about 47 percent[71] of the time, nearly even money at about 1.1 to 1 against. But, is a pair a good hand this point in seven stud, with two cards to come? Well, that depends on your pair and how many players you're up against. Heads up, this pair of queens is a big favorite and will win about 65 percent of the time, well over average (average being 50 percent). If there are four players against you, a pair of queens at this point is just slightly above average winning around 22 percent of the time (average being 20 percent).

Q♠Q♦7♥7♦5♣ (Two Pair + X)

You'll hit a full house or better just under 17 percent of the time, about 5 to 1 against. This hand is a big favorite heads up, winning about 80 percent of the time. Against four opponents it is well above average, winning about 43 percent of the time.

J♠J♦J♥5♣2♦ (Trips + XX)

You'll hit a full house or better about 33 percent of the time, about 2 to 1 against. Most of the time, though, you won't need to improve—your trips will win a lot more often than they lose.

Sixth Street

A♠K♣10♦J♥5♣2♦ (Four connected [one-way], unsuited cards + XX)

[71.] Perhaps this is a good time for a reminder: In this Appendix, whenever I indicate that a hand will win X percent of the time against Y number of players, I'm talking about *random* hands. If you have two pair on fifth street and are heads up with Fred, who never takes a fifth card unless he's already got trips, then you're dead no matter what the random statistics say.

Unless you're going to try to run some kind of bluff, or unless every queen in the deck is still live, forget about trying to improve. Muck it.

A♠K♣10♦7♥5♣2♦ (Three connected [one-way], unsuited cards + XXX)

Even worse. Muck it.

A♠K♠10♠J♠5♣2♦ (Four connected [one-way], suited cards + XX)

Still a heck of a hand, right? Four to a royal flush. In fact, even heads up, this hand at this point is below average: it will lose more than it wins. It's difficult to believe, but the reason is really obvious: anyone with a pair of 2s is beating you right now—you have to hit something to win. You'll hit the straight or better about 26 percent of the time, a little better than 3 to 1 against, and the flush or better will come in about 19 percent of the time, a little worse than 4 to 1 against.

A♠K♠10♠7♦5♣2♦ (Three connected [one-way], suited cards + XXX)

Muck it.

J♦10♣9♥8♦5♣2♦ (Four connected [both-ways], unsuited cards + XX)

Muck it unless just about all of the 7s and queens are live.

J♦10♣9♥5♦2♣6♥ (Three connected [both-ways], unsuited cards + XXX)

Yuck.

J♦10♦9♦8♦5♣2♥ (Four connected [both-ways], suited cards + XX)

This one still may be worth a try. You'll hit the straight or better about 33 percent of the time, around 2 to 1 against, and the flush or better about 20 percent of the time, about 4 to 1 against.

J♦10♦9♦5♣2♥6♥ (Three connected [both-ways], suited cards + XXX)

See ya.

Q♠Q♦7♥5♦2♣6♣ (Pair with XXXX)

Your options here are to hit two pair or trips which will happen about 30 percent of the time, or about 2.3 to 1 against.

Q♠Q♦7♥7♦5♣2♦ (Two Pair + XX)

Your only room for improvement is the full house, which will happen about 9 percent of the time, a little worse than 10 to 1 against.

J♠J♦J♥5♣2♦6♣ (Trips + XXX)

This is a good time to take notice of the advantage of trips over two pair in stud—it is not just a better hand, it is a *much* better hand. With two pair, as above, your other cards are superfluous. You have to hit a queen or a seven to improve, four cards. With trips you can hit a full house or better with ten cards: one jack, three each of the 5s, 2s and 6s. So, you'll hit a full house or better about 22 percent of the time, about 3.5 to 1 against.

Seven Card Stud Low—Razz (Wheel Low)

Third Street

A♠2♥9♣ (Three to a 9-low)

You'll hit a 9-low or better about 62 percent of the time.

A♠2♥8♣ (Three to an 8-low)

An 8-low or better will come in about 48 percent of the time.

A♠2♥7♣ (Three to a 7-low)

You'll hit a seven low or better about 33 percent of the time, or about 2 to 1 against.

A♠2♥6♣ (Three to a 6-low)

The 6-low or better will come in about 19 percent of the time, a bit worse than 4 to 1 against.

A♠2♥5♣ (Three to a wheel)

The elusive wheel is still elusive. It'll happen about 7 percent of the time, or about 13 to 1 against. However, you're still at about even money to hit an 8-low or better.

Fourth Street

A♠2♥9♣5♦ (Four to a 9-low)

It's looking pretty good. You'll hit the 9-low or better about 81 percent of the time.

A♠2♥9♣K♦ (Three to a 9-low + X)

One clinker really gets in the way. You're down to hitting the 9-low or better about 45 percent of the time, a bit less than even money.

A♠2♥8♣5♦ (Four to an 8-low)

You'll get an 8-low or better about 71 percent of the time.

A♠2♥8♣K♦ (Three to an 8-low + X)

We've dropped to about 32 percent, or a bit worse than 2 to 1 against.

A♠2♥7♣5♦ (Four to a 7-low)

You'll hit a 7-low or better about 59 percent of the time.

A♠2♥7♣K♦ (Three to a 7-low + X)

The odds against hitting a 7-low or better have dropped to about 4 to 1 against.

A♠2♥6♣5♣ (Four to a 6-low)

You'll get the 6-low or better about 43 percent of the time, about 1.3 to 1 against.

A♠2♥6♣K♣ (Three to a 6-low + X)

The clinker makes it harder: about 8 to 1 against getting a 6-low or better.

A♠2♥5♣3♦ (Four to a wheel)

The wheel will come in about 23 percent of the time, about 3.3 to 1 against. You'll never have a better shot at a wheel.

A♠2♥5♣K♦ (Three to a wheel + X)

Down to about 4 percent to hit a wheel, or 24 to 1 against. That king really did a number on your hand.

Fifth Street

A♠2♥9♣5♦K♦ (Four to a 9-low + X)

Here, the king hasn't done such devastating damage. You'll still hit a 9-low or better about 67 percent of the time.

A♠2♥9♣K♦Q♣ (Three to a 9-low + XX)

In the first place, with two high cards at this point you're restricted to hitting just the 9-low—there's no longer an "or better." So, you'll hit the 9-low about 22 percent of the time, about 3.5 to 1 against. But will a 9-low win it for you?

A♠2♥8♣5♦K♦ (Four to an 8-low + X)

You'll hit the 8-low or better about 57 percent of the time.

A♠2♥8♣K♦Q♦ (Three to an 8-low + XX)

The 8-low will still come in about 15 percent of the time, a bit better than 6 to 1 against.

A♠2♥7♣5♦K♦ (Four to a 7-low + X)

You'll get a 7-low or better about 45 percent of the time.

A♠2♥7♣K♦Q♣ (Three to a 7-low + XX)

You'll hit the 7-low about 9 percent of the time, a little worse than 10 to 1 against.

A♠2♥6♣5♣K♦ (Four to a 6-low + X)

The 6-low will come in about 31 percent, a bit worse than 2 to 1 against.

A♠2♥6♣K♣Q♣ (Three to a 6-low + XX)

You're probably not going to get a 6-low.

A♠2♥5♣3♦K♦ (Four to a wheel + X)

The wheel is still hard to get, even with two cards to come. It'll come in about 16 percent of the time, about 5 to 1 against.

A♠2♥5♣K♦Q♣ (Three to a wheel + XX)

Forget about trying to hit a wheel.

Sixth Street

A♠2♥9♣5♦K♦Q♣ (Four to a 9-low + XX)

You're still looking pretty good to hit a 9-low, which will come in about 44 percent of the time.

A♠2♥9♣K♦Q♣J♣ (Three to a 9-low + XXX)

There's only one card to come, so what do you want to hit—a J-low? You tried to keep going with two bad cards, but now it's all over.

A♠2♥8♣5♦K♦Q♣ (Four to an 8-low + XX)

You'll hit the 8-low about 35 percent of the time, a bit better than 2 to 1 against.

A♠2♥7♣5♦K♦Q♣ (Four to a 7-low + XX)

> The 7-low will come in about 26 percent of the time, a little better than 3 to 1 against.

A♠2♥6♣5♣K♦Q♣ (Four to a 6-low + XX)

> You'll hit the 6-low about 17 percent of the time, a bit better than 5 to 1 against.

A♠2♥5♣3♦K♦Q♣ (Four to a wheel + XX)

> It's a bit worse than 10 to 1 against hitting the wheel.

Hold'em

A word about Hold'em, about which several volumes could be written. Come to think of it, several volumes *have* been written about it. For our purposes here, however, just remember that Hold'em is like draw in that you only have behavioral deduction available to you to try to figure out what cards are out and, thus, what your chances are. If you're playing in a tight game with competent players and all of a sudden there's a lot of betting, calling, and raising before the flop, you may well deduce that there are a lot of high cards out in the players' pockets. On the one hand, if you have high cards too in this situation, your chances of hitting them are going to drop. On the other hand, it might be a good time to sneak in with medium or low cards. As for hitting straights and flushes after the flop, usually (usually!) you'll be the only one going for your particular straight or flush.

Say you have J♣10♣ and the flop gives you four to a flush with the turn and the river yet to come. Should you be worried about someone else having two clubs with the Q♣, K♣, or A♣? No. You shouldn't be "worried," but you should be cautious, and you should try to discern if someone else seems to be going after the flush too. For one thing, if two (or more) of you do have two clubs in the pocket, then the chances are greater that you'll both miss. (Obviously, since there are fewer clubs in the deck to hit with.)

Having said that, probabilities—odds, chances—in Hold'em are much more straight forward than in stud as there are no obviously dead cards. The cards on the board are for use by everybody.

Pocket (Results considering entire five-card board)

1. Any two cards, not a pair:

    Pair: One or the other of your hole cards will show up on the board to pair about 48 percent of the time, virtually even money. You will end up with *only* one pair (that is, one pair is your best hand) of one or the other of your hole cards about 23 percent of the time.

    Two Pair: You will make two pair *using both of your hole cards* about 5.5 percent of the time, about 17 to 1 against. There is an important distinction here about making two pair using both of your hole cards, and making two pair, one pair of which is on the board. In other words, if you hold A-J and the board gives you another ace and another jack to make two pair, aces and jacks, this is a *much* better two pair than if the board gives you, say, an ace and a pair of queens. In the latter case, statistically you have "improved" to two pair, aces and queens, but this "two pair" is a much weaker hand since those queens belong to everybody.

    Trips: You will make trips of one or the other of your hole cards about 4.5 percent of the time, or about 21 to 1 against.

    Full House: You'll get a full house using one or both of your cards about 1.6 percent of the time, about 61 to 1 against. (This does not count the times there will be trips on the board. Say you hold A-J and the board shows 3 3 3 J 6. Statistically you have a full house, but it is of the "common" variety. To arrive at the figures above, I am only considering full houses of—using the A-J example—AAAJJ, AAAxx, JJJAA, and JJJxx.)

Fours: Four of a kind using one of your hole cards will only happen about 0.2 percent of the time, about 499 to 1 against.

2.   Any Pair

If you start out with a pair you may or may not be the favorite, depending on how high your pair is and how many people are playing. It's tough to improve a pair, that is, actually involving your pair in the improvement. If you hold, say J-J, except for fluke hands here's what is available:

Trips: One more Jack will show up on the board about 12 percent of the time, about 4.5 to 1 against.

Full House: You will make a full house consisting of JJJXX about 6.4 percent—a little better than 15 to 1 against.

Fours: About 0.81 percent—around 120 to 1 against. Once again, what I mean by "involving your pair" is that if a pair comes on the board, sure, you have "improved" to two pair—but so has anyone else who is holding another pair. Statistically, you'll actually "make" a full house about 2 percent more often than I've cited above, but that just means that trips have shown up on the board and your pair, therefore, makes a full house (in this case, say, 333JJ) but so does anyone else's pair.

3.   A♠K♠ or A♣2♣ (Connected [one-way], suited cards)

Straight: You'll hit a straight using one or both of your cards about 3 percent of the time, about 33 to 1 against.

Flush: This, of course, applies to any two suited cards. You'll hit a flush using one or both of your cards (with the A-K suited it would always be both, with the A-2 suited it might sometimes only be the ace) about 6.3 percent of the time, a little better than 15 to 1 against. This is important. Many players see two suited cards in the pocket and think they've got a really good shot at hitting a flush. As you can see here, it's actually a really *bad* shot at hitting a flush, which is why hands like 8♥3♥ are trash.

Straight Flush: The straight flush in this example is limited to the royal flush or the wheel-flush and will occur about 0.05 percent of the time, or about 2,000 to 1 against.

4.   A♠K♦ (Connected [one-way], unsuited cards)

What you sacrifice here, of course, is the flush draw. You'll only hit a flush about 2 percent of the time, about 49 to 1 against. The straight flush is off the charts.

5.   J♠10♠ (Connected [both-ways], suited cards)

Having the straight and the straight flush open ended makes these differences: You'll hit a straight about 9 percent of the time, about 10 to 1 against. The straight flush (including the royal) has dropped to a measly 500 to 1 against.

6.   J♠10♦ (Connected [both-ways], unsuited cards)

Obviously, your potential to hit the straight is the same. Forget about the flush, though (see A♠K♦ above).

7.   A♦7♦ (Unconnected, suited cards)

This is the opposite of A♠K♦ and J♠10♦ above: you have flush potential but no virtually straight potential.

8.   A♦7♣ (Unconnected, unsuited cards)

Practically no straight or flush potential, otherwise like any two cards, not a pair.

The Flop:

9a.   [A♠K♠] 10♣6♦2♥ (No help, two overcards)

You'll pair one or the other of your hole cards about 18 percent of the time, a bit better than 5 to 1 against.

Total options for improving (including fluking the straight) are a little over 25 percent, slightly better than 3 to 1 against.

9b.   [A♠K♠] 10♠6♦2♥ (Three to a flush, two overcards)

Besides being able to pair your hole cards, you'll hit the flush a little more than 4 percent of the time, a little better than 24 to 1 against.

9c.   [A♠K♠] 10♠6♠2♥ (Four to a flush, two overcards)

You're in good shape to hit the flush. It will come in about 35 percent of the time, a bit better than 2 to 1 against. You can also still pair your cards if you miss the flush.

9d.   [A♠K♠] 10♠6♠A♥ (Four to a flush, top pair)

Now this righ-chere is one heck of a hand. Your aces might stand up alone. You'll hit a king or another ace about 21 percent of the time, a bit better than 4 to 1 against. And you've still got your flush draw. You'll beat four opponents about 75 percent of the time.

9e.   [A♠K♠] Q♦10♥2♦ (Four to an inside straight, two overcards)

This is the kind of hand that will drive your less astute opponents nuts. Dogma, of course, is that you should never go after inside straights. Well, if the inside straight is simply one of your several outs, it can be a hell of a draw. Here, with two cards to come, you will hit the inside straight about 16 percent of the time, a little worse than 5 to 1 against. Your other outs, of course, are hitting your overcards. What you'd really like to see is the straight because in this example if you do hit an ace or a king, someone else may have hit the straight.

9f.   [A♠K♠] 10♦A♣2♥ (Pair)

You'll improve to two pair or better, using your hole

cards, about 20 percent of the time.

9g.   [A♠K♠] 10♦A♣K♥ (Two Pair)

You'll improve to a full house or better about 16.5 percent of the time, about 5 to 1 against. If you don't improve, watch out for the straight.

9h.   [A♠K♠] A♦A♥5♣ (Trips)

You'll hit a full house or better, using both your hole cards, about 16.5 percent of the time, about 5 to 1 against. You might think that with a hand like this you wouldn't need to improve, but you could be losing already—to someone with a pair of 5s in the pocket. Hitting an ace or a king on the turn or the river certainly wouldn't hurt.

10.   [A♠K♦] any flop not giving three or four to a flush.

All the above under 9a-9h apply except for flush draws which have become relatively unattainable.

11a.   [J♥10♥] 6♣5♠2♦ (No help, two overcards)

Same as 9a above, except that your overcards aren't so hot.

11b.   [J♥10♥] 6♣5♠A♦ (No help, no overcards)

There *may* not be an ace out against you, but with a tableful of opponents there probably will be. Against three random opponents you're about 7 to 1 canine when average, of course, would be 3 to 1. That means you're a rather large canine at this point. You'll have to hit two running Js or 10s, two running cards to the straight, or a J and a 10 on the turn and river to be in contention, and that's only going to happen around 3 percent of the time, about 33 to 1 against.

11c.   [J♥10♥] 9♣8♦2♠ (Four to a straight, two overcards)

The difference here from 9e above is that your straight

is open on both ends. You'll hit the straight about 31 percent of the time, a little over 2 to 1 against. You also have two overcards to hit.

11d. [J♥10♥] Q♠K♦2♣ (Four to a straight, no overcards)

Although you still have four to an open-ended straight, this hand is not as good as 11c above. There may already be Ks and Qs out against you, which means you *must* hit the straight to win. You no longer have hitting overcards among your outs.

11e. [J♥10♥] 5♥A♥2♣ (Four to a flush, no overcards)

Here again, you probably have to hit the flush to win because there may be aces out against you already.

11f. [J♥10♥] 5♥2♥J♦ (Four to a flush, top pair)

This is the same situation as in 9d above, but your top pair isn't so great and can be outdrawn if a queen, king, or ace shows up. If no cards higher than a J appear, you're okay. Otherwise, better hope you hit the flush.

11g. [J♥10♥] 5♥A♥J♣ (Four to a flush, second pair)

Again, better hope you hit the flush since your Js aren't likely to be good.

11h. [J♥10♥] 9♥8♥2♣ (Four to a straight flush, two overcards)

This is a hand to get excited about. You'll hit the straight or better about 54 percent of the time, plus having the overcards. (By the way, you'd be happier hitting the straight, which would be the nuts, than hitting the flush which could be beaten by higher hearts.)

11i. [J♥10♥] Q♥K♥2♣ (Four to a straight flush, two overcards)

Okay, you've still got four to the straight flush but you're probably going to have to hit at least the straight to win. The advantage here over 11h is that if the flush comes in there is only one card, the A♥, which can beat you.

12. [A♦7♦] 10♣Q♥2♠ (No help, one overcard)

Here's the difference between having a good kicker and having a lousy kicker. In 9a above you have two cards to outdraw possible pairs. Here you have only one—your seven isn't going to do any good at all. You'll hit the ace about 13 percent of the time, a little better than 7 to 1 against.

13a. [Q♣Q♦] 9♣6♦2♥ (No help, overpair)

In a loose game you may be beat already. In a tight game, probably not (probably—not certainly), at least not from anyone having hit the flop. In any case, you'll improve to trip queens about 8.5 percent of the time, or about 11 to 1 against. If you don't improve and an ace or king shows up, then you may well be beat in any sort of game.

14b. [Q♣Q♦] K♣8♠2♥ (No help, overcard on the board)

If you have a pair in the pocket, what you don't want to see is a higher card on the board. Obviously, the lower your pocket pair the more likely it is that a higher card will pop up. When that happens, if anyone starts betting you're probably beat, but that pocket pair can be very difficult to muck. But muck it you should. At 11 to 1 against improving you're just going to waste a lot of money. (Then a queen pops up on the turn and you feel like shooting yourself.)

14c. [Q♣Q♦] K♠A♥2♣ (No help, two overcards on the board)

If you thought you were in trouble in 14b above, you're really in trouble now. Usually best to muck it if anyone starts getting excited.

14d. [Q♣Q♦] Q♥9♣2♥ (Trips, no overcards on the board)

These trips are a far different hand from the trips shown in 9h above wherein the pair is on the board and the trips are made with one of the whole cards. In that case you could conceivably be beaten already. In this case, you have the nuts for the time being. Keep an eye on the straight and flush draws, but against five opponents you'll win this about 80 percent of the time.

14e. [Q♣Q♦] Q♥A♥K♥ (Trips, two overcards on the board, possible straight and possible flush on the board)

In contrast to 7d above, your set of queens could conceivably be in sixth place at this point behind a royal flush, a flush, a straight, a set of aces and a set of kings. When the dust settles, however, you'll have whipped five random opponents about 51 percent of the time.

The Turn

15a. [A♠K♠] 10♣6♦2♥ 9♦(No help, two overcards)

You'll pair one or the other of your hole cards about 13 percent of the time, a bit better than 7 to 1 against. Be careful. There are now a possible straight, a straight draw and a flush draw on the board.

15b. [A♠K♠] 10♠6♠A♥5♦ (Four to a flush, top pair)

You'll hit the flush about 19.5 percent of the time, or a bit over 4 to 1 against. In 9d above you'd beat four random opponents about 75 percent of the time. The turn hasn't helped you and you'll still win about 70 percent of the time. That ace with top kicker is a goodie. How much difference does that king kicker make? If you have A♠2♠—which means you still have top pair and the flush draw—you'll only beat four opponents about 60 percent of the time, and your losses are going to be very expensive.

15c. [A♠K♠] Q♦10♥2♦3♥ (Four to an inside straight, two overcards)

At this point your inside-straight plus your overcard draws have diminished somewhat to 8 percent plus 13 percent which is 21 percent, or a bit better than 4 to 1 against.

15d. [A♠K♠] 10♦A♣2♥6♠ (Pair)

If you need to, you'll improve to two pair or trips, using your hole cards, about 11 percent of the time, or about 8 to 1 against. Now here's an interesting phenomenon: Having lost the flush draw, in contrast to 15b above, you're down to beating four opponents about 65 percent of the time. Here, if you lose the kicker as well and are playing with, say, A♠3♠, you're down to beating four opponents about 50 percent of the time. The kicker alone makes a 30 percent difference in numbers of wins.

15e. [A♠K♠] 10♦A♣K♥3♦ (Two Pair)

You'll improve to a full house about 8.7 percent of the time, about 10.5 to 1 against.

15f. [A♠K♠] A♦A♥5♣3♦ (Trips)

You'll hit a full house or better using your hole cards, about 8.7 percent of the time, about 10.5 to 1 against. Now, sure, if another 5 or another 3 comes on the river you'll have a full house too, but anyone else with an ace will tie you, i.e., your king kicker becomes useless, and you could be in third place behind four 5s and four 3s. Remember that when discussing improvement I'm talking about using your hole cards, not playing cards that everyone gets to use.

16a. [J♥10♥] 6♣5♠2♦9♥ (No help, two overcards)

Same as 15a above, except that your overcards aren't so good.

16b. [J♥10♥] 6♣5♠A♦9♥ (No help, no overcards)

There *may still* not be an ace out against you, but there

often will be. Now, there's also a possible straight out there as well. That means you're a Great Dane at this point. The best you can do is a pair of Js and you probably want to just get out now.

16c. [J♥10♥] 9♣8♦2♠3♦ (Four to a straight, two overcards)

The difference here from 15c above is that your straight is open on both ends. You'll hit the straight about 17 percent of the time, a little under 5 to 1 against. You also have two overcards to hit, but if you hit one of them someone else may have hit the straight.

16d. [J♥10♥] Q♠K♦2♣3♦ (Four to a straight, no overcards)

Although you still have four to an open-ended straight, this hand is definitely not as good as 16c above. There may already be Ks and Qs out against you, which means you *must* hit the straight to win. You no longer have hitting overcards among your outs.

16e. [J♥10♥] 5♥A♥2♣9♦ (Four to a flush, no overcards)

Here again, you probably have to hit the flush to win because there may be aces out against you already.

16f. [J♥10♥] 5♥2♥J♦9♠ (Four to a flush, top pair)

If no card higher than a jack appears on the river, you may be okay. Otherwise, you'll need to hit the flush. Watch out: there are six (count 'em) straight draws out there.[72]

16h. [J♥10♥] 9♥8♥2♣3♦ (Four to a straight flush, two overcards)

This hand isn't quite as exciting as it was in 11h. You'll hit the straight or better about 32 percent of the time, about 2 to 1 against, plus having the overcards. (You'd

[72] I hope you've tried counting them first. A-2-3-4-5, 2-3-4-5-6, 5-6-7-8-9, 7-8-9-10-J, 8-9-10-J-Q, 9-10-J-Q-K

still be happier hitting the straight, for the same reason as mentioned before—your hearts can be beaten by bigger hearts.)

16i.   [J♥10♥] Q♥K♥2♣3♦ (Four to a straight flush, two overcards on the board)

You've still got four to the straight flush but, again, you're probably going to have to hit at least the straight to win.

17.   [A♦7♦] 10♣Q♥2♠6♦ (No help, one overcard)

To win anything you're probably going to have to hit the ace. That will happen about 6.5 percent of the time, a bit worse than 14 to 1 against. Two bad you don't have two overcards.

18a.   [Q♣Q♦] 9♣6♦2♥J♠ (No help, overpair)

You still have a good shot at being best hand at this point. It's 22 to 1 against your hitting trip queens, so you'd better hope you still have the best hand. Note, however, that if a queen does come up you may lose to a straight.

18b.   [Q♣Q♦] K♣9♠2♥3♦ (No help, overcard on the board)

Are you still in this hand with that king on the board? Well, maybe no one has the kings. Are you sure?

18c.   [Q♣Q♦] K♠A♥2♣ (No help, two overcards on the board)

If you're still in this hand with a king *and* an ace on the board then you must be playing heads up against a pretty loose player. *You're* not the one making the mistake, are you?

18d.   [Q♣Q♦] Q♥9♣2♥3♦ (Trips, no overcards on the board)

Now the foot is in the other shoe: If you still have

opponents at this point, they must be pretty loose.

18e. [Q♣Q♦] Q♥A♥K♥3♦ (Trips, two overcards on the board, possible straight on the board)

If you still have opponents at this point you're either going to lose a big one or win a big one. It may be that the only improvement you want to see is the fourth queen, 45 to 1 against. If someone has been hanging in there with you to this point, you probably don't want to see another ace or king come up—it would be a shame to lose to aces or kings full. The only card besides the queen I would really like to see on the river would be a 3, preferably a 3♥.

Appendix 2

Poker Notes, Anomalies and Misconceptions

Rank of Poker Hands

Have you ever wondered why that when you make a low flush, say 10-high, it always seems that someone has a higher one, say an ace-high flush? Well, you've been cheated, that's why. The thing is, it isn't your opponent who cheated you, it's poker itself.

Like gems, the rarer a poker hand is the more valuable it's supposed to be. That's how we get the overall ranking of hands: beginning with the royal flush, each successive class of hands occurs with increasing frequency, as follows:

Number of Hands Possible in a 52-Card Deck	
Straight Flush	40
Four of a Kind	624
Full House	3,744
Flush	5,108
Straight	10,200
Three of a Kind	54,912
Two Pair	123,552
One Pair	1,098,240
No Pair	1,302,540
TOTAL	2,598,960

So, if there are only forty ways to make a straight flush and over a million ways to make one pair, we say that a straight flush beats one pair because it is statistically less likely to occur.

But there is another way we rank hands: by an arbitrary ranking of the cards. There are four 2s in a deck of cards and there are four aces in a deck of cards, but we have decided that an ace beats a 2—and all the other cards in between for that matter. This, of course, is why it makes so much difference in games like stud and Hold'em when you hold high cards: they're just as easy to get as low cards, but they win.

So why were you being cheated when your 10-high flush lost to an ace-high flush? Because the way we have things set up, it's much, much easier to get an ace-high flush! There are 1,972 ways to make an ace-high flush and only 276 ways to make a ten-high flush. A 10-high flush is therefore more than seven times more difficult to get than an ace-high flush! If a 10-high flush is a diamond, an ace-high flush is road gravel—but we've declared it more valuable.

Were we to rank individual hands *truly* following their rarity of occurrence, the list would look like this on the following page.

So now you know: when your two pair kings-up loses to three of a kind, you've lost to a hand that is over three times easier to get! I doubt that the publication of this list will change the way the world ranks poker hands, so what this means is that you have to be extra cautious. Go for the high cards and the bigger hands: they're easier to get—and they win!

Impossible

How many times have you had a hand like trips, an opponent has drawn one card to a flush, has made his hand and beaten you? Lots, right? Well, that's pretty strange because the odds against that happening are enormous. Four to a flush will show up in a five-card hand about 4 percent of the time. Then the player has to draw and hit, which as we all know will happen about 19 percent of the time. For both of those events to occur— one, get four to a flush, and two, hit on the draw—the combined

True Rank of Hands in Order of Difficulty to Hold		
Ways to make		
1	7-high flush	16	Inverted: 75-high beats 76-high, etc.
2	straight flush	40	By traditional arbitrary rank
3	8-high flush	56	Inverted: 85-high beats 86-high, etc
4	9-high flush	136	Inverted
5	10-high flush	276	Inverted
6	Jack-high flush	500	Inverted
7	four of a kind	624	By traditional arbitrary rank
8	Queen-high flush	836	Inverted
9	King-high flush	1,316	Inverted
10	Two-pair 3's	1,584	By traditional arbitrary rank
11	Ace-high flush	1,972	Inverted
12	Two-pair 4's	3,168	By traditional arbitrary rank
13	Full House	3,744	By traditional arbitrary rank
14	No pair 7-high	4,080	Inverted
15	Two-pair 5's	4,752	By traditional arbitrary rank
16	Two-pair 6's	6,336	By traditional arbitrary rank
17	Two-pair 7's	7,920	By traditional arbitrary rank
18	Two-pair 8's	9,504	By traditional arbitrary rank
19	Straight	10,200	By traditional arbitrary rank
20	Two-pair 9's	11,088	By traditional arbitrary rank
21	Two-pair 10's	12,672	By traditional arbitrary rank
22	Two-pair Jacks	14,256	By traditional arbitrary rank
23	No pair 8-high	14,280	Inverted
24	Two-pair Queens	15,840	By traditional arbitrary rank
25	Two-pair Kings	17,424	By traditional arbitrary rank
26	Two-pair Aces	19,008	By traditional arbitrary rank
27	No pair 9-high	34,680	Inverted
28	Three of a kind	54,912	By traditional arbitrary rank
29	No pair 10-high	70,380	Inverted
30	No pair Jack-high	127,500	Inverted
31	No pair Queen-high	213,180	Inverted
32	No pair King-high	335,580	Inverted
33	No pair Ace-high	502,860	Inverted
34	One Pair	1,098,240	Inverted kickers: AAQJ10 beats AAKQJ, etc.

probabilities are about 0.0076, or 0.8 percent of the time, which is about 130 to 1 against. For that to happen in conjunction with your having trips, which will happen a little over 2 percent of the time, the odds are over 6,000 to 1 against. But it happens (seems to happen) all the time.

Just remember: much of what mathematics tells you about poker, well, it ain't necessarily so.

How bad was your beat?

Back on page 83 of the main text I mentioned that a player had gone into a stupor, having been busted out on a 4 to 1 shot. Before discussing that getting beat on a 4 to 1 shot should not be stupor-inducing to a poker player, I mentioned that, actually, he had lost to a less than 2 to 1 shot. It was really about 1.84 to 1. Here's why it looked one way but was really another.

Our hero, we'll call him Tom, was playing Hold'em and had flopped the two top pair. However, the flop also contained two cards to a flush. There was about $3,000 in the pot, which was also about what Tom still had in front of him. He bet it all and one opponent (we'll call him Jerry), who had much more than that on the table and who turned out to have the flush draw, called. The turn was a blank, and the river brought the flush. Stupor. Since the turn had been a blank, Tom figured he had lost on the river, a 4 to 1 shot. Wrong.

All the betting was over with *two* cards to come. In terms of probabilities, that makes those two cards a unit; it doesn't matter if the desired card comes on the first or second draw, it was a two-card draw. A two-card draw to a flush gives you odds of 1.84 to 1 against hitting. With $6,000 in the pot and Jerry calling $3,000 he got a good deal, a little better than exact odds to make the call. That wasn't a bad beat at all, it was just business.[73]

[73.] If you include the times that Jerry will hit his flush and still lose because Tom has hit the full house, Jerry's odds go to about 1.88 to 1. Not enough difference to quibble over.

Imagine you're playing six-card draw (sure, home games often play six-card draw). You have four to a heart flush and draw two cards. Tom would say that if you look first at one card and it's not a heart, then you look at the other card and it *is* a heart, that you've made a 4 to 1 shot. He'd say you have to look at your cards simultaneously and see that one of them is a heart in order for two-card-draw odds to apply.

Going back to our original situation, let's say that Tom had had $12,000 on the table and that Jerry had at least that much as well. Now there are a couple of possible scenarios. In a no limit game, if Tom had bet the entire $12,000 into the $3,000 pot, Jerry would have only been getting 15,000 to 12,000, or 1.25 to 1 odds. It would have been a mistake for him to call. But why pick exactly $12,000? Because it's convenient to our next example.

If the game were pot limit, Tom could still only bet the $3,000 that was in the pot. However, Jerry is now facing a much different situation. Now he has to figure on:

1. Facing two, one-card draws, each at about 4 to 1 against, and each giving him pot odds of only 2 to 1 against. That is, he has to call $3,000 against $6,000 to make his flush on the turn. If he doesn't get it, he'll surely (if Tom does the right thing) be facing a $9,000 call to win $18,000 if he hits on the river. Both are bad business.

2. Calling all Tom's money, $12,000, to draw two cards to his flush, in other words, turning two one-card draws into one two-card draw. As we've seen before, Jerry's potential pot odds are short for trying to do that, 1.25 to 1.

Either way it would have been a mistake for Jerry to call—had Tom had more money on the table. Which brings us to our point: *Tom didn't have enough money left to protect his hand* and THAT is a situation that defeats short-money players over and over again. But what was poor Tom to do? He couldn't put more money on the table (in fact, he was in a tournament: not only could he not put more money on the table, he was going to be busted out if he lost what he had) and he was facing a situation in which he didn't have enough money to protect himself.

Here's the strategy, folks, and the thought process: Tom should have thought, "If someone has a flush draw, my betting what's in the pot will simply give him correct odds to go ahead and make the draw. My bet will be high-risk—I could be busted out—and will be meaningless in terms of protecting my hand." By now you, the reader, know what Tom should have done: he should have *checked*. Tom has to check and: (1) *hope* Jerry checks along (Jerry would probably be so thrilled to get a free draw to his flush that, in fact, he almost certainly would check along); (2) *hope* the flush doesn't hit on the turn. In this case, Tom could now bet his $3,000 before the river, creating 2 to 1 pot odds for what is now, really and truly, a 4 to 1 shot. If Jerry calls and hits on the river, well, he's made a mistake and just gotten lucky, that's all.

If the flush comes on the turn, Tom has saved his $3,000. If Jerry bets out on his flush draw, thus "inviting" Tom to give him proper odds by calling, Tom should just fold. Yes, even with the best hand at this point, he should just fold. Not having enough money in front of you to protect your hand is a helluva fix. You've got to bob and weave all over the place because your fists—your chips—are not strong enough to do any damage.

Short-handed Games

If you're playing in a game that incorporates some sort of fixed cost per round, either an ante or a blind, a short-handed game is a much different animal from a full-table game. In casino games the blinds stay the same whether there are ten players or three players. Take a $10–$20 game where the blinds total $15 per round. With ten players at the table each hand is costing you $1.50. With first and second round bets at $10 this lets you play pretty tightly if you want to. With three players, however, you are now paying $5.00 to get a hand. If you don't loosen up, your cost-per-hand is going to eat up all your chips.

In the limit game described in the main text, the dealer antes $5 for all players. When there are eight players in the game, each hand is costing 62.5 cents per player. When there are four players in the game, each hand is costing $1.25. Not only that, but . . .

With eight players, the limit game manages about 100 hands a session, therefore a player's "overhead" in antes for the session is $62.50. With four players, the limit game manages about 150 hands per session, which means that each player is paying out $187.50 in antes for the evening. That's what you have to win back just to break even. Tight play is going to kill you, not just because of the antes, but also . . .

In a full game, there will usually be enough action for a tight player to make some money when he plays. In a short-handed game this isn't necessarily true. So the tight player in this situation has two strikes against him: waiting to get "good" hands is too expensive, and when he gets them he doesn't make any money. Double whammy.

Median Hands

Here's some poker trivia that might win some bar bets for you.[74] Many poker books speculate over median hands. For example, "What's the median two pair hand?" often comes up. Well, I have some definitive answers for you.

It turns out there is no median two pair. How can that be? Well, the median two pair is in a nether world between JJ552 and JJ44A. There are 61,632 configurations of two pair that will beat JJ552, and 61,632 configurations of two pair that will lose

---

[74.] Modern law-suit mania, however, requires me to disclaim that this information might be wrong. So if you lose your bar bet you should have counted all the hands yourself and I don't want to hear about it—you have only yourself to blame.

to the next lower hand, JJ44A. In other words, the median is somewhere between these two hands.

The median overall poker hand lives in the same nether world. There are 1,298,460 hands that will beat AKQJ7, and there are 1,298,460 hands that will lose to AKQJ6.

This should help dissuade you should you ever be tempted to play Caribbean stud in a casino. Wow, is that game a rip-off! The way Caribbean stud works, you play a pat hand against the house. To receive your hand you must "ante"—we'll call it $10. If you look at your hand and decide it's a winner you must double your ante to "stay." If you "fold," you lose your ante. The problem is that the house will fold, declaring a "push" if the house doesn't have at least an A-K high to play with. When the house folds, of course, it doesn't lose anything.

Now, the lowest possible A-K high hand is AK432 which is in the 56.3187th percentile of all hands, meaning that over 43 percent of all poker hands are lower than AK432. Therefore, the house will NOT PAY YOUR WINNER as much as 43 percent of the time. Say you look at your hand and have trip 3s. You double your ante. The house dealer looks at his/her hand and 43 percent of the time will not have an A-K high and won't have to pay you off. Do you still want to play a game in which the house doesn't have pay up to 43 percent of your winners? Remember, if you have folded the house gets your "ante" whether or not it has a hand.

Limit Shock

Limit shock can hit a player both ways, either going up or coming down. If you're used to playing, say, $2–$4 limits and all of a sudden find yourself in a $20–$40 game or higher, the money, the game, the cards themselves often seem to take on a sinister, frightening personality. The cards are the cards—they don't know if you're betting $2 or $1,000 to see the flop and, theoretically, that's how you should look at it, too. But human nature dictates otherwise.

I said back on page 296 of the main text that one of the mistakes the pros make is to assume that a $20–$40 game is just as mechanical as a $3–$6 game. What I meant is that no one, repeat, no one faces a $40, $80, or $120 bet the same way he would face a $4, $8, or $12 bet. You *can* bluff someone out with a raise to $80 when that same person would have pooh-poohed a raise to $8 and called. I don't care *what* you try to tell me about pot odds, about forgetting the "real" value of money when you play, about its just being only chips: eighty bucks is eighty bucks and it simply *means* more—not just in terms of the game but to our entire being, our entire view of the material world—than does a measly eight bucks. We all have a built-in respect for the value of money that, even when we try to deny it, is always lurking somewhere inside us.

Now the other side of the coin: limit shock on the way down. Sometimes, when I get back from Vegas, or wherever I've been playing in $20–$40 games and higher, I'll sit down at the limit game with its $2–$5 spread and lose my shirt. Why? Because I haven't adjusted to the little stakes, don't take them seriously, get bored, don't pay attention—and overall play a really lousy game. This, obviously, is a disastrous attitude and I have to fight with myself to overcome it. You, at least, are now forewarned to be on the lookout for this attitude in yourself.

More about Knowing the Rules

There is, or was, a funny game played in British casinos called Irish. Irish is like Omaha in that you must use two cards from your hand and three from the board, but each player receives *six* cards down! I first ran into Irish at the Victoria Casino in London. The game was pot limit and dealer's choice within a range of allowable choices. One of the players chose Irish, and all of a sudden I find myself with six cards in my hand. Now, wait a minute, six cards? I'd better find out what this is all about. The dealer explained to me that I had to use two from my hand. Oh, like Omaha but with a shit-load of cards? That's right. Not having the slightest idea what a "good" starting hand might be, with all those cards to choose from, I call the opening bets to see the flop. The flop comes three spades and among my fistful of cards I have the K♠ and 3♠. It looks good so I bet out and get a few calls. The turn comes the 2♠, and I figure it's time for a question. "Now, hold on," say I, "If this is like Omaha, then one spade in my hand is not going to make a flush, right?" "Right," says the dealer. My concern is obvious: My K♠3♠ looks pretty good unless all someone else needed was one A♠. Feeling happier I bet out again. To shorten the story, the river was a dud, I bet out again, was called, and I had the winning hand.

Now here's the point of the story: The guy who called and lost immediately accused me of a "moody." Before getting into that, suffice it to say that I successfully explained the logical need for my questions and was ruled the winner.

Now, what's a "moody"? Specific to this example, in British poker you are not allowed to "coffeehouse", which is one of the finer points of American poker. You are not allowed to mislead the other players as to the value of your hand by talking about it. You can have a heart attack, you can wet your pants, you can faint, you can break into a cold sweat, you can pull out your rosary, but you *can't talk* about it. If you do, it's a "moody." The guy who accused me of a moody was alleging that I had deliberately made him think I only had one spade in my hand by asking if one spade could be used. In Las Vegas or California, or just about anywhere else, he would have been laughed out of the casino, but in Britain he had a valid and serious point: had the dealer (or floorman) ruled in his favor as to the moody, my hand would have been dead. I bring this up not as a strategic point for Omaha or Irish, but once again to point out: MAKE SURE YOU KNOW THE DAMN RULES. There are some really bizarre and unexpected rules out there that you'd never be able to guess—you have to ask.

An odd final word about Irish. When I was again in England

a couple years later they were still playing Irish, but Irish wasn't Irish any more; it had mutated into a kind of super-pineapple Hold'em. Each player still initially receives six cards but then ends up throwing four of them away. Progress, I guess.

Appendix 3

Europoker

have often been accused of not playing with a full deck, but the only times I'm likely to admit that this is true are when I've been playing poker abroad. Although the title of this section is "Europoker", stripped-deck poker is played throughout the world. In fact, just about the only place I know of where it is exceedingly rare to find stripped-deck poker being played is in the United States. Sort of like soccer, I guess, and even that is changing. Who knows? Maybe Europoker will catch on in the U.S. as well, although I sort of doubt it. Nonetheless, as part of your well-rounded poker education you should at least be aware of what it's all about.

The first thing to remember is the number eleven. That is what determines how many cards are removed from a fifty-two card deck. If there are four players, the 2s through 6s will be removed, leaving 7 as the lowest card. 7 (card) + 4 (players) = 11. See? So, if there are five players, the 6 will be the lowest card and so forth. It is rare to find a Europoker game with more than five players. Usually, there are only two types of game played: five card draw, often called "closed" poker, and five card stud, often called "open" poker. Either way, the stripped deck presents some anomalies that require some getting used to.

The first thing is to be able to recognize A-7-8-9-10, or A-6-7-8-9 as the lowest straight, the Europoker equivalent of the wheel. It just doesn't look right, does it?

A far more serious difference is that *a flush beats a full house,* which to most Americans is like having the batter run to third base first. The reason a flush beats a full house is that as soon as you take even one number, like the 2s, out of a fifty-two card deck, a flush becomes statistically more difficult to get than a full house. So it makes sense. Believe me, though, if you're not used to this and don't keep reminding yourself, you can make some very serious mistakes. The complete chart on page 365 shows all the various statistical differences.

In terms of strategy, Europoker is often much more of a straight *card* game than is "normal" poker. With fewer cards it becomes much easier and much more obvious to make estimates of probabilities. Not only is it easier to figure out what your opponent may have, but it becomes easier to predict what they—and you—are likely to get. Let's say there are four of you playing stud so you're playing with thirty-two cards, 7 to the ace. By the fourth card, you're sitting on trips and one of your opponents clearly has four to a straight. Say he needs a queen or a 7. You can see thirteen cards and no queens nor 7s. That leaves nineteen unknown cards, as many as eight of which may still be live to help your opponent. He's looking at less than 1.4 to 1 against hitting. You'd better hope that your cards are live too. Say he needs a jack for an inside straight. In "normal" poker his situation would almost be laughable; in Europoker it may not be. If there are no jacks out, he's still only looking at less than 4 to 1 against hitting.

If you're playing five card draw, here are some more surprises, as compared to the "normal" fifty-two card deck:

Approximate Odds Against					
Hand	Draw	Hit	28 cards	32 cards	52 cards
1 pair	3 cards	2 pair	2.5 to 1	3 to 1	5+ to 1
		trips	4.5 to 1	5 to 1	8 to 1
		full house	26 to 1	35 to 1	97 to 1
		fours	108 to 1	142 to 1	359 to 1
2 pair	1 card	full house	5 to 1	6 to 1	11 to 1
trips	2 cards	full house	7 to 1	8.5 to 1	15.5 to 1
		fours	11.5 to 1	13.5 to 1	22.5 to 1
4-straight	1 card	straight	2 to 1	2.5 to 1	5 to 1
4-flush	1 card	flush	7 to 1	6 to 1	4+ to 1

EUROPOKER—HANDS AS COMPARED TO FULL DECK

Cards Used	# of Players*	St. Flushes	Quads	Full Houses	Flushes**	Straights	Trips	Two Pair	One Pair	No Pair	All Hands
2 to the A	9	40	624	3,744	5,108	10,200	54,912	123,552	1,098,240	1,302,540	2,598,960
% of all hands		0.0015%	0.0240%	0.1441%	0.1965%	0.3925%	2.1128%	4.7539%	42.2569%	50.1177%	100.0000%
3 to the A	8	36	528	3,168	3,132	9,180	42,240	95,040	760,320	798,660	1,712,304
% of all hands		0.0021%	0.0308%	0.1850%	0.1829%	0.5361%	2.4669%	5.5504%	44.4033%	46.6424%	100.0000%
4 to the A	7	32	440	2,640	1,816	8,160	31,680	71,280	506,880	463,080	1,086,008
% of all hands		0.0029%	0.0405%	0.2431%	0.1672%	0.7514%	2.9171%	6.5635%	46.6737%	42.6406%	100.0000%
5 to the A	6	28	360	2,160	980	7,140	23,040	51,840	322,560	249,900	658,008
% of all hands		0.0043%	0.0547%	0.3283%	0.1489%	1.0851%	3.5015%	7.8783%	49.0207%	37.9783%	100.0000%
6 to the A	5	24	288	1,728	480	6,120	16,128	36,288	193,536	122,400	376,992
% of all hands		0.0064%	0.0764%	0.4584%	0.1273%	1.6234%	4.2781%	9.6257%	51.3369%	32.4675%	100.0000%
7 to the A	4	20	224	1,344	204	5,100	10,752	24,192	107,520	52,020	201,376
% of all hands		0.0099%	0.1112%	0.6674%	0.1013%	2.5326%	5.3393%	12.0133%	53.3927%	25.8323%	100.0000%
8 to the A	3	16	168	1,008	68	4,080	6,720	15,120	53,760	17,340	98,280
% of all hands		0.0163%	0.1709%	1.0256%	0.0692%	4.1514%	6.8376%	15.3846%	54.7009%	17.6435%	100.0000%
9 to the A	2	12	120	720	12	3,060	3,840	8,640	23,040	3,060	42,504
% of all hands		0.0282%	0.2823%	1.6940%	0.0282%	7.1993%	9.0344%	20.3275%	54.2067%	7.1993%	100.0000%

indicates flushes beat full house

* Number of players + lowest card = 11
** Excluding Straight Flushes

Appendix 4

Glossary of Standard Poker English

ace-high: A flush or a no-pair hand in which the ace is the high card.

ace-to-five: Another name for a low game in which the wheel is low. Usually refers to low five card draw. See *wheel*.

action: Betting. A tight game has little action; a loose game has a lot.

active player: A player who is still involved in the pot. A player who has not folded.

advertise: To bluff in order to get caught, thus showing the other players that you do bluff.

ahead: Winning.

all in: To bet, or to have bet, all the money a player has on the table. An *all-in* player has no more money with which to bet.

American Airlines: A pair of aces in the *pocket* in Hold'em.

ante: An amount of money put in the pot by each player, or by the dealer on behalf of all the players, before receiving any cards.

anything opens: See *Guts*.

back door: A hand made unexpectedly by a player who was trying to hit some other hand.

backer: A person who stakes a poker player to a particular game, or to play in general.

back into: To win a pot unexpectedly: "I had a busted flush, but I *backed into* the low."

back to back: Usually refers to the first two cards in five card stud, when paired, as in: a pair of aces, *back to back*.

bad beat: To lose against the odds.

Baskin-Robbins: A 3 and an ace (thirty-one flavors) in the pocket in Hold'em.

belly-buster: See *Gutshot*.

bet blind: To bet without having seen one's cards. Different from *blind,* which see.

bet into: To bet first against an opponent whose hand seems, *a priori,* to be better than the bettor's hand.

bet the pot: To bet the same amount of money as contained in the pot at the moment the bet is made.

betting limit: The maximum amount that may be bet at any given time or during any given betting round.

betting rounds: When playing a hand, the intervals during which each active player has the opportunity to bet, check, raise, or fold.

bicycle: A somewhat antiquated synonym for *the wheel,* A-2-3-4-5, which is either the lowest possible straight in high poker, or the best possible hand in low poker when straights and flushes are not considered.

Big Slick: The A-K off suit in the *pocket* in Hold'em.

blind: Especially in casino or public card room games, a "blind" bet is often required of the first player, or the first two players, to the left of the dealer. Those players are required to "bet" without having as yet received any cards. These blind bets not only take the place of the ante, but preclude checking in the first betting round as each player must either *call* or *raise* the blind, or fold. When two players are required to make this "bet" the first usually must put in one-half of a full betting unit; this is the *small blind*. In a $10–$20 game, in which the minimum bet is $10, the *small blind* would be $5. The *big blind,* required of the player immediately to the left of the *small blind,* is a full betting unit, in this case $10.

bluff: Reread Chapter 6 if you don't know what a bluff is.

board: (1) The cards turned face up on the table for common use by all players in games such as Hold'em and Omaha. (2) In stud, a player's face-up cards.

board games: Poker variations such as Hold'em and Omaha in which the players use common cards turned face up on the table.

boat: Full house.

bobtail: An *open-ended straight,* which see.

boss hand: The strongest hand at the moment but, usually, with more cards to come which may lower its status. Sometimes used interchangeably with *the nuts,* which see.

bottom dealer: A card cheat who is skilled at dealing cards off the bottom of the deck.

break: To cause a player to lose all his money, usually necessitating his withdrawal from the game, or worse: "That one hand broke John and he had to move into the YMCA."

break up: (1) To end the poker session, all or most players having left. (2) To discard from and draw to a previously pat hand: "I broke up my pat 8-low to draw to a 6."

bring it in: Especially in casino stud games, the first player required to bet is said to *bring it in.*

Broderick Crawford: A 10 and a 4 in the pocket in Hold'em.

buck: When a professional dealer is dealing the cards in games such as Hold'em, Omaha, or Draw—that is, games other than Stud—the putative dealer among the players is designated by what in modern times is called *the button.* In times past, this was known as the *buck.* Many writers ascribe this name to the fact that *the buck* was a knife with a buckhorn handle that was unceremoniously stuck in the table in front of the dealer. Thus, the expression "passing the buck" refers not to dollars, but to the buckhorn-handled knife. Whether or not this is accurate depends upon whom one asks.

bullet: An ace.

bump: To raise.

burn: To deal the top card off the deck into the discards, rather than put it into play. This is done in stud and *board games* to preclude the possibility of a player's being able to discern the next card from, perhaps, markings on the cards.

burp: A soniferous expulsion of gasses from the body which is allowed at poker games but is not allowed at home nor in fancy restaurants.

bust: (1) A worthless hand. (2) To cause a player to lose all his money.

busted: Said of a player who has lost all his money and has, therefore, had to leave the game.

busted hand: Usually referring to an unsuccessful flush or straight draw, a *come hand* which has missed and is therefore worthless.

buy-in: (1) The minimum amount of money required to enter a particular game. (2) The recommended amount of money required to enter a particular game. For example: The buy-in requirement in most casinos for a $10–$20 limit game is $100. That won't get you very far. The recommended—by me—buy-in for any game is four times the maximum bet. If you can't beat a $10–$20 game with $800, or a $5–$10 game with $400, better find another game.

by me: A phrase used synonymously with *"check"* or *"pass."*

California low: Synonym for *the wheel,* which see.

call: To put money in the pot in response to another player's bet which does not exceed the amount of that player's bet.

calling station: A player who *calls* too often, failing to recognize or believe that he's beaten.

card odds: The ratio of the favorable chances of improving a hand to the unfavorable chances. A function of the number cards that will improve the hand against the number of cards that will not.

card shark: A popular—though not inappropriate—malapropism for *card sharp*.

card sharp: (1) A cheater. (2) An expert player.

cards speak: (1) The principle that a player's inability to discern and/or announce the proper rank of his hand in the showdown is of no detriment to the true value of his hand. (2) In high-low poker, the method of determining the (usually) two winners by simply showing the hands.

case (card): The last of a particular rank or suit of cards available. In stud, if the A♦, A♥ and A♠ are showing, the A♣ is the *case* ace.

cash in: To leave a poker game and change one's chips back into currency.

cash game: Modern terminology used to differentiate from a tournament.

cash out: Same as *cash in*. In what other language in the world would cash *in* and cash *out* mean the same thing? Have you ever noticed that "to run *up* a bill" is not the opposite of "to run *down* a pedestrian"?

catch-up: See *playing catch up*.

chase: To try to *outdraw* a better hand.

check: (1) To bet nothing. (2) A poker chip.

check copping: A method by which a player (or a dealer) can pass his hand over the pot and surreptitiously remove chips. This is done either by crimping the palm in such a way as to hold the chip, or by actually putting sticky stuff on the palm of the hand which makes the chips adhere to the palm. A $100 chip is the same size and weight as a $1 chip. Keep an eye out: in a big game with many hundreds or thousands of dollars in the pot, it's easy to overlook one measly $100 chip.

check-raise: To check, hoping to induce another player to bet so that the player who checked can then raise.

chip runner: An employee of a casino or public card room who will take players' cash at the table and exchange it for chips to be used in the game.

cinch: A synonym for *nuts*.

coffeehouse: To mislead opponents as to the value of your hand by talking about it. (Whether this is written as one word or two—*coffee house*—in Standard Poker English depends upon who you ask. I prefer it as one word.)

cold: Used to describe a player on a losing streak, or the cards that seem to be causing that streak: "My cards have been running cold."

cold call: To call a raised bet, not having previously called the unraised bet. If a player has called a $10 bet which is subsequently raised to $20, this is not a *cold call*. If the player has yet to call any bet because the action has not yet gotten around to him, then he calls when the bet has been raised ahead of him, that is a *cold call*.

cold deck: A stacked deck brought into the game by a cheat.

come bluff: A bet which is made when the bettor holds a *come hand*. The strategy of the bet is to try to win the pot without actually having to hit the hand. The added *out,* if the *come bluff* is called, is that the bettor may actually hit the hand and win on the hand's merit.

come hand: A hand which is incomplete at a given moment, e.g., a four-flush or a four-straight, but may become complete if there is still opportunity to draw.

come, on the: see *on the come*.

connectors: Two cards in the pocket in Hold'em that can combine to make a straight, e.g., J-10, 7-6. See also *gapped connectors* and *suited connectors*.

court card: Any face card: jack, queen, or king.

cowboy: (1) A wild and loose player. (2) slang for a king.

cracked (to get): To lose with a hand that at one point was a favorite. "My pocket rockets got *cracked* three times in a row."

cutter: The person in a casino game, usually but not always the house dealer, in charge of taking the house *rake* from the pot.

dead card: (1) A card that is no longer in play because it has been discarded or is so far down in the deck as to be superfluous to the deal. For example: "The dealer flashed the ace of spades on the bottom so I knew it was dead." (2) In stud, a card which is no longer available for use in a player's hand because it is already showing in another player's hand.

dead cert: Principally a British expression, synonymous with "sure thing" or *nuts*.

dead hand: A hand which, usually as a consequence of one or another breach of the rules, is no longer playable.

dead man's hand: On August 2, 1876, James Butler "Wild Bill" Hickok was shot from behind and killed by a man named Jack McCall while playing poker in a saloon in Deadwood, Dakota Territory. Legend has it he was holding two pair, aces, and 8s, as he died. Some say the aces and the 8s were all black (no one seems to know what the kicker was). Over 120 years later, at this writing, two pair, aces, and 8s, are still known as the *dead man's hand*. Some have adapted this sobriquet to Hold'em for A-8 in the pocket.

dead money: Money left in the pot by players who are no longer active.

dealer's choice: A poker session in which either the actual dealer (as in a home game) or the putative dealer (as in a casino game with a house dealer present) may choose which variation of poker is to be played. Sometimes the choice applies to a particular hand, changing with the next deal; sometimes it applies to one round in which case if there are six players in the game that particular variation of poker will be played seven times, back to the dealer who called for it.

defensive bet: Different from the *defensive bluff*, which see, this is a small bet made in an attempt to stop an opponent from making an even bigger bet.

defensive bluff: A bet made by a player whose cards might, just might, win on their own but, in that player's opinion, need a boost in the form of a bet. In other words, that player is hoping his opposition will fold, not necessitating a showdown.

deuce: Slang for a 2.

deuce-to-the-seven: The system for ranking low hands whereby the lowest possible hand is 7-5-4-3-2 off suit. The ace is always high and straights and flushes are considered as high hands.

dog: Short for *underdog,* which see.

dog it: To fold the winning hand, or the leading hand at the moment.

door card: In stud games, the first card dealt face up.

double belly buster: A simultaneous draw to two inside straights, which, therefore, gives the player the same odds as drawing to one, open-ended straight. For example: In Stud or Hold'em (which of these cards may be in the hole or in the pocket is irrelevant to this example) on the sixth card, you hold: Q J 9 8 6 5. Either a 7 or a 10 will make a straight, even though both are *inside straights.*

double pop: To reraise a first raise.

down cards: In stud, the *hole cards,* which see.

down the river: Another name for seven card stud. Also, sometimes refers to the last, seventh, card.

down to the green: Out of money.

draw: (1) In draw poker, to discard cards from the hand and replace them with others from the deck. (2) In stud poker or board games, to keep playing in the attempt to hit a particular hand.

draw dead: To attempt to improve a hand which, even when improved to its maximum potential, will still lose. For example:

to try to improve to a flush when another player already has a full house.

draw light: To take chips from the pot in a limit game to indicate how much a player who is out of money on the table owes to the pot.

draw out: To improve a hand and beat an opponent whose hand was previously superior. Same as *outdraw*.

draw poker: A game in which none of a player's cards are exposed, and which may be exchanged for cards from the deck.

draw to: To draw, referring to a specific hand the player wants to improve: to draw to a pair, to draw to a flush, etc.

driver's seat: A player who apparently has the strongest hand at the moment is "in the driver's seat."

drop: (1) Same as to *fold*. (2) To lose: "I *dropped* $500 in that game."

early position: The first player(s) to have to act in a betting round.

edge: (1) A player's advantage over other players due to his superior skill. (2) A somewhat archaic term for an ante made by the dealer on behalf of all the players.

face card: Any king, queen or jack.

false cut: Used by cheaters to return the deck to its original, stacked, order.

false openers: A hand which does not contain the required minimum for opening but which has been used to open the pot, nonetheless, either by mistake or design.

false shuffle: Used by cheaters who appear to be shuffling the deck, but who are actually keeping the cards in the desired order.

family pot: A hand in which all the players at the table remain active.

fart: see *burp*.

fast company: Wily, experienced gamblers.

fatten (the pot): To increase the amount of money in the pot.

favorite: The likely winner.

Fifth Street: (1) In stud, the fifth card. (2) In Hold'em and Omaha, the fifth card on the board (which is actually the seventh card in active hands).

fill: To complete a hand, such as a flush, straight or full house.

fill up: Usually refers to completing a full house.

fish: A sucker.

flat limit: A betting limit that does not vary throughout the betting rounds.

floorman, floorperson, floorwoman: A supervisor in a casino or public poker room.

flop: (1) The first three common, or board, cards dealt simultaneously in Hold'em or Omaha. (2) To make a particular hand or come hand using those cards and the hole cards: to flop a set; to flop a straight; to flop a flush draw.

flush: see *poker hands*

fold: To opt not to play by refusing to call another player's bet.

four flush, four straight: Four cards to a flush or a straight

four of a kind: see *poker hands*

Fourth Street: (1) In stud, the fourth card dealt. (2) In Hold'em and Omaha, the fourth card on the board (which is actually the sixth card in active hands).

free card: A card received by a player, usually in stud or board games, without his having had to pay or call a bet to receive it.

free ride: To be able to stay in a hand without having to call a bet. Usually occurs when all players check.

freeze-out: A game (poker session) in which a player must quit when he has lost all his table stake. Usually, all players are required to stay in the game (as in a tournament) until one player has won all the chips.

full house: see *poker hands*

geese: More than one goose.

goose: A *sucker*.

guts (to open): Five card draw with no opening requirements. As different from "Jacks or better."

gutshot: A draw to an inside straight, or having successfully made that draw.

heads up: Poker between just two players.

help: To improve a hand.

high-low: A variation of poker in which the pot is divided between the high winner and the low winner.

high roller: A gambler for very high stakes.

hit: To make the hand or receive the card a player was hoping for.

hole: In stud or board games, the collection of cards in a player's hand which are not visible to the other players.

hole card: A card in the hole.

hook: Slang for a jack.

house: A full house.

ignorant end: The low end of a straight; same as *suck end*.

implied pot odds: Same as *potential pot odds*.

in: To be active during a hand, to call a bet: "I'm in."

in the dark: Same as to bet blind; to bet without seeing one's cards.

in the middle: Used to describe a player who is caught between two raising players.

in the pocket: Same as *in the hole*.

inside straight: Four cards to a straight, with the missing card being in the middle of the sequence: 8 9 _ J Q.

iron ass: Same as *leather ass*.

jacks-back: A variation of draw in which a pair of jacks or better is required to open for high. If no player opens, the hand is played for low.

jam pot: A pot in which several players are creating a lot of action by raising and reraising.

kibitzer: A nonplaying spectator who takes a seemingly unwarranted interest in the game.

kick: To raise

kicker: (1) The extra card in a hand such as two pair: in AAKK3 the 3 is the kicker. (2) Your next highest card after considering your hand. In Hold'em, if a player holds AQ and hits a pair of aces, the queen is his kicker. If he hits a pair of queens, the ace is his kicker.

knave: Antiquated slang for a jack.

knock: Same as *knuckle,* but less anatomically specific.

knuckle: (1) To rap the table (ostensibly with the knuckles) to check. (2) To rap the table to indicate *pat.*

Ku Klux Klan: Slang for three kings, used principally in the southern U.S.

lady: Slang for a queen.

late position: At a full table, the last two or three players to have to act.

lay down: (1) Usually means to *fold.* (2) Can also mean to show one's hand at the end of a hand.

lead off: Same as *bring it in.*

leak: (1) A weakness in a player's playing style or strategy. (2) A nonpoker gambling habit by which a player loses his poker winnings.

leather ass: (1) A tight, patient player. (2) Patience itself: "You need a leather ass to play in that game."

legging: Same as *slow playing.*

light: To have insufficient money to call one or more bets during a hand. See *draw light.*

little blind: Same as *small blind.* See *blind.*

limit poker: A game in which the maximum, and sometimes the minimum, bet is stipulated by rule or agreement of the players.

limp in: To call with a weak or marginal hand.

live card: A card which is still in play, apparently still available for use in improving a hand.

live one: Same as *sucker,* but a rich one.

lock: Same as *nuts.*

long run (the): The period of time required (infinity) for theoretical probabilities to be accurate.

look: To call a bet.

looking down s.o.'s throat: To have an opponent *nutted.*

looking out the window: Describes a player who is not paying attention to the game.

loose: Describes a player who (or a style of play that) apparently attempts to defy the odds.

lowball: A variation of poker in which the lowest hand wins. Sometimes used only to refer to ace-to-five low draw.

low poker: The general term for the variation of poker in which the lowest hand wins.

make: (1) To shuffle the deck. (2) To fill a hand: "I *made* a flush on the river."

main pot: In table stakes games, the pot created by all the active players before one or more of them ran out of money thus necessitating the creation of a *side pot.*

mark: (1) To use illegal means to render cards identifiable. (2) A *sucker.*

marker: An IOU, but normally used specifically to refer to gambling debts.

matching card: A card that helps a player's hand.

mechanic: A cheater whose specialty is manipulating the deck.

mechanic's grip: The peculiar way a mechanic tends to hold the deck when dealing, can be a giveaway.

middle position: In between the first and last players to have to act.

misdeal: A deal which is sufficiently incorrect, for one reason or another, to necessitate redealing the cards. Rules on what constitutes a *misdeal* vary greatly.

miss: To fail to complete one's hand.

moody: In British poker: (1) A move such as betting or calling out of turn which is made to influence another player's actions. (2) *Coffeehousing* or other misleading talk concerning the value or potential of one's hand.

move in: (1) To bet all one's money, to go *all in*. (2) What you have to do with your brother-in-law when you've lost your house in a poker game.

muck: (1) To throw away, *fold,* one's hand. (2) The discard pile.

mug: A *sucker*.

no limit: A game in which the only restriction as to the amount a player can bet, or be required to call, is the amount of money he has on the table.

nut: A gambler's overhead or living expenses.

nut flush: In Hold'em and Omaha, the best possible flush.

nut player: A player who tends to play only very strong hands.

nuts (the): (1) The certain winner, the unbeatable hand. (2) The best possible hand at a given moment in a hand.

nutted: In stud, a player who has an apparently inferior hand to that of another player is said to be *nutted*.

odds: The ratio of favorable chances to unfavorable chances. See also *card odds* and *pot odds*.

odds on: Odds in favor. That is, there is a greater than 50 percent chance of a favorable outcome.

off-suit: Cards that are not of the same suit.

on the come: To hold an incomplete hand such as a four-flush and hoping for improvement from cards yet to be received.

one-way straight: Four to a straight that can only be completed by hitting one card on the end: AKQJ or 432A.

on tilt: Used to describe a player whose judgment and ability have become diminished, usually as the result of a series of losses or *bad beats*.

open: To make the first bet.

open-ended straight: Four to a straight that can be completed by hitting a card on either end: 9876 (the 10 or the 5 will complete the straight).

outdraw: To improve one's hand and beat an opponent whose hand was previously superior. Same as *draw out*.

outs: The cards available to improve a hand. When a player starts counting his *outs* it usually indicates that he is currently a big *dog*.

overcard: A card in the hole or pocket that is of higher rank than any card showing on the board. Conversely, a card on the board that is of higher rank than any cards in a player's hole or pocket.

overlays: In stud, cards that are higher in rank than any opponent's cards.

overpair: In Hold'em, a pair in the pocket that is of higher rank than any card on the board.

pace: The overall speed with which a game progresses.

paint: Any king, queen or jack.

pass: (1) To check. (2) To fold.

pat hand: A complete poker hand dealt before the draw.

picked off: To get caught bluffing.

play back: To reraise.

play behind: In a table stakes game, usually in a casino or public card room, if a player has asked for more chips the *chip runner* will count the player's money and announce to the dealer that player so and so is "*Playing* X dollars *behind.*" In other words, he is playing money that is not yet on the table. The casino will enforce that player's obligation to put whatever money he subsequently bets into the pot.

play catch-up: Same as *chase*.

pocket: Usually refers to the first two cards dealt face down to each player in Hold'em. Sometimes refers to the *hole cards* in stud.

pocket rockets: A pair of aces in the *pocket*.

poker hand: A poker hand is made up of five cards, never more. In the 160 years or so that poker has been around, many different combinations of five cards have been recognized as ranked hands. With virtually no exceptions, when using a deck of fifty-two cards modern poker recognizes *only* the following hands, in descending order of rank:

Royal flush: The highest of the straight flushes, 10 J Q K A of the same suit.

Straight flush: Any cards in consecutive sequence from A 2 3 4 5 (lowest) to 9 10 J Q K (highest), of the same suit.

Four of a kind: Any four cards of the same rank plus a fifth card, from 2 2 2 2 X (lowest) to A A A A X (highest).

Full house: Any three cards of the same rank combined with any two cards of another rank from 2 2 2 3 3 (lowest) to A A A K K (highest).

Flush: Any five cards not in sequence, of the same suit, from 7 5 4 3 2 (lowest) to A K Q J 9 (highest)

Straight: Any five cards in consecutive sequence, not of the same suit from A 2 3 4 5 (lowest) to 10 J Q K A (highest).

Three of a kind: Any three cards of the same rank combined with any two other cards that are not a pair, from 2 2 2 X Y (lowest) to A A A X Y (highest).

Two pair: Any two cards of the same rank combined with any two other cards of the same rank plus an extra card, from 3 3 2 2 4 (lowest) to A A K K Q (highest).

One pair: Any two cards of the same rank combined with any three other cards of different ranks, from 2 2 5 4 3 (lowest) to A A K Q J (highest).

No pair: Any five nonsequential cards that are not suited nor

are any of the same rank, from 7 5 4 3 2 (lowest) to A K
Q J 9 (highest).

pony up: To ante.

position: (1) A player's place in the order of betting. (2) Where
a player is seated in relation to other players.

pot: The total money bet during a hand.

potential pot odds: The amount of money already in the pot,
plus the amount which may be added to the pot by other
players, usually in subsequent betting rounds, as a ratio to
the amount of money a player is contemplating putting in
the pot at the moment.

pot limit: A system of restricting the maximum allowable bet to the
equivalent of the size of the pot at the moment the bet is made.

pot odds: The amount of money already in the pot as a ratio to the
amount of money a player is contemplating putting in the pot.

prop: A professional poker player who receives a salary from a
casino or public card room (in the case of California card
rooms he may also be exempted from paying the seat rental),
but who plays with his own money. A *prop* will usually have
a particular variety of games and range of stakes within which
the house uses him to shore up short-handed games or to get
games started. Short for "proposition player." See also *shill*.

quads: Slang for four of a kind

quorum: The assumed requisite number of players to start a
poker game. "Assumed" because poker can be played quite
happily by two people, but many players will refuse to begin
a game unless there are four, five, or more.

rabbit: A timid *sucker*.

rabbit hunting: (1) To go through the *muck* to see what cards
have been discarded. (2) After folding, to ask to see the next
card off the deck, the card that would have gone to that player
had he not folded.

rag: A card of low denomination.

railbird: A spectator.

raise: To increase the amount of a bet made previously by another player.

rake: The percentage of each pot the house takes as a fee.

rap pat: To indicate by rapping on the table that one doesn't wish to draw any cards.

rat hole: To take money off the table in a table stakes game.

read: To try to discern the value of an opponent's hand through analysis of his behavior.

readers: Marked cards. Cards which have been tampered with in some way to make them identifiable from the back.

represent: To attempt to create the illusion of having a particular hand when one doesn't actually have it.

reraise: To increase a bet which has already been increased by at least one raise. To raise the raiser.

ring game: Used to indicate a "regular" poker game as different from tournament play.

river: (1) The fifth and last board card in Hold'em. (2) To make a hand using that card.

rock: A tight player.

rolled up: In seven card stud, refers to the first three cards when they are all of the same rank: *rolled up* jacks.

sandbag: To *slow play* a strong hand, usually with the intention of *check-raising* if someone bets.

scoop: To win both halves of the pot in a high-low game.

see: to call a bet.

semi-bluff: Same as a *come bluff.*

set: Slang for three of a kind, usually in Hold'em, when the three of a kind consist of a pair in the pocket and one card from the board.

set (a player) in: To bet an amount sufficient to make a player go *all in* if he calls.

shill: Same as a *prop*, except that a *shill* plays with the house's money.

short money: A lesser amount of money than is necessary to contend on an equal financial footing in a poker game.

shorts: A pair of lower rank than jacks in five card draw, jacks or better to open.

showdown: The final act, showing the hands, that determines the winner and loser of a hand.

shy: Same as *light*

sidecard: Same as *kicker*.

side pot: In a table stakes game, the pot that is contested by the active players who have continued to bet once one player has gone *all in*.

Sixth Street: In seven card stud, the sixth card.

sixty-four: The system for ranking low hands in low poker whereby the ace is considered the lowest card, but straights and flushes are counted as high hands. The best low hand therefore is 6 4 3 2 A off-suit.

slowplay: To disguise a very strong hand by checking or simply calling a bet rather than raising, thereby hoping to keep as many players in the hand as possible and, thus, win more money.

small blind: Same as *little blind*. See *blind*.

snapped off: Same as *picked off*.

soup: Same as *muck*.

squeeze: To look slowly at one's cards.

stack: The chips a player has in front of him.

stake: (1) The amount of money a player has with which to play. (2) To furnish a player with money with which to play.

stand pat: In draw, to refuse to draw cards to one's hand.

stay: To remain active in a hand by calling a bet.

steal a pot: To bluff and win by virtue of not being called.

steaming: Same as *on tilt*.

stranger: A card that does nothing to help one's hand.

string bet: A call and raise made in two parts with a pause before announcing the intention to raise. Considered illegal in most casino and many private games as it is often a ploy to gauge other players' reactions to the call before deciding to raise.

stuck: Slang for losing.

sucker: They say that if you can't spot the sucker at the table, it's you.

suited: Cards of the same suit.

sweep: Same as *scoop*.

swing: In high-low to declare both ways in an attempt to win both halves of the pot.

table stakes: Whether in *limit poker, pot limit,* or *no limit,* the general principle that a player may not bet nor be forced to call more money than he has on the table.

tap: (1) To bet all one's money. (2) To force another player to bet all his money.

tapped out: Out of money.

tell: An unconscious habit or mannerism which betrays the strength or weakness of one's hand.

Third Street: In stud, the third card dealt.

three of a kind: See *poker hand*.

ticket: Slang for a card.

tight: Conservative, cautious play.

tilt: See *on tilt*.

time: Refers to the charge for seat rental in some casinos and public card rooms.

toke: To tip the dealer.

trey: Slang for a 3.

trips: Slang for three of a kind.

turn: The fourth board card in Hold'em.

two pair: See *poker hand*.

underdog: A player who is facing unfavorable odds and is likely to lose.

under the gun: The first player required to act in a given betting round.

unglued: Same as *on tilt*.

up card: In stud, the cards which are dealt face up to each player.

walk: To let the blind bettor win unchallenged.

wheel: (1) The lowest possible straight in high poker. (2) The system for ranking the hands in low poker whereby the ace is low and straights and flushes are not considered. Therefore, the best low hand is 5 4 3 2 A, suited or not.

whipsaw: The situation a player is in when he is between two players who are betting and raising aggressively.

wired: Same as *back to back* and *rolled up*.

zombie: An inscrutable poker player who never shows any emotion.

Bibliography

his list represents but a bare fraction of books about poker. The Library of Congress lists 166 titles going back only ten years! If you are really interested in pursuing the subject, the Gambler's Book Club in Las Vegas will provide you with a catalogue of about 100 titles.

Anonymous. *Maverick's Guide to Poker*. Boston: Charles E. Tuttle Company, Revised Edition, 1994; 169 pages.

This book was originally published in 1962 under the name *Poker According to Maverick* (Dell). The main differences in the new edition are that Mel Gibson's face is on the cover instead of James Garner's, and there is an added section about Hold'em. The truly interesting thing about this book is that it's not a bad book at all in terms of serious poker advice. Whoever actually wrote it knew what he was doing. It's also fun to read.

Bobby Baldwin. *Tales out of Tulsa*. (Hollywood: Gambling Times/ Lyle Stuart, 1984; 167 pages)

This book mixes poker lessons with glimpses of the gambler's life in a way that is both informative and fun to read.

Jon Bradshaw. *Fast Company*. Vintage paperback edition: New York, Random House, 1975; preface, 1987 by Nik Cohn; 239 pages.

Jon Bradshaw, who died in 1986, was an extremely well-known and respected journalist in the 1960s and 70s and here produced an entertaining and insightful study of gamblers and their mentality. He did this through in-depth interviews with and reports on Puggy Pearson, Bobby Riggs, Minnesota Fats, Tim Holland, Johnny Moss, and Titanic Thompson, famous gamblers all. It's a very interesting look at the gambler's world.

Doyle "Texas Dolly" Brunson, et al. *Super/System A Course in Power Poker*. Las Vegas: B&G Publishing, 1978–1994; 605 pages.

The fact that this book was originally published as *How I Made over $1,000,000 Playing Poker* and was subsequently retitled and marketed as *Super/System: A Course in Power Poker* shows some of the changes in Pokerdom over the last twenty years or so. The old braggadocio has given way to the new pseudo-techy, pseudo-yuppie (*power* lunches, *power* ties, self em*power*ment) facade. As far as I know, however, the text has not changed, at least not much. In any case, the sections actually written by Doyle Brunson are candid, entertaining, and informative. Bobby Baldwin's section on limit Hold'em is equally informative and worthwhile. The rest is, well, it's okay, I guess. Brunson is amazingly candid when writing of his life as a gambler and admitting that his next book could be titled *How I Lost over $1,000,000 Playing Golf*. Many—if not most—of the pros one encounters in Pokerdom have "leaks", which means they will win it at the poker table and then lose it betting on something else, but not a lot of them will admit it. Be that as it may, Brunson's lessons on winning at poker are must reading: what he describes is essentially poker as a people game much as (ahem) I do.

John Fox. *Play Poker, Quit Work and Sleep till Noon!* Seal Beach: Bacchus Press, 1977; third edition, 1978; 343 pages.

This is one of my all-time favorite poker books. It is funny, clever and loaded with much more advice than anyone could possibly absorb in a couple of lifetimes. However, it is limited now in that it only refers to Old-Gardena-style, public, five card draw. Some of its basic strategies are applicable to other forms of poker, so it is still worth reading. Furthermore, it is definitely a book by a pro of the "never give a sucker an even break" school. For that reason alone it is worth reading—to find out how the hardcore pros think.

Anthony Holden. *Big Deal: One Year as a Professional Poker Player*. London: Bantam Press, 1990; Paperback edition, 1995; 366 pages.

In Pokerdom, this is probably the most famous book published in the last twenty years. This is partly due to the fact that it was written by a real-world (as opposed to poker-world) person of considerable cachet as an author and scholar, and partly, of course, because it is a hell of an interesting book. Earlier in this book, I referred to this book as "surprisingly influential." What I meant by this was that most poker books are of the "how to" variety of one sort or another. This one is not, yet it is mentioned and referred to repeatedly in just about every book published in the last five years. It's the autobiographical account of an avid amateur poker player who one day decides to follow his rainbow and try to make it as a pro, finds out he's not cut out for it, and goes back to civilian life. His descriptions of Pokerdom and its denizens are priceless and timeless.

Lee Jones. *Winning Low Limit Hold'em*. Pittsburgh: ConJelCo, 1994; 176 pages.

As I mentioned in the main text, this book is reputed to be perhaps the definitive work on low limit Hold'em. If you're planning on playing $3–$6 Hold'em in casinos, better read it.

Lou Krieger. *Hold'em Excellence: From Beginner to Winner*. Las Vegas: B&F Enterprises, 1995; 169 pages.

This is a very concise yet thorough book for the beginner who wants to learn low- to medium-stake casino Hold'em. Easy to read and understand.

A. D. Livingston. *Advanced Poker Strategy and Smart Winning Play*. North Hollywood: Wilshire Book Company, 1977; 227 pages.

A book of the old school, this is solidly in the "never-stay-unless-you-think-you-have-the-best-hand" category, and although it claims to be "advanced", it is really quite a good book for beginners. It'll give a beginner a solid foundation in the play of the cards and the overall tenor of hard-nosed, though amateur, poker. The book's best feature, in my opinion, is its 189 pages of poker variations—a veritable encyclopedia for home players. Unfortunately, it was written when Hold'em was in the cradle and doesn't have much to say about it, except that it seems to be "the game of the future."

John Scarne. *Scarne on Cards*. Signet paperback edition: Chicago: New American Library, 1973; 433 pages.

Scarne's Guide to Modern Poker. New York: Simon & Schuster, 1984; 307 pages.

Play of the cards; psychology; public and private poker; rules; variations for home games; methods of cheating and dealing with cheaters—you can't play poker or any kind of card game seriously without reading Scarne. That's all there is to it.

Tex Sheahan. *Wins, Places & Pros*. Hollywood: Gambling Times/ Lyle Stuart, 1984; 155 pages.

I wish I were acquainted with Tex Sheahan because he's one of the very few active pros who writes and presumably thinks like a human being. Although this book won't improve your poker game, Sheahan's tales of games and people and life in Pokerdom are witty and have a philosophical charm that is sorely lacking in most contemporary poker publications. Fun to read.

David Spanier. *Inside the Gambler's Mind*. Reno: University of Nevada Press, 1994; 240 pages.

The Pocket Guide to Gambling. New York: Simon & Schuster, 1980; 144 pages.

Total Poker. New York: Penguin, 1977; 221 pages.

Mr. Spanier is a political journalist and author who is also one of the most respected writers of gambling and game subjects on the planet. His books are all extremely informative and a pleasure to read.

Peter O. Steiner. *Thursday-Night Poker*. New York: Random House, 1996; 426 pages.

Steiner is a retired professor of economics at the University of Michigan and has an assortment of other academic titles and credentials. His book is written from the point of view of an amateur who enjoys playing in both private and public games, has long and varied experience, and who must be a very meticulous player. His knowledge of poker is thorough, and his advice on play of the cards is sound. However, he has a strange attitude about money and its role in poker. For one thing, he seems to think it's all right to lose—not just lose occasionally, mind you, but lose regularly. I feel this shows very little sympathy for the losers. He, Steiner, is clearly a winner at poker and can afford to shrug off the fact that, as he says, the swings even in a "high stakes" private game would rarely represent more than 1 percent of the players' annual income. The poor sod who's blowing that much money (as much as 50 percent of his annual income!) on a regular basis, however, could be in a lot of trouble.

Frank R. Wallace. *A Guaranteed Income for Life/Advanced Concepts of Poker*. New York: Warner Books, 1978; 368 pages.

This is the book that gave birth to John Finn, comic book superhero (or arch villain) of poker. He doesn't, perhaps, truly deserve the sobriquet of Arch Villain because he doesn't actually cheat—but he does everything else imaginable to squeeze, browbeat, sweet talk, manipulate, and slime his way to poker profits, and he's *never* distracted or sloppy or on tilt or . . . human. Well, any and every poker player should read this book, but if you're looking for John Finn, I'm sure you'll find him drinking Sterno under a bridge somewhere, or perhaps he's joined a monastery and is busy fleecing the monks. Unfortunately, to be fair (one doesn't want to be Finn-ish, after all), I must say there is quite a lot of interesting and useful statistical information in the book which makes it worth reading for that reason.

Herbert O. Yardley. *The Education of a Poker Player*. New York: Simon & Schuster, 1957; 129 pages.

This is the all-time classic, the book that everyone who is even *thinking* about playing poker seriously should read—many times. My aged copy is just about worn out from innumerable thumb-throughs and re-reads. If any book will make the light bulb go on in your head as you exclaim "This is poker!" it is this one.

Mason Malmuth. *Poker Essays*. Las Vegas: Two Plus Two Publishing, 1991; 262 pages.

Gambling Theory and Other Topics. Las Vegas: Two Plus Two Publishing, 1987, Fourth Edition, 1994; 313 pages.

Mason Malmuth and Lynne Loomis. *Fundamentals of Poker*. Las Vegas: Two Plus Two Publishing, 1992; 70 pages.

David Sklansky. *The Theory of Poker*. Las Vegas: Two Plus Two Publishing, 1987; Third Edition, 1994; 276 pages.

Sklansky on Poker. Las Vegas: Two Plus Two Publishing, 1981; Second Edition, 1994; 215 pages.

Getting the Best of It. Las Vegas: Two Plus Two Publishing, 1982; Second Edition, 1993; 248 pages.

David Sklansky, and Mason Malmuth. *Hold'em Poker for Advanced Players*. Las Vegas: Two Plus Two Publishing, 1988, Second Edition, 1994; 212 pages.

I have lumped all these Sklansky/Malmuth/et al. books together because these and others of their books are pretty much of a type: if you want to be Karl Malden in the *Cincinnati Kid* ("Oh, you know. I just play the percentages—never win much and never lose much") these are the books to read. These are also the books to read to find out what the middle- to lower-echelon pros are thinking. (The only exception to this is the last book, *Fundamentals of Poker,* which is actually a very good "starter pamphlet" for a new poker player.) I am not, mind you, saying that these books do not contain good advice about how to play (professional) poker, they do. They are just very technical, very self-important, and no fun at all. It does seem to me from time to time that Mason Malmuth could be a candidate for a title of "Poker Philosopher"—certainly much more so than Sklansky. But then he gets into totally incomprehensible mathematics which are going to be of value to about 0.000001 percent of the poker-playing population, and that's being generous, and gives one the impression that he's writing to impress rather than to educate. In any case, if you're new to poker, please read some of the other books (like Yardley) first: these will make you wonder why anyone bothers.